Practice *Planners*

Arthur E. Jongsma, Jr., Series Editor

Helping therapists help their clients...

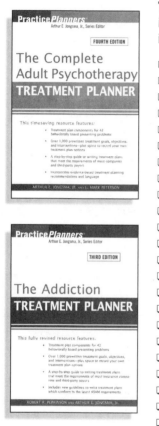

Treatment Planners cover all the necessary elements for developing formal treatment plans, including detailed problem definitions, long-term goals, short-term objectives, therapeutic interventions, and DSM-IV™ diagnoses.

❏ The Complete Adult Psychotherapy Treatment Planner, Fourth Edition ......978-0-471-76346-8 / $55.00
❏ The Child Psychotherapy Treatment Planner, Fourth Edition ....978-0-471-78535-4 / $55.00
❏ The Adolescent Psychotherapy Treatment Planner, Fourth Edition ....978-0-471-78539-2 / $55.00
❏ The Addiction Treatment Planner, Third Edition ....978-0-471-72544-2 / $55.00
❏ The Couples Psychotherapy Treatment Planner...................................978-0-471-24711-1 / $55.00
❏ The Group Therapy Treatment Planner, Second Edition ....978-0-471-66791-9 / $55.00
❏ The Family Therapy Treatment Planner...978-0-471-34768-2 / $55.00
❏ The Older Adult Psychotherapy Treatment Planner...............................978-0-471-29574-7 / $55.00
❏ The Employee Assistance (EAP) Treatment Planner...............................978-0-471-24709-8 / $55.00
❏ The Gay and Lesbian Psychotherapy Treatment Planner ....978-0-471-35080-4 / $55.00
❏ The Crisis Counseling and Traumatic Events Treatment Planner..............978-0-471-39587-4 / $55.00
❏ The Social Work and Human Services Treatment Planner........................978-0-471-37741-2 / $55.00
❏ The Continuum of Care Treatment Planner ....978-0-471-19568-9 / $55.00
❏ The Behavioral Medicine Treatment Planner ....978-0-471-31923-8 / $55.00
❏ The Mental Retardation and Developmental Disability Treatment Planner......978-0-471-38253-9 / $55.00
❏ The Special Education Treatment Planner ....978-0-471-38872-2 / $55.00
❏ The Severe and Persistent Mental Illness Treatment Planner ....978-0-471-35945-6 / $55.00
❏ The Personality Disorders Treatment Planner......................................978-0-471-39403-7 / $55.00
❏ The Rehabilitation Psychology Treatment Planner ....978-0-471-35178-8 / $55.00
❏ The Pastoral Counseling Treatment Planner ....978-0-471-25416-4 / $55.00
❏ The Juvenile Justice and Residential Care Treatment Planner.................978-0-471-43320-0 / $55.00
❏ The School Counseling and School Social Work Treatment Planner.........978-0-471-08496-9 / $55.00
❏ The Psychopharmacology Treatment Planner.......................................978-0-471-43322-4 / $55.00
❏ The Probation and Parole Treatment Planner ....978-0-471-20244-8 / $55.00
❏ The Suicide and Homicide Risk Assessment
   & Prevention Treatment Planner ....978-0-471-46631-4 / $55.00
❏ The Speech-Language Pathology Treatment Planner ....978-0-471-27504-6 / $55.00
❏ The College Student Counseling Treatment Planner..............................978-0-471-46708-3 / $55.00
❏ The Parenting Skills Treatment Planner..978-0-471-48183-6 / $55.00
❏ The Early Childhood Education Intervention Treatment Planner ....978-0-471-65962-4 / $55.00
❏ The Co-Occurring Disorders Treatment Planner ....978-0-471-73081-1 / $55.00
❏ The Sexual Abuse Victim and Sexual Offender Treatment Planner...........978-0-471-21979-8 / $55.00
❏ The Complete Women's Psychotherapy Treatment Planner.....................978-0-470-03983-0 / $55.00

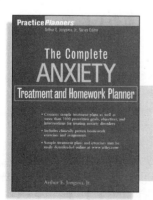

The **Complete Treatment and Homework Planners** series of books combines our bestselling *Treatment Planners* and *Homework Planners* into one easy-to-use, all-in-one resource for mental health professionals treating clients suffering from the most commonly diagnosed disorders.

❏ The Complete Depression Treatment and Homework Planner ....978-0-471-64515-3 / $44.95
❏ The Complete Anxiety Treatment and Homework Planner......................978-0-471-64548-1 / $44.95

Over 500,000 Practice*Planners* sold ...

PracticePlanners®

Homework Planners feature dozens of behaviorally based, ready-to-use assignments that are designed for use between sessions, as well as a disk or CD-ROM (Microsoft Word) containing all of the assignments—allowing you to customize them to suit your unique client needs.

❑ Brief Couples Therapy Homework Planner ....978-0-471-29511-2 / $55.00
❑ Child Psychotherapy Homework Planner, Second Edition............................978-0-471-78534-7 / $55.00
❑ Child Therapy Activity and Homework Planner ....978-0-471-25684-7 / $55.00
❑ Adolescent Psychotherapy Homework Planner, Second Edition ....978-0-471-78537-8 / $55.00
❑ Addiction Treatment Homework Planner, Third Edition................................978-0-471-77461-7 / $55.00
❑ Brief Employee Assistance Homework Planner ....978-0-471-38088-7 / $55.00
❑ Brief Family Therapy Homework Planner...978-0-471-38512-7 / $55.00
❑ Grief Counseling Homework Planner ....978-0-471-43318-7 / $55.00
❑ Divorce Counseling Homework Planner ....978-0-471-43319-4 / $55.00
❑ Group Therapy Homework Planner ....978-0-471-41822-1 / $55.00
❑ School Counseling and School Social Work Homework Planner ....978-0-471-09114-1 / $55.00
❑ Adolescent Psychotherapy Homework Planner II ....978-0-471-27493-3 / $55.00
❑ Adult Psychotherapy Homework Planner, Second Edition ....978-0-471-76343-7 / $55.00
❑ Parenting Skills Homework Planner...978-0-471-48182-9 / $55.00

Progress Notes Planners contain complete prewritten progress notes for each presenting problem in the companion Treatment Planners.

❑ The Adult Psychotherapy Progress Notes Planner.....................................978-0-471-76344-4 / $55.00
❑ The Adolescent Psychotherapy Progress Notes Planner ....978-0-471-78538-5 / $55.00
❑ The Severe and Persistent Mental Illness Progress Notes Planner..........978-0-471-21986-6 / $55.00
❑ The Child Psychotherapy Progress Notes Planner.....................................978-0-471-78536-1 / $55.00
❑ The Addiction Progress Notes Planner..978-0-471-73253-2 / $55.00
❑ The Couples Psychotherapy Progress Notes Planner ....978-0-471-27460-5 / $55.00
❑ The Family Therapy Progress Notes Planner ....978-0-471-48443-1 / $55.00

Client Education Handout Planners contain elegantly designed handouts that can be printed out from the enclosed CD-ROM and provide information on a wide range of psychological and emotional disorders and life skills issues. Use as patient literature, handouts at presentations, and aids for promoting your mental health practice.

❑ Adult Client Education Handout Planner ....978-0-471-20232-5 / $55.00
❑ Child and Adolescent Client Education Handout Planner..........................978-0-471-20233-2 / $55.00
❑ Couples and Family Client Education Handout Planner ....978-0-471-20234-9 / $55.00

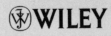

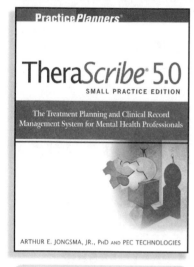

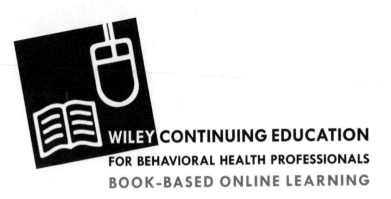

Adolescent Psychotherapy
Homework Planner,
Second Edition

PRACTICE*PLANNERS*® SERIES

Treatment Planners

The Adult Psychotherapy Treatment Planner, Fourth Edition
The Child Psychotherapy Treatment Planner, Fourth Edition
The Adolescent Psychotherapy Treatment Planner, Fourth Edition
The Addiction Treatment Planner, Third Edition
The Continuum of Care Treatment Planner
The Couples Psychotherapy Treatment Planner
The Employee Assistance Treatment Planner
The Pastoral Counseling Treatment Planner
The Older Adult Psychotherapy Treatment Planner
The Behavioral Medicine Treatment Planner
The Group Therapy Treatment Planner, Second Edition
The Gay and Lesbian Psychotherapy Treatment Planner
The Family Therapy Treatment Planner
The Severe and Persistent Mental Illness Treatment Planner
The Mental Retardation and Developmental Disability Treatment Planner
The Social Work and Human Services Treatment Planner
The Crisis Counseling and Traumatic Events Treatment Planner
The Personality Disorders Treatment Planner
The Rehabilitation Psychology Treatment Planner
The Special Education Treatment Planner
The Juvenile Justice and Residential Care Treatment Planner
The School Counseling and School Social Work Treatment Planner
The Sexual Abuse Victim and Sexual Offender Treatment Planner
The Probation and Parole Treatment Planner
The Psychopharmacology Treatment Planner
The Speech-Language Pathology Treatment Planner
The Suicide and Homicide Risk Assessment & Prevention Treatment Planner
The College Student Counseling Treatment Planner
The Parenting Skills Treatment Planner
The Early Childhood Education Intervention Treatment Planner
The Co-Occurring Disorders Treatment Planner

Progress Notes Planners

The Child Psychotherapy Progress Notes Planner, Third Edition
The Adolescent Psychotherapy Progress Notes Planner, Third Edition
The Adult Psychotherapy Progress Notes Planner, Third Edition
The Addiction Progress Notes Planner, Second Edition
The Severe and Persistent Mental Illness Progress Notes Planner
The Couples Psychotherapy Progress Notes Planner
The Family Therapy Progress Notes Planner

Homework Planners

Brief Therapy Homework Planner
Brief Couples Therapy Homework Planner
Brief Employee Assistance Homework Planner
Brief Family Therapy Homework Planner
Grief Counseling Homework Planner
Group Therapy Homework Planner
Divorce Counseling Homework Planner
School Counseling and School Social Work Homework Planner
Child Therapy Activity and Homework Planner
Addiction Treatment Homework Planner, Third Edition
Adolescent Psychotherapy Homework Planner, Second Edition
Adult Psychotherapy Homework Planner, Second Edition
Child Psychotherapy Homework Planner, Second Edition
Parenting Skills Homework Planner

Client Education Handout Planners

Adult Client Education Handout Planner
Child and Adolescent Client Education Handout Planner
Couples and Family Client Education Handout Planner

Complete Planners

The Complete Depression Treatment and Homework Planner
The Complete Anxiety Treatment and Homework Planner

PracticePlanners®

Arthur E. Jongsma, Jr., Series Editor

Adolescent Psychotherapy
Homework Planner

Second Edition

Arthur E. Jongsma, Jr.

L. Mark Peterson

William P. McInnis

WILEY

John Wiley & Sons, Inc.

Note about Photocopy Rights

The publisher grants purchasers permission to reproduce handouts from this book for professional use with their clients.

ISBN-13: 978-0-471-78537-8
ISBN-10: 0-471-78537-7

Printed in the United States of America.

10 9 8 7 6 5 4

This book is dedicated to our mothers and mothers-in-law:

Phyllis McInnis
Joan Wieringa
Harmina Doot
Evelyn Landis
Dorothy Peterson

We recognize and appreciate the love, support, and guidance they provided through our adolescence and into our adulthood.

CONTENTS

PRACTICE*PLANNERS*® SERIES PREFACE

Accountability is an important dimension of the practice of psychotherapy. Treatment programs, public agencies, clinics, and practitioners must justify and document their treatment plans to outside review entities in order to be reimbursed for services. The books and software in the Practice*Planners*® series are designed to help practitioners fulfill these documentation requirements efficiently and professionally.

The Practice*Planners*® series includes a wide array of treatment planning books including not only the original *Complete Adult Psychotherapy Treatment Planner, Child Psychotherapy Treatment Planner,* and *Adolescent Psychotherapy Treatment Planner,* all now in their fourth editions, but also *Treatment Planners* targeted to a wide range of specialty areas of practice, including:

- Addictions
- Co-occurring disorders
- Behavioral medicine
- College students
- Couples therapy
- Crisis counseling
- Early childhood education
- Employee assistance
- Family therapy
- Gays and lesbians
- Group therapy
- Juvenile justice and residential care
- Mental retardation and developmental disability
- Neuropsychology
- Older adults
- Parenting skills
- Pastoral counseling
- Personality disorders
- Probation and parole
- Psychopharmacology
- School counseling
- Severe and persistent mental illness
- Sexual abuse victims and offenders

- Special education
- Suicide and homicide risk assessment

In addition, there are three branches of companion books which can be used in conjunction with the *Treatment Planners,* or on their own:

- ***Progress Notes Planners*** provide a menu of progress statements that elaborate on the client's symptom presentation and the provider's therapeutic intervention. Each *Progress Notes Planner* statement is directly integrated with the behavioral definitions and therapeutic interventions from its companion *Treatment Planner.*
- ***Homework Planners*** include homework assignments designed around each presenting problem (such as anxiety, depression, chemical dependence, anger management, eating disorders, or panic disorder) that is the focus of a chapter in its corresponding *Treatment Planner.*
- ***Client Education Handout Planners*** provide brochures and handouts to help educate and inform clients on presenting problems and mental health issues, as well as life skills techniques. The handouts are included on CD-ROMs for easy printing from your computer and are ideal for use in waiting rooms, at presentations, as newsletters, or as information for clients struggling with mental illness issues. The topics covered by these handouts correspond to the presenting problems in the *Treatment Planners.*

The series also includes:

- **Thera*Scribe*®**, the #1 selling treatment planning and clinical record-keeping software system for mental health professionals. Thera*Scribe*® allows the user to import the data from any of the *Treatment Planner, Progress Notes Planner,* or *Homework Planner* books into the software's expandable database to simply point and click to create a detailed, organized, individualized, and customized treatment plan along with optional integrated progress notes and homework assignments.

Adjunctive books, such as *The Psychotherapy Documentation Primer* and *The Clinical Documentation Sourcebook* contain forms and resources to aid the clinician in mental health practice management.

The goal of our series is to provide practitioners with the resources they need in order to provide high quality care in the era of accountability. To put it simply: we seek to help you spend more time on patients, and less time on paperwork.

ARTHUR E. JONGSMA, JR.
Grand Rapids, Michigan

ACKNOWLEDGMENTS

We want to acknowledge and express appreciation to our wives—Judy, Cherry, and Lynn—who have supported us through the many years of the Practice*Planners* series. We appreciate their willingness to read the manuscripts and offer helpful suggestions. And, speaking of manuscript preparation, this project has had the benefit of many hours of perseverance by our dedicated typist, Sue Rhoda. She has organized our chaotic, scribbled details into a meaningful manuscript with a spirit of kindness and generosity. Thank you, Sue, for your loyalty and good work.

A.E.J.
L.M.P.
W.P.M.

HOMEWORK PLANNERS INTRODUCTION

ABOUT PRACTICE*PLANNERS*® HOMEWORK PLANNERS

In today's era of managed care, which often requires shorter and fewer treatment sessions, therapists can assign between-session homework to help maximize the effectiveness of briefer treatment. Homework provides continuity to the treatment process and allows the client to work between sessions on issues that are the focus of therapy. Many clients feel empowered by doing something on their own to facilitate the change process, and this reinforces their sense of control over their problems. The purpose of the *Homework Planner* series is to help you quickly put together homework assignments, so you can spend less time on paperwork and more time with your client.

Each *Homework Planner:*

- Saves you hours of time-consuming paperwork.
- Offers the freedom to develop customized homework assignments.
- Includes dozens of copier-ready exercises that cover the most common issues, situations, and behavioral problems encountered in therapy.
- Provides expert guidance on how and when to make the most efficient use of the exercises.
- Features assignments that are cross-referenced to each corresponding *Treatment Planner*—allowing you the right exercise for a given situation or behavioral problem.
- Includes a computer disk or CD-ROM that allows you to customize each exercise to fit your particular needs.

HOW TO USE THIS HOMEWORK PLANNER

The assignments in this *Homework Planner* are grouped by presenting problems and cross-referenced to every presenting problem found in its companion *Treatment Planner*. Although these assignments were created with a specific presenting problem in mind, don't feel limited to a single problem-oriented chapter when searching for an appropriate assignment. Included with each exercise is a cross-referenced list of suggested presenting problems for which the assignment may also be appropriate and useful. A broader cross-referenced list of assignments is found in the Appendix, where you can find relevant assignments beyond the exercises found in any specific presenting problem chapter.

Assigning therapy homework is just a beginning step. Carrying out the assignment requires a follow-up exploration of the impact of the assignment on the client's thoughts, feelings, and behavior. What are the results? Was this assignment useful to the client? Can it be redesigned or altered for better results? We encourage you to examine and search for new and creative ways to actively engage your client in participating in the homework process.

ARTHUR E. JONGSMA, JR.
L. MARK PETERSON
WILLIAM P. MCINNIS

BREAK IT DOWN INTO SMALL STEPS

GOALS OF THE EXERCISE

1. Complete large projects or long-term assignments on time.
2. Improve organizational skills by breaking down projects into smaller steps.
3. Receive rewards for successfully completing projects.
4. Avoid the pattern of procrastinating or "waiting until the last minute" to begin working on a large or long-term project.

ADDITIONAL PROBLEMS FOR WHICH THIS EXERCISE MAY BE MOST USEFUL

- Attention-Deficit/Hyperactivity Disorder (ADHD)
- Mania/Hypomania
- Oppositional Defiant

SUGGESTIONS FOR PROCESSING THIS EXERCISE WITH THE CLIENT

This homework assignment is designed to assist adolescents with a learning disability, history of underachievement, or an Attention-Deficit/Hyperactivity Disorder to complete their large or long-term projects. The therapist, parents, and client are encouraged to sit down as a team to break down projects into smaller steps and then set a deadline for each step. Consultation with the client's teacher is strongly encouraged to help identify the different steps. Encourage the parents and client to implement a reward system to positively reinforce the client for successfully completing each step. It is recommended that the final reward for completing the entire project on time be of greater value or significance than the rewards for completing the smaller steps. Negative consequences may also be used if the client fails to complete a step by the specified time period.

BREAK IT DOWN INTO SMALL STEPS

Are you tired of rushing around at the last minute or cramming the night before to complete a long-term project that you have been given plenty of time to complete? If so, then this exercise will assist you in completing your large or long-term projects in a more timely and efficient manner. You are encouraged to meet with your parents, teachers, and therapist shortly after you are assigned a large project to help break down the task into smaller steps. In this way, you will avoid the pattern of procrastinating or putting the project off until the last minute. The project will become more manageable and you will experience less anxiety or stress in the long run. Place this assignment sheet in your notebook or post it in a prominent place to remind you of the steps that need to be completed before you turn in the entire project.

1. First, identify the project that needs to be completed.

   Name of project: _____

   _____

   _____

   Class: _____

   Final deadline: _____

2. Break the project down into several smaller steps. Establish a deadline for each separate step.

   Step   **Target Deadline**

   1. _____   _____

   2. _____   _____

   3. _____   _____

   4. _____   _____

   5. _____   _____

   6. _____   _____

   7. _____   _____

   8. _____   _____

9. _____ _____

10. _____ _____

3. Sit down with your parents, teachers, or therapist and identify a reward for successfully accomplishing each step on or before the deadline. The reward may be the same for each step. Record the date you completed each step and the reward you received in the following spaces.

Actual Completion Date **Reward**

1. _____ _____

2. _____ _____

3. _____ _____

4. _____ _____

5. _____ _____

6. _____ _____

7. _____ _____

8. _____ _____

9. _____ _____

10. _____ _____

4. Develop a list of negative consequences for the times when you do not meet your deadline. Record the date you completed the step and the negative consequence you received for not completing it on time in the following spaces.

Late Completion Date **Negative Consequence**

1. _____ _____

2. _____ _____

3. _____ _____

4. _____ _____

5. _____ _____

6. _____ _____

7. _____ _____

8. _____ _____

9. _____ _____

10. _____ _____

5. Identify a grand reward for completing the entire project on or before the final deadline:

    _____

    _____

    _____

    _____

    _____

6. Please respond to the following questions after you have completed and turned in your entire project (and also if you were not successful in turning the assignment in on time).

    A. What motivated you to complete each step? _____

        _____

        _____

    B. Were you more motivated by trying to get the rewards or trying to avoid the negative consequences? _____

        _____

        _____

    C. What obstacles or frustrations did you face along the way? _____

        _____

        _____

    D. What helped you overcome or work around the obstacles or frustrations?

        _____

        _____

    E. How did you feel about yourself after you completed each step? How about after you completed the entire project? _____

        _____

        _____

        _____

    F. What did you learn about yourself and about organization in doing this project?

        _____

        _____

        _____

        _____

GOOD GRADE/BAD GRADE INCIDENT REPORTS

GOALS OF THE EXERCISE

1. Explore factors contributing to either good or bad grades on an assignment or test.
2. Identify effective strategies or positive study skills that will help to improve academic performance.
3. Take ownership or assume personal responsibility for academic performance.
4. Attain and maintain a level of academic performance that is commensurate with level of ability.

ADDITIONAL PROBLEMS FOR WHICH THIS EXERCISE MAY BE MOST USEFUL

- Anxiety
- Attention-Deficit/Hyperactivity Disorder (ADHD)
- Conduct Disorder/Delinquency
- Oppositional Defiant

SUGGESTIONS FOR PROCESSING THIS EXERCISE WITH THE CLIENT

In this assignment, the client is asked to complete either a Good Grade or Bad Grade Incident Report to identify the factors that contributed to him/her receiving either a good or bad grade. The incident forms will help the client to identify the strategies or positive study skills that he/she will need to utilize on a regular basis to achieve and/or maintain a level of performance that is equal to his/her ability level. The assignment will also help the client begin to take ownership of his/her grades or school performance. The client should be reinforced for taking personal responsibility for doing what is necessary to receive good grades. The assignment may also identify emotional factors or social pressures that contribute to the client's poor grades. The therapist should consider using the incident reports in the therapy sessions with clients who have a learning disability. Teachers or school officials can also be asked to help the client complete these forms.

GOOD GRADE INCIDENT REPORT

1. Please give a recent example of when you received a good grade on a test or assignment. What grade did you receive? What class did you receive the good grade in?

    _____

    _____

2. Which of these factors and/or strategies helped you to receive the good grade? (Please check all that apply.)

    ____ Motivation/desire to do well

    ____ Studied in advance

    ____ Reviewed material more than once

    ____ Broke assignment down into small steps over time

    ____ Studied with a friend or other student

    ____ Received help from an adult tutor

    ____ Received tutoring from another peer

    ____ Asked teacher in class for help to better understand subject

    ____ Met with teacher after class or before school

    ____ Asked parent for help

    ____ Called a friend for help

    ____ Other (please identify)

    _____

    _____

3. How did you feel after receiving the good grade?

    _____

    _____

    _____

4. How did your parent(s) or teacher(s) react to your good grade?

    _____

    _____

    _____

5. In what other class(es) can you use these strategies to improve your grade?

    _____

    _____

    _____

    _____

BAD GRADE INCIDENT REPORT

1. Please give a recent example of when you received a bad grade on a test or assignment. What grade did you receive? What class did you receive the poor grade in?

   _____

2. What factors contributed to your bad grade on the test or assignment? (Please check all that apply.)

   ____ Lack of study or preparation

   ____ Did not study properly

   ____ Laziness/lack of interest

   ____ Forgot to study for the test

   ____ Studied at last minute or did not give self enough time to complete assignment

   ____ Chose to have fun instead of study

   ____ Rushed through assignment or test/failed to review answers

   ____ Made careless mistakes

   ____ Do not want to be viewed as nerd or geek if I make a good grade

   ____ Did not understand material or subject

   ____ Did not seek out help from teachers/parents

   ____ Too much homework in other class(es)

   ____ Distracted by outside problems or stress

   ____ Test anxiety

   ____ Too much pressure to achieve by parents or others

   ____ Do not want to be expected to get good grades all the time

   ____ Other (please describe)

   _____

   _____

3. How did you feel about yourself after receiving the bad grade?

   _____

   _____

4. How did your parent(s) or teacher(s) react to your bad grade?

   _____

   _____

5. What could you do differently in the future to receive a better grade in this class?

   _____

   _____

   _____

QUESTIONS AND CONCERNS AROUND BEING ADOPTED

GOALS OF THE EXERCISE

1. Increase the level of openness and dialogue with new parents.
2. Decrease level of anxiety by answering questions surrounding the adoption process.
3. Identify potential areas of concern that need to be further addressed and resolved.
4. Promote honest and direct communication between adoptee and new parents.

ADDITIONAL PROBLEMS FOR WHICH THIS EXERCISE MAY BE MOST USEFUL

- None

SUGGESTIONS FOR PROCESSING THIS EXERCISE WITH THE CLIENT

Adopted adolescents are typically from family systems where they have rarely had the opportunity to share their concerns or dare to ask any questions. This exercise is designed to promote open communication between the adoptee and his/her new parents. The adoptee is given permission to share his/her concerns and ask questions that he/she may have about the adoption process. The first part of the processing should be done individually with the adoptee, focusing on the items rated with a number three. The processing should be encouraging and supportive of the need for questions to be verbalized. Also, barriers, fears, and defenses to questioning need to be addressed and hopefully reduced. The second part of the processing would be done with adoptee and parents together if the adoptee is willing. If the adoptee is not willing, the questions and concerns can be given to the parents for them to respond in writing. The parents' responses would then, in turn, be processed with the adoptee. The emphasis in both stages of the processing needs to be on the value of asking questions to promote openness and to build trust.

QUESTIONS AND CONCERNS AROUND BEING ADOPTED

Expressing our concerns and asking questions can make us feel less anxious and more open and trusting of new situations. Listed are several concerns and questions that teens and others have around adoption. Rate each question and/or concern you have as follows:

1. Not a question/concern I have

2. Maybe a question/concern I have

3. Definitely a question/concern I have

_____ Why do you want to adopt, and why do you want to adopt me?

_____ What will happen if I mess up a lot?

_____ I don't know if you can really like me.

_____ If I like your family, will that mean I cannot still like my other family?

_____ How will I be disciplined when I do something wrong?

_____ What will you do if I embarrass you?

_____ When I turn 18, what will happen? Will it be the end of our relationship?

_____ What will happen if you find out how bad I really am?

_____ I'm afraid I will be too much for you to handle.

_____ What should I do if I really don't like something you are doing?

_____ How much will you want to know about my parents and family?

_____ How will I know when you are upset and when you are upset with me?

_____ Will you get mad at me if I talk or don't want to talk about my family?

_____ If I love you, will that mean that I no longer love my family?

_____ What will happen if I can't be like you want me to be?

_____ Do I have to be perfect to be accepted by you?

_____ If I mess up, will you get rid of me?

_____ Will you ask me questions about my birth family?

_____ Will you back off and leave me alone if I need space?

_____ Other questions:

_____

_____

SOME THINGS I'D LIKE YOU TO KNOW . . . (ADOLESCENT AND ADULT)

GOALS OF THE EXERCISE

1. Promote dialogue between the client and new adoptive parents.
2. Increase the client and parents' knowledge of each other.
3. Identify and acknowledge key things about each other.

ADDITIONAL PROBLEMS FOR WHICH THIS EXERCISE MAY BE MOST USEFUL

- Blended Family
- Low Self-Esteem
- Social Phobia/Shyness

SUGGESTIONS FOR PROCESSING THIS EXERCISE WITH THE CLIENT

More often than not, we can be slow or hesitant to learn the small, but important things about each other. We gather them in a hit or miss fashion when a situation opens up for us to do so. This information exchange is key as each of us recognizes, affirms, and builds an understanding of each other. There are two forms in this exercise, one for the adolescent and one for parents. The therapist can begin by having the client share his/her information in an individual session, and then move to a family session. It would be beneficial if the therapist models asking nonprobing questions of clarification to obtain further information from the parties and then encourages them to do the same. If all the exercise cannot be completed in a single session, the client and parents could be assigned to complete the assignment at home and then report back the next session on what they learned.

SOME THINGS I'D LIKE YOU TO KNOW . . .
(ADOLESCENT)

Please complete the following items about yourself.

1.   Identify your favorite things:

GAMES

Card Games _____ _____

Board Games _____ _____

Video Games _____ _____

ENTERTAINMENT

TV Shows _____ _____

Movies _____ _____

Activities (sports/hobbies) _____ _____

Music Types _____ _____

Music Groups/Performers _____ _____

SCHOOL

Favorite Subject _____

Least Favorite Subject _____

Easiest Subject _____

Hardest Subject _____

FOODS

Likes _____ _____

Dislikes _____ _____

Desserts _____ _____

Restaurants _____ _____

2. Circle one of the following that is most like you:

    Quiet   or Talker

    Cautious   or Risk taker

    Thinker   or Doer

    Giver   or Receiver

    Yes   or No

    Optimist   or Pessimist

    Morning person or Night person

3. Complete the following sentences:

    I get excited about _____

    I worry when _____

    I get embarrassed when _____

    I get upset when _____

    I like _____

    I get mad when _____

    I feel stupid when _____

    I feel loved when _____

    The worst thing that could happen to me is _____

    _____

    What I like most about a dad is _____

    _____

    What I like most about a mom is _____

    _____

    The thing that bugs me most about younger brothers and sisters is _____

    _____

    I get down when _____

    I feel lonely when _____

    The thing I like the best about family is _____

    _____

4. Circle your preference:

    A. In the morning I prefer to:

        Get up myself   Be called   Not get up until the last minute

    B. On weekdays, a good bedtime for someone my age is:

        9:00 PM   9:30 PM   10:00 PM   10:30 PM   11:00 PM

C. On weekends, a good bedtime is:

    10:30 PM   11:00 PM   11:30 PM   12:00 AM   Whenever I'm tired

D. I prefer:

    My own room   Share a room   Either is okay

E. I prefer to do homework:

    Right after school   Right after dinner

    Whenever I decide to   At an agreed-upon time

F. In terms of attention, I prefer:

    A little   Some   Quite a bit   A lot

G. Regarding my family, I prefer to:

    Not answer questions   Tell very little

    Answer any questions asked   Tell only what I want to

    Share my story with those I feel comfortable with

SOME THINGS I'D LIKE YOU TO KNOW . . .
(ADULT)

Please complete the following items about yourself.

1.   Identify your favorite things:

GAMES

Card Games   _____   _____

Board Games   _____   _____

Video Games   _____   _____

ENTERTAINMENT

TV Shows   _____   _____

Movies   _____   _____

Activities (sports/hobbies)   _____   _____

Music Types   _____   _____

Music Groups/Performers   _____   _____

SCHOOL

Favorite Subject   _____

Least Favorite Subject   _____

Easiest Subject   _____

Hardest Subject   _____

FOODS

Likes   _____   _____

Dislikes   _____   _____

Desserts   _____   _____

Restaurants   _____   _____

2.   Circle one of the following that is most like you:

    Quiet   or Talker

    Cautious   or Risk taker

    Thinker   or Doer

    Giver   or Receiver

    Yes   or No

    Optimist   or Pessimist

    Morning person or Night person

3.   Complete the following sentences:

    I get excited about _____

    I worry when _____

    I get embarrassed when _____

    I get upset when _____

    I like _____

    I get mad when _____

    I feel stupid when _____

    I feel loved when _____

    The worst thing that could happen to me is _____

    _____

    The thing I like best about being a parent is _____

    _____

    The thing I like least about being a parent is _____

    _____

    One thing that bugs me about teenagers is _____

    _____

    I get down when _____

    I feel lonely when _____

    The thing I like the best about family is _____

    _____

ANGER CONTROL

GOALS OF THE EXERCISE

1. Express anger through appropriate verbalizations and healthy physical outlets on a consistent basis.
2. Reduce the frequency and severity of aggressive and destructive behaviors.
3. Increase the frequency of statements that reflect acceptance of responsibility for aggressive behaviors.
4. Identify core issues that contribute to the emergence of the angry outbursts or physically aggressive behaviors.

ADDITIONAL PROBLEMS FOR WHICH THIS EXERCISE MAY BE MOST USEFUL

- Attention-Deficit/Hyperactivity Disorder (ADHD)
- Mania/Hypomania
- Oppositional Defiant

SUGGESTIONS FOR PROCESSING THIS EXERCISE WITH THE CLIENT

This homework assignment is designed for clients who demonstrate poor control over their anger. Instruct the client to use the positive and negative incident reports on the following pages to record times when he/she displays both good and poor control of his/her anger. Praise the client for occasions when he/she demonstrates good control of his/her anger. Reinforce the positive coping strategies that the client uses to control his/her anger. If, on the other hand, the client displays poor control of his/her anger, the therapist should assist the client in finding more effective ways to control his/her anger. In discussing the client's angry outbursts, be sensitive and attuned to any core issues that might precipitate the angry outbursts or acts of aggression. Identification of the core issues will hopefully lead to a discussion of ways that the client can more effectively manage his/her stress or meet his/her needs.

ANGER CONTROL

The goal of this assignment is to help you improve your control of your anger. Poor anger control can create a variety of problems in your life. Your angry outbursts or aggressive behaviors can place a strain on your relationships with parents, siblings, teachers, peers, friends, and so on. Other people may grow tired of your angry outbursts and begin to pull away or respond with anger. If you have problems controlling your anger, then you will likely be punished more often. Anger control problems can affect your self-esteem and cause you to feel unhappy, insecure, or guilty. This program seeks to help you gain greater control over your emotions and behavior and, in turn, help you feel better about yourself.

1. The first step in solving any problem is to recognize that a problem exists and to identify it. Sit down with your parents and therapist and identify the specific aggressive behaviors that you want to learn to control more effectively. Following is a list of aggressive behaviors, both verbal and physical, that a person may exhibit. Circle or underline the aggressive behaviors that you have had in the past. Blank spaces have been provided to write any other aggressive behaviors that have not been included on this list:

    - Throwing objects
    - Breaking things
    - Name calling
    - Cursing or swearing
    - Disrespectful talk
    - Critical remarks
    - _____
    - _____

    - Hitting
    - Kicking
    - Punching
    - Taunting
    - Pulling hair
    - Spitting
    - _____
    - _____

2. Now that your specific aggressive behaviors have been identified, you can join together with your parents and therapist as a team to find effective ways to control your anger. Remember, everyone becomes angry from time to time. The goal of this program is not to prevent you from ever experiencing any anger, but to help you learn to express your anger through talking and healthy physical outlets. Between therapy sessions, you and your parents are encouraged to record times when you show both good and poor control over your anger. Use the positive incident reports to identify times when you show good control. The positive incident reports can remind you of what you did

right in controlling your anger. On the other hand, use the negative incident report when you display poor control over your anger. The negative incident reports can help you think of better ways to control your anger if you are faced with similar problems in the future. Bring the positive and negative incident reports to the next therapy session so the therapist can discuss the incidents with your parents and you.

3. A reward system can be set in place to reinforce you for showing good control of your anger. You will also receive a consequence if you show poor control. Use the contract form on the following pages to make the contract official. Talk with your parents and therapist about appropriate rewards that can be used to reinforce positive anger control. The following is a list of potential rewards:

    - Extra time to spend watching television or playing video games
    - One-on-one time with mother or father (e.g., attend a movie, exercise together, play a board game)
    - Extended bedtime
    - Extra time on telephone
    - Invite a friend over or go over to a friend's house after school
    - Invite a friend to sleep over at your house
    - Outing to favorite fast-food restaurant
    - Money
    - Snacks
    - Tokens that can be cashed in for a larger reward or privilege at a later date

POSITIVE INCIDENT REPORT

1. Describe an incident where you showed good anger control.

    _____
    _____
    _____
    _____

2. How did you show your anger?

    _____
    _____
    _____
    _____

3. What strategies did you use to control your anger?

    _____
    _____
    _____
    _____

4. How did you feel about yourself after the incident?

    _____
    _____
    _____

5. How did other people respond to how you showed your anger?

    _____
    _____
    _____
    _____

6. What, if anything, would you do differently if you were faced with a similar problem in the future?

    _____
    _____
    _____

NEGATIVE INCIDENT REPORT

1. Describe an incident where you showed poor control of your anger.

    _____

    _____

    _____

    _____

2. What were you angry about?

    _____

    _____

    _____

    _____

3. How did other people respond to your anger?

    _____

    _____

    _____

    _____

4. What were the consequences of your angry outburst or aggressive behavior?

    _____

    _____

    _____

    _____

5. What would you do differently if you had to do it all over again? How would you handle your anger?

    _____

    _____

    _____

6. What can you do to solve the problem with the other person(s) in the future?

    _____

    _____

    _____

ANGER CONTROL CONTRACT

I, _____, would like to work on controlling my aggressive behaviors. Ag-
    (Name)
gressive behaviors are defined as the following: _____
                                                      (List specific behaviors)

_____

_____

_____

If _____ displays good control of his/her anger and demonstrates
      (Name of client)

_____ aggressive behavior(s) or less per day/week (circle one), then
      (Frequency)

_____ will receive the following reward: _____
      (Name of client)

_____

_____

_____

_____

_____

If _____ shows poor control of his/her anger and becomes aggressive
      (Name of client)

_____ or more time(s) in the next day/week (circle one), then _____
 (Frequency)   (Name of client)

will receive the following consequence: _____

_____

_____

_____

In witness of this contract, we have signed our names on this date: _____
                                                                        (Month/Day/Year)

_____   _____

Signature of Client   Signature of Parent

_____   _____

Signature of Parent   Signature of Teacher or Therapist

STOP YELLING

GOALS OF THE EXERCISE

1. Decrease frequency and severity of angry, verbal outbursts (e.g., yelling, screaming, swearing).
2. Identify the consequences that yelling and screaming have on self and others.
3. Explore underlying emotions that contribute to angry outbursts.
4. Express anger through appropriate verbalizations and/or healthy physical outlets.

ADDITIONAL PROBLEMS FOR WHICH THIS EXERCISE MAY BE MOST USEFUL

- Attention-Deficit/Hyperactivity Disorder (ADHD)
- Conduct Disorder
- Mania/Hypomania
- Oppositional Defiant

SUGGESTIONS FOR PROCESSING THIS EXERCISE WITH THE CLIENT

This exercise is specifically designed for clients who frequently yell, scream, and swear when they are angry. In processing the client's responses, the therapist should help the client identify what he/she hopes to accomplish by yelling. The client is asked to consider both the potential benefits and negative consequences of yelling. It is hoped that the client will also be able to identify other underlying emotions that he/she may be experiencing other than anger. Finally, the assignment will help the client identify more adaptive ways to express and/or manage his/her anger and other emotions.

STOP YELLING

Please answer the following questions to help your therapist, family members, and yourself gain a greater understanding of the factors contributing to your angry outbursts. The exercise may also help to identify other emotions you may feel when you yell, scream, or swear at others. Finally, it is hoped that this exercise will help you find better ways to express your anger and other emotions.

1. What do you often hope to accomplish by yelling or screaming at others? What message are you trying to send by yelling?

_____

_____

_____

_____

2. What, if any, are the positive consequences of your yelling? (For example, parents back down to avoid argument or you are able to intimidate siblings.)

_____

_____

_____

_____

3. What are the negative consequences of your yelling at others?

_____

_____

_____

_____

4. How do your parents react to your angry outbursts?

_____

_____

_____

_____

5. It is not unusual for people to experience other emotions when they are feeling very angry. Take a few minutes to consider what other emotions you commonly feel when you get so angry that you yell. Please check the other emotions that you feel.

____ Sadness	____ Nervousness
____ Hurt	____ Tension
____ Disappointment	____ Fear
____ Loneliness	____ Insecurity
____ Rejection	____ Inferiority
____ Emptiness	____ Embarrassment
____ Jealousy	____ Shame
____ Confusion	____ Guilt

6 Please describe a recent incident when your anger masked a deeper feeling (such as sadness, hurt, fear, etc.).

_____

_____

_____

_____

7. Unfortunately, other people often fail to recognize these other feelings because they are reacting to your yelling or screaming. What is a better way to express these other feelings?

_____

_____

_____

_____

8. What are other more effective ways to express your anger besides yelling and screaming?

_____

_____

_____

_____

9. What could your parents, family members, or teachers say or do (or not say or stop doing) that could help you express your anger better and not yell as much?

_____

_____

_____

_____

FINDING AND LOSING YOUR ANXIETY

GOALS OF THE EXERCISE

1. Identify what precipitates the feelings of anxiety.
2. Increase the ability to verbalize thoughts and feelings about what brings on anxiety.
3. Explore options for coping with or resolving the feelings of anxiety.
4. Develop two specific ways to cope with anxious feelings.

ADDITIONAL PROBLEMS FOR WHICH THIS EXERCISE MAY BE MOST USEFUL

- Panic/Agoraphobia
- Runaway
- Social Phobia/Shyness

SUGGESTIONS FOR PROCESSING THIS EXERCISE WITH THE CLIENT

Anxiety, or nervousness, can often be something that is hard to pin down. It can certainly be seen in adolescents, but getting at just what might be the specific cause is difficult and often elusive. Anxieties often disappear and change with time. The important thing is for adolescents to develop the ability to talk about their anxieties with someone they trust and someone who will take what they have to say seriously. Therefore, it is important not to say that feelings do not make sense or to offer some rational explanation as to why this cannot be. Instead, it is essential to just listen, accept, and encourage. Acceptance and encouragement of sharing of feelings can either help specifically identify what the source of the anxiety is or help reduce the anxiety through desensitization and extinction.

FINDING AND LOSING YOUR ANXIETY

There are many things that can make a person feel anxious or nervous. In order to feel better, it is important to identify exactly what makes you anxious. Find in the following word search these items that can make some of us feel anxious or nervous:

Monsters	Storms	Death	Mistakes	Fighting
Bugs	Dark	Yelling	Divorce	
Snakes	Strangers	Noises	Arguing	

Complete the following word search.

S	T	O	R	M	S	K	R	A	D	S
R	P	E	V	J	O	S	S	Y	I	E
E	R	L	K	F	E	N	T	G	V	K
T	D	E	A	T	H	A	R	N	O	A
S	L	U	K	W	R	K	A	I	R	T
N	P	S	R	G	N	E	N	T	C	S
O	I	B	U	G	S	S	G	H	E	I
M	T	I	A	C	E	D	E	G	B	M
C	N	O	I	S	E	S	R	I	U	T
G	N	I	L	L	E	Y	S	F	K	O

1. Name three things that make you feel anxious or nervous.

    A. _____

    B. _____

    C. _____

2. Choose one of the three things that makes you feel the most anxious.

3. When you experience this anxious feeling, which of the following things happen to you? (Circle at least one.)

    Hands sweat

    Get angry

    Become fearful

    Call for help

    Run to a safe place

    Heart beats faster

    Feel physically sick

    Try to think or do something else quick

    Start talking to anyone who is nearby

    Become short of breath

    Freeze and do nothing

    Try not to let others know by acting okay

    Other reactions to feeling anxious are: _____

4. What have you tried that helps you get over feeling nervous?

    _____
    _____
    _____
    _____
    _____

5. What has worked the best?

    _____
    _____
    _____
    _____
    _____

6. Now ask two people who you trust the following questions:

    A. Do you ever feel anxious?   1. Yes   No
                                          2. Yes   No

    B. What makes you anxious?   1. _____
                                          2. _____

C. How do you handle the anxiety
you feel?

1. _____

_____

2. _____

_____

7. Either from the input you received from others or from an idea you have, create another possible way to handle your anxious feelings.

_____

_____

_____

_____

GETTING IT DONE

GOALS OF THE EXERCISE

1. Complete school and homework assignments on a regular, consistent basis.
2. Develop positive study skills and work habits.
3. Parents maintain regular communication with the teacher(s) to increase the client's compliance with completion of school and homework assignments.
4. Parents and teacher(s) structure reinforcement of client's completion of school and homework assignments by utilizing reward system.

ADDITIONAL PROBLEMS FOR WHICH THIS EXERCISE MAY BE MOST USEFUL

- Academic Underachievement
- Conduct Disorder/Delinquency
- Low Self-Esteem
- Oppositional Defiant

SUGGESTIONS FOR PROCESSING THIS EXERCISE WITH THE CLIENT

It is not uncommon for adolescents with an Attention-Deficit/Hyperactivity Disorder (ADHD) to have difficulty completing their school or homework assignments on a regular, consistent basis. Many clients with ADHD require increased structure or supervision to complete their schoolwork regularly. The increased supervision or structure often requires frequent communication between the home and school. In this program, the parents and teacher(s) are asked to maintain open lines of communication through the use of daily or weekly progress reports. The teacher(s) is asked to send home a daily or weekly progress report to the parents, informing them as to how well their son or daughter is doing at keeping up with and completing school assignments. The frequency of the progress reports, either daily or weekly, should depend on several factors: the child's age, motivation, and how responsible he/she is about completing his/her school or homework assignments. Encourage the parents and teacher(s) to implement a reward system to reinforce the client for completing the work.

GETTING IT DONE

PARENTS' INSTRUCTIONS

Adolescents who have been diagnosed as having an Attention-Deficit/Hyperactivity Disorder (ADHD) often have difficulty completing school assignments on a regular basis. They may have trouble completing their work for a variety of reasons. Adolescents with ADHD frequently display problems with their organizational skills. Their short attention spans and distractibility interfere with their ability to stay focused on tasks for long periods of time. They may not be listening well when the teacher provides important instructions or assigns homework. The adolescent with ADHD may forget to record important school assignments or may fail to bring home the books or materials necessary to complete the assignment. Perhaps, even more frustrating for some parents, they may actually complete the assignment, but then they forget to turn it in or misplace it along the way. If this sounds familiar to you, then try this program to increase your child's compliance with completing school and homework assignments.

1. The goal of this program is to help your adolescent complete his/her school or homework assignments on a regular basis. This program recognizes your adolescent's need for increased structure and supervision in accomplishing this goal. In this plan of action, parents and teachers are encouraged to maintain open lines of communication with one another. The teachers are requested to send home a daily or weekly progress report, informing you as to how well your adolescent is doing at completing his/her school/homework assignments. Review this progress report at the end of each day or week. The frequency of the progress reports will depend on your child's age, attitude, and degree of responsibility in completing the schoolwork.

    In order for the program to be effective, cooperation among the parents, teacher(s), and adolescent is important. Teachers are encouraged to fill out the Daily or Weekly School Report, which is provided on the following pages. They should check whether the adolescent has completed his/her expected amount of work or note any uncompleted school assignments. A space is also provided for the teacher to record any additional homework. Parents should review the report with the adolescent, initial the form, and send it back to the teacher. Space is provided on the Daily or Weekly School Report form for teachers or parents to record any additional comments. The adolescent's cooperation is an important ingredient in the success of this program. The adolescent should be informed in advance that the program is starting. He/she should be told that he/she will be responsible for bringing the progress report home at the end of each day or week. He/she will also be expected to bring home any books, important papers, or materials necessary to complete his/her assignments. Failure to do so should result in a consequence or loss of reward.

2. Parents and teachers are encouraged to use a reward system to reinforce the adolescent for completing his/her school/homework assignments. The adolescent should be positively reinforced for completing all school or homework assignments at the end of each day or week. Use the following contract form as a means of formalizing the agreement with your adolescent. Post the contract prominently in the adolescent's room or on the refrigerator as a reminder to complete his/her work. Talk with your adolescent about appropriate rewards that can be used to reinforce responsible behavior. A list of potential rewards follows:

   • Allow extra time to spend watching television or playing video games

   • Spend one-on-one time with mother or father (e.g., attend a movie, exercise together, play a board game)

   • Extended bedtime

   • Extra time on telephone or computer

   • Purchase extra cell phone minutes

   • Allow adolescent to invite a friend over or go over to a friend's house after school

   • Allow adolescent to invite a friend to sleep over at house

   • Outing to favorite fast-food restaurant

   • Money

   • Snacks

   • Tokens that can be cashed in for a larger reward or privilege at a later date

DAILY SCHOOL REPORT

Name: _____   Date: _____

_____

School: _____   Grade: _____

_____

Subject	Teacher	Classroom Work Check if completed (✓); note uncompleted assignments	Homework

Additional Comments:

_____

_____

_____

_____

_____

_____

_____

_____

_____

_____

WEEKLY SCHOOL REPORT

Name: _____ Week from: _____ to: _____

Grade: _____

Subject	Teacher	Classroom Work Check if completed (✓); note uncompleted assignments	Homework

Additional Comments:

_____

_____

_____

_____

_____

_____

_____

_____

_____

_____

_____

_____

SCHOOL CONTRACT

If _____, a student at _____, completes all of
          (Name of client)   (School name)

his/her school or homework assignments by the end of each day/week (circle one),

then _____ will receive the following reward:
          (Name of client)

_____

_____

_____

_____

_____

_____

_____

_____

_____

In witness of this contract, we have signed our names on this date: _____
                                                                          (Month/Day/Year)

_____   _____

Signature of Client   Signature of Parent

_____   _____

Signature of Parent   Signature of Teacher or Therapist

SOCIAL SKILLS EXERCISE

GOALS OF THE EXERCISE

1. Develop more appropriate social skills.
2. Increase positive interactions with peers and authority figures.
3. Learn self-monitoring techniques to help assess social skills.
4. Identify and reinforce positive behaviors that will enable the establishment and maintenance of peer friendships.

ADDITIONAL PROBLEMS FOR WHICH THIS EXERCISE MAY BE MOST USEFUL

- Autism/Pervasive Developmental Disorder
- Conduct Disorder/Delinquency
- Mania/Hypomania
- Oppositional Defiant
- Peer/Sibling Conflict
- Social Phobia/Shyness

SUGGESTIONS FOR PROCESSING THIS EXERCISE WITH THE CLIENT

This exercise is designed to teach self-monitoring techniques to adolescents with an Attention-Deficit/Hyperactivity Disorder (ADHD) to improve their social skills. The parent(s), teacher(s), client, and therapist are encouraged to sit down as a team to identify specific social behaviors that the client needs to work on and improve. The client, with the assistance of his/her team, selects various social skills that he/she would like to practice each day or over the course of a week. Model the appropriate social behaviors for the client in the therapy sessions through the use of role-playing and behavioral rehearsal. Encourage the client to use a self-monitoring form as a reminder to practice the desired social skills and to assess his/her performance.

SOCIAL SKILLS EXERCISE
PARENT/TEACHER INSTRUCTIONS

Adolescents with an Attention-Deficit/Hyperactivity Disorder (ADHD) often experience problems in their interpersonal relationships with both peers and adults. They become entangled in more arguments and disputes with others because of their impulsivity, intrusiveness, aggressive behaviors, and poor social skills. They annoy or antagonize others with their silly behaviors, teasing, and name-calling. The ADHD adolescent, in turn, is frequently teased or picked on by his/her peers because of his or her own annoying behaviors. In this exercise, the adolescent will use a self-monitoring form to focus on improving specific social skills.

1. Meet with the adolescent to identify and select the specific social skills that you would like him or her to practice each day or over the course of a week. Be specific in defining the desired social behaviors so that the adolescent clearly understands what is expected of him/her. Model the positive social behaviors through the use of role-playing. The following is a list of suggested social skills that the adolescent can practice.

    *   Compliment peers or siblings
    *   Accept compliments from others
    *   Show respect for thoughts, feelings, and needs of others
    *   Express feelings in an appropriate and assertive manner
    *   Apologize for misbehaviors
    *   Respond to losing or failure by displaying good self-control
    *   Perform a favor for someone without expecting anything in return
    *   Demonstrate kindness to peers
    *   Express thanks and appreciation
    *   Ignore teasing or name-calling
    *   Share personal items
    *   Cooperate in a game or activity without arguing
    *   Give others a turn or allow others to go first
    *   Start conversations

- Introduce yourself to new or unfamiliar peers
- Raise hand before blurting out answers in the classroom

2. Instruct the adolescent to use the Social Skills Self-Monitoring Form on the following page to help improve his/her social skills. Place the self-monitoring form in a readily accessible place, such as in his/her notebook or on the refrigerator. Space is also provided on the form to record when and how effective the adolescent was in practicing the skill.

3. Use a reward system to reinforce the adolescent for his/her positive social behaviors. The reward system will help maintain his/her interest and motivation for practicing the social skills. Please use the Social Skills Contract to identify the specific target behaviors.

SOCIAL SKILLS SELF-MONITORING FORM

Name:_____ Date:_____

Choose a social skill from the following list or write in one of your own ideas to practice.

Suggested Social Skills

- Compliment others
- Ignore teasing or name-calling
- Do a favor for someone
- Start a conversation
- Share your personal items
- Wait your turn patiently
- _____

- Express feelings in an appropriate manner
- Show kindness to peers
- Cooperate in a game or activity
- Introduce yourself to a new person
- Listen to others' concerns or problems
- _____
- _____

I will practice this skill today:

_____

_____

_____

Record incidents in which you practiced the social skill:

1. Name of person:_____ Location:_____

    Comments: _____

    _____

    _____

2. Name of person:_____ Location:_____

    Comments: _____

    _____

    _____

3. Name of person:_____ Location:_____

    Comments: _____

    _____

    _____

SOCIAL SKILLS CONTRACT

If _____ practices the following social skill _____
       (Child's name)   (Social skill)

_____ time(s) in the next day or week (circle one), then _____
(Frequency)   (Child's name)

will receive the following reward:

_____

_____

_____

_____

_____

In witness of this contract, we have signed our names on this date: _____
                                                                                   (Month/Day/Year)

_____   _____

Signature of Child   Signature of Parent

_____   _____

Signature of Parent   Signature of Teacher or Therapist

STOP, THINK, AND ACT

GOALS OF THE EXERCISE

1. Develop coping strategy to inhibit the tendency toward impulsive responding.
2. Increase awareness on how impulsive behaviors lead to negative consequences for self and others.
3. Identify problem and explore alternative courses of action before making final decision to act.
4. Learn to evaluate own behavior and how it affects self and others.

ADDITIONAL PROBLEMS FOR WHICH THIS EXERCISE MAY BE MOST USEFUL

- Anger Management
- Conduct Disorder/Delinquency
- Mania/Hypomania
- Oppositional Defiant

SUGGESTIONS FOR PROCESSING THIS EXERCISE WITH THE CLIENT

Adolescents with an Attention-Deficit/Hyperactivity Disorder (ADHD) are characterized by their tendency to exercise poor judgment and act without considering the consequences of their actions. The ADHD client frequently finds him/herself in trouble without realizing what caused him/her to get there, and fails to recognize the antecedents of his/her negative consequences. In this exercise, the client is taught a basic problem-solving strategy to help inhibit impulses. The client first identifies a problem and then works through the subsequent problem-solving stages. This exercise can be used with other adolescents who do not have ADHD, but who have problems with impulse control.

STOP, THINK, AND ACT

Adolescents with an Attention-Deficit/Hyperactivity Disorder (ADHD) often find themselves in trouble without realizing what caused them to get there. It is not uncommon for the ADHD teenager to try to solve problems by quickly rushing into a situation without stopping and thinking about the possible consequences of his/her actions. The failure to stop and think causes negative consequences for both self and others. If this sounds all too familiar and you are tired of finding yourself in trouble because of your failure to stop and think, then this exercise is designed for you. In this exercise, you are taught to use basic problem-solving steps to deal with a stressful situation. By following these steps, you will hopefully find yourself in less trouble with others and feel better about yourself.

1. The first step in solving any problem is to realize that a problem exists. At this beginning stage, you are asked to identify either a major problem that you are currently facing or a common recurring problem that troubles you. Talk with your parents, teachers, friends, or peers if you have trouble selecting a problem that you would like to focus on solving.

    Identify the problem:

    _____

    _____

    _____

    _____

    _____

2. After identifying the problem, consider three different possible courses of action to help you solve or deal with the problem. List the pros and cons of each possible course of action. Record at least three different pros and cons for each course of action.

    First possible course of action to be taken:

    _____

    _____

    _____

Pros   **Cons**

_____   _____

_____   _____

_____   _____

_____   _____

Second possible course of action to be taken:

_____

_____

_____

Pros   **Cons**

_____   _____

_____   _____

_____   _____

_____   _____

Third possible course of action to be taken:

_____

_____

_____

Pros   **Cons**

_____   _____

_____   _____

_____   _____

_____   _____

3. Next, review the pros and cons of each one of your possible courses of action. At this point, you are encouraged to talk with a teacher, parent, friend, or peer to help you choose a final plan of action.

4. Identify the course of action that you plan to follow:

_____

_____

_____

5. What factors influenced you to choose this course of action?

_____

_____

_____

_____

6. What advice or input did you receive from others that influenced your decision?

_____

_____

_____

_____

7. Now it is time to follow through on your plan of action. In the space provided, describe the events that occurred when you followed through with your plan of action.

_____

_____

_____

_____

_____

_____

_____

_____

_____

_____

You are in the final stage of this exercise. You have identified the problem, considered different possible courses of action, made a decision, and followed through on your plan of action. Your final task is to evaluate the results or success of your plan of action. Please respond to the following questions.

8. What were the results of your plan of action?

_____

_____

_____

_____

9.   How do you feel about the results?

_____

_____

_____

_____

10. How did your plan affect both you and others?

_____

_____

_____

_____

11. What did you learn from this experience?

_____

_____

_____

_____

12. What, if anything, would you do differently if you were faced with the same or a similar problem in the future?

_____

_____

_____

_____

_____

_____

MANAGING THE MELTDOWNS

GOALS OF THE EXERCISE

1. Parents identify the frequency, intensity, and nature of the client's emotional outbursts or meltdowns.
2. Parents develop an understanding of the precipitating events or factors that contribute to the emergence of the emotional outbursts or meltdowns.
3. Parents implement effective coping strategies or disciplinary techniques to help them manage or deal with the client's emotional outbursts.
4. Decrease the frequency and intensity of emotional outbursts or meltdowns.

ADDITIONAL PROBLEMS FOR WHICH THIS EXERCISE MAY BE MOST USEFUL

*   Anger Management
*   Attention-Deficit/Hyperactivity Disorder (ADHD)
*   Mania/Hypomania
*   Psychoticism

SUGGESTIONS FOR PROCESSING THIS EXERCISE WITH THE CLIENT

It is recommended that this assignment be utilized in the early stage of treatment to help the therapist gain a clearer picture of the nature of the client's emotional outbursts or meltdowns. In the assignment, the parents are asked to step back and reflect on the precipitating events or factors that contribute to the emergence of their son/daughter's emotional outbursts or meltdowns. The assignment will hopefully help the parents recognize what strategies have been useful in managing the client's meltdowns. At the same time, it is hoped that the parents will cease using any strategies or interventions that have not proven to be effective over time. The assignment concludes with the parents being given the opportunity to ask any specific questions that they may have about how to manage their son/daughter's emotional outbursts or meltdowns.

MANAGING THE MELTDOWNS

It is not uncommon for children or adolescents with an Autistic Disorder, Asperger's Disorder, or Pervasive Developmental Disorder to exhibit emotional outbursts or meltdowns. At times, the outbursts may seem to come out of the blue. Please respond to the following items or questions to help your therapist gain a clearer picture of the nature and context of your son/daughter's emotional outbursts or meltdowns.

1. Please describe a typical emotional outburst or meltdown by your son/daughter.

    _____

    _____

    _____

    _____

    _____

2. On the average, how often do the outbursts occur? (For example, how many times per day, week, or month?)

    _____

    _____

    _____

3. What factors or events frequently cause your son/daughter to experience an emotional outburst or meltdown? Review the following list and place a checkmark next to all the events or factors that contribute to the emergence of your son/daughter's outbursts.

    ____ Negative reaction to change

    ____ Excessive stimulation in surrounding environment

    ____ Loud noises

    ____ Interrupting child's routine or stopping his/her repetitive behavior

    ____ Difficulty in shifting from engaging in pleasurable activity to being required to work

    ____ Difficulty accepting "no"

    ____ Being told to do something he/she does not want to do

    ____ Teasing or name-calling by siblings and peers

    ____ Losing or failure

____ Failure to perform a new task

____ Exposure to a feared object

____ Unable to shift response to meet demands of new situation

4. If the items listed do not identify the factors contributing to your son/daughter's emotional outbursts or meltdowns, then what other factors or events frequently cause your son/daughter to lose control of his/her emotions?

    _____

    _____

    _____

    _____

5. How do you generally respond to your son/daughter's emotional outbursts or melt-downs?

    _____

    _____

    _____

    _____

6. What have you found to be helpful in managing or dealing with your son/daughter's outbursts?

    _____

    _____

    _____

    _____

7. On the other hand, what strategies or interventions have you not found to be helpful in dealing with your son/daughter's emotional outbursts or meltdowns?

    _____

    _____

    _____

    _____

8. What specific questions do you have for your therapist about how to deal with your son/daughter's emotional outbursts?

    A. _____

    B. _____

    C. _____

    D. _____

    E. _____

PROGRESS SURVEY

GOALS OF THE EXERCISE

1. Parents rate level of satisfaction with the client's progress in different areas of functioning.
2. Parents establish specific goals for the client to strive to achieve in therapy and/or at school.
3. Parents arrange for the client to receive appropriate resources and services to address areas of weakness or concern.

ADDITIONAL PROBLEMS FOR WHICH THIS EXERCISE MAY BE MOST USEFUL

- Academic Underachievement
- Mental Retardation
- Psychoticism

SUGGESTIONS FOR PROCESSING THIS EXERCISE WITH THE CLIENT

In this assignment, the parents are asked to complete a survey assessing their satisfaction with the client's progress or growth in different areas of adaptive functioning. The parents' responses will also shed insight into their degree of satisfaction or frustration with the support services or resources that the client has already received. The therapist can help assess whether the client has been receiving sufficient or appropriate services. The therapist and parents together can identify what services they would like the client to receive in the future. Use the survey to establish specific goals for the client in therapy or at school. The therapist should consult with the parents about whether they want to share their thoughts, feelings, or concerns with school officials. The parents' responses may be helpful in formulating specific goals for the client at his/her next Individualized Educational Planning (IEP) meeting.

PROGRESS SURVEY

This survey gives you the opportunity to share your thoughts and feelings about your son or daughter's progress or growth in different areas of functioning. Please respond to the following questions or items.

1. Using the scale that follows, rate your level of satisfaction with your son/daughter's progress or growth in the identified areas. Place the appropriate number in the blank space next to each area.

1	2	3	4	5	6
Very satisfied	Satisfied	Neutral	Dissatisfied	Very dissatisfied	Not applicable (or not area of concern)

____ Overall Academic Performance

____ Reading

____ Mathematics

____ Written Language

____ Speech/Language Development

____ Expressive Language Skills

____ Receptive Language Skills

____ Daily Communication Skills

____ Overall Motor/Physical Development

____ Gross Motor Skills (e.g., running, jumping)

____ Fine Motor Skills (e.g., writing, eating)

____ Daily Living Skills

____ Vocational Skills Development

____ Adaptation Skills (e.g., ability to adapt to change in routine or to new social situations)

____ Overall Social Development

____ Daily Social Skills (e.g., eye contact, greeting others)

____ Peer Relationships

___ Ability to Establish/Maintain Friendships

___ Family Relationships

___ Behavior at School

___ Behavior at Home or in Community

___ Overall Emotional Development

___ Stability of Moods

___ Ability to Control Emotions or Impulses

2.   In what area(s) are you most pleased with your son/daughter's growth or progress?

_____

_____

_____

_____

3.   What factors have contributed to your son/daughter's progress in these area(s)? (For example, what services, resources, or individuals have helped your child grow?)

_____

_____

_____

4.   In what area(s) are you most concerned or frustrated with your son/daughter's lack of progress?

_____

_____

_____

_____

5.   What factors have contributed to your son/daughter's lack of progress?

_____

_____

_____

6.   What specific behavior or skills would you like to see your son/daughter improve on in therapy or the current school year? or, What goals would you like to see your child attempt to achieve?

_____

_____

7. What resources or support services do you think your child will need in the next year?

_____

_____

_____

_____

8. What stressors or obstacles do you foresee your son/daughter as having to face or overcome in order to achieve his/her identified goals?

_____

_____

_____

9. What worries or concerns do you have for your son/daughter as he/she moves through the teenage years toward becoming a young adult?

_____

_____

_____

_____

A FEW THINGS ABOUT ME

GOALS OF THE EXERCISE

1. Exchange information between old and new family members.
2. Begin to develop connections between old and new family members.
3. Increase openness and sharing between family members.

ADDITIONAL PROBLEMS FOR WHICH THIS EXERCISE MAY BE MOST USEFUL

*   Adoption
*   Low Self-Esteem
*   Social Phobia/Shyness

SUGGESTIONS FOR PROCESSING THIS EXERCISE WITH THE CLIENT

The mutual sharing of things about ourselves is a significant way in which we make connections to others and for others to feel connected to us. This exercise is a way of promoting the beginning of that process in a nonthreatening manner. It can be done with one family and a new stepparent or both families and stepparents. Members should be encouraged to ask questions about their shared responses. This questioning may need to be modeled to members by the therapist at the start of the session. As the process proceeds, the therapist should step back, be less actively involved, and be more of a facilitator. If all the information cannot be shared in a session, the family can be given an assignment of setting a time to finish it at home and report how it went at the next session.

A FEW THINGS ABOUT ME

Each family member should complete all of the following sections and attach pictures of themselves to the center of the paper. You may share the information in a family therapy session or family gathering at home.

FAVORITES

Food: _____

Restaurant: _____

Sport/hobby: _____

DATES
(3 important dates in your life)

1. _____

2. _____

3. _____

← Past Picture   Present Picture →

LIKES/DISLIKES

BEST	**Likes**	**Dislikes**
Best friend: _____	1. _____	1. _____
Best holiday: _____	2. _____	2. _____
Best vacation: _____	3. _____	3. _____

STEPPARENT AND SIBLING QUESTIONNAIRE

GOALS OF THE EXERCISE

1. Identify thoughts and feelings about having new family members and a new family unit.
2. Verbalize acceptance of the new family arrangement and commitment to making it work.
3. Increase awareness and commitment to what can be done to help make this new family arrangement work.

ADDITIONAL PROBLEMS FOR WHICH THIS EXERCISE MAY BE MOST USEFUL

*   Divorce Reaction
*   Parenting

SUGGESTIONS FOR PROCESSING THIS EXERCISE WITH THE CLIENT

The processing of this exercise is best directed toward expanding the client's overall awareness of his/her thoughts and feelings about having new members in his/her family. The exercise can also help to identify the barriers the client has regarding the members coming together as a new family unit. Finally, the last portion of the exercise is directed toward eliciting a commitment from the client to do what he/she can to bring everyone together as a working family unit. The exercise could be shared and processed in a family session if the client is not overly resistant to the idea.

STEPPARENT AND SIBLING QUESTIONNAIRE

Complete the following questionnaire and then discuss your responses with your therapist.

1. What are some of the things that you like and dislike about having a stepparent?

    Likes: Dislikes:

    _____   _____
    _____   _____
    _____   _____

2. What are some of the things that you like and dislike about having stepbrothers and stepsisters (if there are any)?

    Likes: Dislikes:

    _____   _____
    _____   _____
    _____   _____

3. How comfortable are you at this point in time being a part of this "new" family?

Uncomfortable	A little	So-so	Quite comfortable	Very comfortable

    Explain: _____

    _____

4. How comfortable do you think your stepparent is with the new family?

Uncomfortable	A little	So-so	Quite comfortable	Very comfortable

    Explain: _____

    _____

5. If I like my stepparent, how disloyal will that be to my parent?

Not at all	A little	Some	Quite	A lot

6. How much time/attention do you want from a stepparent?

Very little	A little	Some	Quite a lot	A lot

7. How would you like your stepparent to introduce you to others? (check one)

____ My son/daughter   ____ My stepson/stepdaughter   ____ Just my first name

8. How do you plan to introduce your stepparent to others? (check one)

____ My stepparent   ____ First name

____ My dad/mom   ____ Avoid if possible

9. What I would not like my stepparent to do is:

____ Talk negatively about my dad

____ Talk negatively about my mom

____ Act like he/she is my "real" parent

____ Try too hard to make me like him/her

____ Be too affectionate with my parent in front of me

____ Be the "boss" or main disciplinarian

____ Mention often how much I am costing him/her

10. One thing my parent could do to make us feel more like a family is:

_____

_____

11. One thing my stepparent could do to make us feel more like a family is:

_____

_____

12. One thing my stepbrother/stepsister could do to make us feel more like a family is:

_____

_____

13. One thing I could do to make us feel more like a family is:

_____

_____

KEEPING STRAIGHT

GOALS OF THE EXERCISE

1. Increase understanding of the nature of relapse triggers.
2. Identify specific personal relapse triggers.
3. Develop strategies for dealing effectively with each identified trigger.
4. Increase skill of recognizing and expressing feelings.

ADDITIONAL PROBLEMS FOR WHICH THIS EXERCISE MAY BE MOST USEFUL

- Anxiety
- Depression
- Panic/Agoraphobia
- Sexual Abuse Perpetrator

SUGGESTIONS FOR PROCESSING THIS EXERCISE WITH THE CLIENT

Relapse is a major component of chemical dependence. The chemically dependent person must be aware of the "Big Bad Wolf" always waiting at the door and plan how to effectively deal with that reality. Go over this homework in a thorough manner since the client's sobriety depends on it, and it is important to bring that very point home. Encourage and challenge the client to expand his or her awareness of what triggers are and to develop alternative ways to handle them. Give positive verbal feedback when the client identifies a major trigger and develops solid, creative ways of dealing with that trigger.

KEEPING STRAIGHT

To avoid relapsing, you must be aware of your triggers and have some constructive ways to handle them when they confront you, as they surely will. A trigger is, according to *Webster's 9th New Collegiate,* "something that acts like a mechanical trigger in initiating a process or reaction." Of course, your process or reaction is wanting to drink or use a drug again. To reduce this risk, you need to become more aware of what triggers exist for you and how you might deal effectively with each of them. Complete the following exercise to help you to do just that.

People, Places, and Things

Each of the these can in many different ways be a trigger. Under each, list two ways you can imagine it being a trigger for you. Then think of two things or ways with which you can effectively handle the trigger.

1. People

    Example: An old friend who I drank or used drugs with drops by.

    a. Keep visit short.
    b. Change subject or say I don't care to talk about using.

    _____

    _____

2. Places

    Example: Invited to attend a rock concert.

    a. Go with a nonusing friend.
    b. Take your own transportation so you can leave if you feel uncomfortable.

    _____

    _____

3. Things

   Example: The first warm Friday night of summer vacation.

   a. Have plans to do something with sober friends or family.
   b. Attend an AA or NA meeting and spend time afterward with sponsor.

   _____   _____

   _____   _____

   _____   _____

   _____

Thinking Errors

4. Having old thoughts or thought patterns come back is a trigger. Recall two thoughts you need to be aware of and two ways to effectively handle them.

   Example: There's no fun without partying.

   a. Remember the negative results of the partying.
   b. I need to find how others have fun without partying.

   _____   _____

   _____   _____

   _____   _____

   _____

Feelings

5. Recovering from chemical dependence involves coming to recognize how we feel and to cope with feelings in ways that are not self-defeating. Since this is new territory and very important in terms of avoiding a relapse, we will begin with the AA saying "HALT," which stands for not allowing yourself to become too Hungry, Angry, Lonely, or Tired. Each of these are feelings that need to be taken care of. You can begin to do so by developing two ways you can positively deal with each of them.

   Hungry a. _____

   b. _____

   Angry a. _____

   b. _____

   Lonely a. _____

   b. _____

   Tired a. _____

   b. _____

6. Also, you need to be aware of what are commonly referred to as *negative feelings,* feelings that make us uncomfortable. Select two feelings from the following group that you have difficulty handling. Then list one way you can start to cope with the feeling more directly.

Hurt	Pain	Depression	Sadness
Guilt	Worry	Embarrassment	Joy

Feeling   **Coping Mechanism**

_____   _____

                                                _____

                                                _____

_____   _____

                                                _____

                                                _____

Now that you have completed this exercise, you can make it a working part of your relapse prevention plan.

TAKING YOUR FIRST STEP

GOALS OF THE EXERCISE

1. Decrease level of denial about the ways in which substance abuse has affected life.
2. Increase openness and honesty about self and how abuse of substances has negatively impacted life.
3. Verbally identify self as chemically dependent.
4. Make a verbal commitment to total abstinence.

ADDITIONAL PROBLEMS FOR WHICH THIS EXERCISE MAY BE MOST USEFUL

- Attention-Deficit/Hyperactivity Disorder (ADHD)
- Conduct Disorder/Delinquency
- Mania/Hypomania
- Oppositional Defiant

SUGGESTIONS FOR PROCESSING THIS EXERCISE WITH THE CLIENT

Arriving at the point of looking at yourself, your substance abuse, and how it has affected the totality of your life is a momentous step. In processing this assignment, the most important thing to keep up front is the need to expand the client's openness and willingness to disclose. This will most likely require a balance of encouragement/positive feedback and gentle open-ended questions that will promote increased disclosure and recognition of the effect of substance use on the client's life. Remember, these clients are often from family units where someone is chemically dependent, making them very guarded. If you encounter a situation where honesty is minimal, encourage the client to take and share this section with an AA/NA member or as a topic at an AA meeting to gain the input of others. Then have the client bring what input he/she has gathered back to your next session for additional processing. In addition to avoiding a strong area of denial, this will offer an opportunity, if he/she follows through, to affirm the client's seriousness about being drug-free.

TAKING YOUR FIRST STEP

None of us remember the first step we took walking, but we know intellectually what it meant and can recall our parents' recounting of that momentous occasion. Mao Tse-tung said of his Chinese people's Long March that it would never have happened without the first step being taken. The same is true for you as you start down a new road without the aid of alcohol or drugs, and this exercise will help.

Personal History

1. Give a description of the family and home you were a part of as a child (0–12), and then describe your childhood.

   _____

   _____

   _____

   _____

   _____

   _____

   _____

2. How did you feel about yourself as a child, and how do you feel about yourself as a teen?

   _____

   _____

   _____

   _____

   _____

   _____

   _____

3. Which of the following things have happened to you or a member of your family?

    ___ Divorce   ___ Physical abuse   ___ Prison

    ___ Sexual abuse   ___ Mental illness   ___ Untimely death

    ___ Loss of job   ___ ADHD   ___ Depression

    ___ Chronic illness   ___ Bankruptcy   ___ Learning disability

4. How old were you when you experimented with alcohol or drugs for the first time? Describe the situation and what happened.

    _____

    _____

    _____

    _____

    _____

5. List all the substances you have experimented with and asterisk (*) the ones you have used on a regular basis.

    _____

    _____

    _____

    _____

    _____

    _____

6. At what age did you start to use alcohol or drugs on a *regular* basis (at least ten times per month)?

    _____

7. Have any of your family members now or in the past had a problem with alcohol or drugs? If yes, list each and what substance is or was that person's drug of choice.

    _____

    _____

    _____

    _____

Powerlessness

Definition: being unable to stop the alcohol or drug use behavior in spite of the negative consequences that are happening to you.

8. What experiences have you had that convince you that you are powerless over alcohol or drugs?

_____

_____

_____

_____

_____

9. Give two examples in each of the following areas:

A. **Progression** (i.e., the amounts or types of drinking/drug use that have changed over time)

Example: Consuming more alcohol or drugs on each occasion of using.

1. _____
2. _____

B. **Attempts to Control** (i.e., attempting to limit what substance you use each time)

Example: Changing drugs or types of alcohol.

1. _____
2. _____

C. **Preoccupation** (i.e., most of your thinking centers on using or planning the next occasion)

Example: Planning your life around the next party or not being without one to attend.

1. _____
2. _____

D. **Loss of Control** (i.e., can no longer predict how much or how long you will use once you start drinking/drugging)

Example: Using or drinking more than you planned to on a consistent basis.

1. _____
2. _____

E. **Self-Destructive Behaviors** (i.e., jumping into impulsive, foolish, and often dangerous behaviors or activities once you start using or drinking)

Example: Starting aggressive arguments with others.

1. _____
2. _____

F. **Justifying Using** (i.e., creating seemingly logical reasons for your drinking or drugging)

Example: I'm depressed or nervous and need to settle myself down.

1. _____
2. _____

Unmanageability

Definition: the addiction to drugs and/or alcohol has caused your life to be chaotic and damaged.

10. In what ways have you seen your life become unmanageable related to your use of drugs or alcohol?

_____

_____

_____

_____

_____

_____

11. Again, give two examples in each of these areas to show you how unmanageable your drinking/drugging has become:

   A. **Social Life**

   Example: Avoiding or spending just a little time with nonusing friends.

   1. _____

   2. _____

   B. **Physical Health**

   Example: Frequently sick and lack of energy.

   1. _____

   2. _____

   C. **Financial**

   Example: Lack of savings or are frequently broke.

   1. _____

   2. _____

   D. **School**

   Example: Frequently absent, tardy, or sleeping during class.

   1. _____

   2. _____

   E. **Emotional Problems**

   Example: Frequent angry outbursts.

   1. _____

   2. _____

F. **Family Problems**

   Example: No longer see yourself as part of the family.

   1. _____

   2. _____

Now that your have completed this exercise, share it with your sponsor and/or therapist for their feedback and questions. Remember their questions and feedback are given to help strengthen your program and make further growth possible. Work to keep your mind open to what they have to offer.

WELCOME TO RECOVERY

GOALS OF THE EXERCISE

1. Learn the terms that are commonly used in recovery and their meanings.
2. Increase knowledge and understanding of the key elements involved in a successful recovery program.
3. Decrease fear and anxiety about joining recovery support groups.

ADDITIONAL PROBLEMS FOR WHICH THIS EXERCISE MAY BE MOST USEFUL

- Attention-Deficit/Hyperactivity Disorder (ADHD)
- Conduct Disorder/Delinquency
- Grief/Loss Unresolved
- Low Self-Esteem
- Runaway
- Social Phobia/Shyness

SUGGESTIONS FOR PROCESSING THIS EXERCISE WITH THE CLIENT

When one is first sober, it can be frightening for him/her to think of living without the use of alcohol. It is important to reduce that anxiety as much as possible in order to make it easier for him/her to join support groups and to understand the key things that need to be done to stay sober. Subsequently, in processing this exercise, work to develop and encourage an attitude of learning and questioning that can add an element of fun and possibility to this "simple but not easy" program.

WELCOME TO RECOVERY

When getting involved in a recovery program, it can be helpful to be introduced to the terms, language, and concepts that make up the program core. Then, at meetings or with other recovering people, you won't feel so in the dark or out of place. The following exercise will provide you with such an introduction.

1. Terms: Use the following terms to fill in the blanks.

Trigger	Enabler	Higher power	Denial
Relapse	Twelve steps	Recovery	Big book
Sponsor	Sober	Powerlessness	

    A. _ _ _ _ _ _ _ _ _ _ _ _ _

    Inability to have control over stopping the use of alcohol or a drug. (13 letters)

    B. _ _ _ _ _ _   _ _ _ _ _

    Name used by most members to refer to God in a 12-step program. (2 words, 11 letters)

    C. _ _ _ _ _

    State of not using or not being under the influence of alcohol or drugs. (5 letters)

    D. _ _ _   _ _ _ _

    A guide for staying sober. (2 words, 7 letters)

    E. _ _ _ _ _ _   _ _ _ _ _

    Guiding principles of AA/NA that members work in order to stay sober and grow personally. (2 words, 11 letters)

    F. _ _ _ _ _ _ _

    A member of AA/NA, who, upon request of a newer member, acts as a guide/supporter in helping the new member learn the program and stay sober. (7 letters)

    G. _ _ _ _ _ _ _

    A person, place, activity, or feeling that could start the urge to drink or drug. (7 letters)

H. _ _ _ _ _ _

The primary defense used by an addict that keeps him/her using by refusing to admit the truth or acknowledge reality. (6 letters)

I. _ _ _ _ _ _ _

Return to using alcohol and drugs after being sober. (7 letters)

J. _ _ _ _ _ _ _ _

State in which one has stopped using alcohol or drugs for a significant period of time and is involved in a 12-step program. (8 letters)

K. _ _ _ _ _ _ _

A person who is usually a close friend or family member that either knowingly or unknowingly helps make it easier for the addict to continue using. (7 letters)

2. Complete the following word search.

Recovery Groups	**Types of Meetings**
AA (Alcoholics Anonymous)	Open
NA (Narcotics Anonymous)	Closed
Al-anon	First Step
RR (Rational Recovery)	Stag
GA (Gamblers Anonymous)	Barefoot
OA (Overeaters Anonymous)	

F	G	B	C	D	A	A
I	D	A	O	P	E	N
R	D	R	T	L	B	O
S	T	E	P	S	U	N
T	R	F	S	G	M	A
S	C	O	F	O	A	L
T	G	O	L	N	L	A
E	A	T	R	R	W	C
P	B	J	Z	Y	H	I

Sayings of AA, NA, and Other Programs

3. Recovery programs have created many sayings that members often use to help them. These sayings encompass key principles of the program. To help you begin to get familiar with them and what they mean, take your best thoughtful guess at the following sayings. Afterward, see how close you came by asking an AA member, sponsor, or your counselor for an exact meaning.

    A. "Keep it simple" _____

    _____

    _____

    B. "One day at a time" or "Just for today" _____

    _____

    _____

    C. "Avoid slippery places" _____

    _____

    _____

    D. "Let go and let God" or "Turn it over to your Higher Power" _____

    _____

    _____

    E. "Stinking thinking" _____

    _____

    _____

    F. "Progress not perfection" _____

    _____

    _____

    G. "Talking the talk, walking the walk" _____

    _____

    _____

HEADED IN THE RIGHT DIRECTION

GOALS OF THE EXERCISE

1. Demonstrate empathy, concern, and sensitivity toward the thoughts, feelings, and needs of others.
2. Identify and recognize how acting out behaviors negatively impact others.
3. Make restitution for past acting-out and antisocial behaviors.
4. Assist in establishing constructive goals for the future.

ADDITIONAL PROBLEMS FOR WHICH THIS EXERCISE MAY BE MOST USEFUL

- Attention-Deficit/Hyperactivity Disorder (ADHD)
- Chemical Dependence
- Oppositional Defiant
- Sexual Abuse Perpetrator

SUGGESTIONS FOR PROCESSING THIS EXERCISE WITH THE CLIENT

In this assignment, the client is asked to read a case study that chronicles how one troubled youth was able to turn his life around. The client is subsequently asked to respond to some process questions and perform some altruistic acts. The homework assignment seeks to build the client's empathy toward others, while helping him/her to recognize how his/her actions affect others. Use this assignment with those youths who experience some remorse over their past misbehaviors and also have the capacity to care for others. This assignment may not be successful in working with the hardened delinquent who exhibits little remorse or empathy for others. Consider the option of reading the case study and reviewing the suggestions for processing this exercise with the client in the therapy session, and then assign the task of performing the altruistic behaviors outside of the session.

Note: The story in this assignment was taken from a sermon by the Reverend Robert Schuller. A similar story appears in the book *Chicken Soup for the Soul* (Canfield and Hansen, Health Communications, Inc., 1993). The story has been modified to meet the needs of this assignment.

HEADED IN THE RIGHT DIRECTION

Carefully read the following case study and then respond to the questions after reading the story. Please take a few minutes to reflect on the story before responding to the questions. Consider how the story applies to your life experiences. After reflecting on the story, you will be given the additional task of performing a positive social behavior.

1. Read this story carefully.

A sociology class for Johns Hopkins University once conducted a scientific study in one of the worst slums in Baltimore. The results of the original study were quite discouraging. The sociology class collected a case history for 200 juvenile delinquents who had committed a variety of serious offenses. The data was tabulated on 200 cards, each marked "Headed to jail." On each card, a description was given of the troubled youth whose background, negative attitude, and future prospects all indicated that this young boy or girl was headed to jail.

Twenty-five years later, another sociology class found the original report filed in the university archives. This class conducted a follow-up study and decided to see what actually happened to the young people identified in the first research project. Surprisingly, the very first card they investigated belonged to a boy named Joe, who was a respectable physician in Baltimore. The research team inquired, "Joe, you were described 25 years ago as an incorrigible kid headed for jail. How come you never got there?"

"It's true," the physician acknowledged, "I was the worst kid in the neighborhood, but Aunt Hannah changed all that."

"Who's Aunt Hannah?" the students asked. The physician explained that Aunt Hannah had been a teacher in the slums. One day, Aunt Hannah had invited Joe over to her house for Sunday dinner, and she told the young man, "Look, Joe, I've been studying you, and I've discovered something in you that I want to tell you about. You have the capacity to be a terrific surgeon. I foresee the time when you will be one of the greatest men in medicine in the city of Baltimore. I'm going to follow you, Joe, all the way."

The physician said, "I walked out of Aunt Hannah's house feeling like I couldn't let her down. She sees me as a great surgeon, and I remember saying to myself, what do you know, what do you know? I made up my mind that day to start attending school every day and finishing my work on time. I had opportunities to get in trouble with some of my old friends, but I walked away or turned them down because I remembered what Aunt Hannah said to me. I didn't want to get into any more trouble. I found out that I was actually happier staying out of trouble and becoming involved in positive activities at school. So I missed jail because of Aunt Hannah."

2. Please take a few moments to reflect on this story to see how it relates to your present life situation and then respond to the following questions.

A. What plans or goals do you have for yourself in the future?

_____

_____

_____

B. What steps must you take now to start you on the right path so you can reach your goal?

_____

_____

_____

C. What hopes do you think other important people in your life have for your future?

_____

_____

_____

D. In the preceding case study, Joe was able to turn his life around and become a respectable physician because of Aunt Hannah's belief in him. Identify some of the important people in your life who have demonstrated concern or caring for you.

_____

_____

_____

E. On the other hand, perhaps you have felt disappointed and let down by some significant people in your life. Identify the important people in your life who you feel have disappointed you. Describe how you were disappointed.

_____

_____

_____

F. How have you hurt others who care for you by either stealing, fighting, skipping school, or breaking the law?

_____

_____

_____

3. In the story, Joe turns his life around and makes a positive contribution to society by studying hard to become a physician. He learns to use his hands to treat and heal others. As part of your assignment, perform three positive tasks in the coming week where you use your hands to show caring and concern for others. Please describe the caring behaviors in the following spaces.

    A. _____
    _____
    _____
    _____
    _____

    B. _____
    _____
    _____
    _____
    _____

    C. _____
    _____
    _____
    _____
    _____

MY BEHAVIOR AND ITS FULL IMPACT

GOALS OF THE EXERCISE

1. Expand the view of how acting out or rebellious behavior has affected others as well as self.
2. Recognize and identify specifically how behavior has negatively impacted others.
3. Accept the ways behavior has harmed others.
4. Identify ways, in addition to apologizing, to restore the relationships that were damaged by behavior.

ADDITIONAL PROBLEMS FOR WHICH THIS EXERCISE MAY BE MOST USEFUL

- Anger Management
- Oppositional Defiant
- Sexual Abuse Perpetrator
- Sexual Acting Out

SUGGESTIONS FOR PROCESSING THIS EXERCISE WITH THE CLIENT

This assignment is constructed around the principle of restorative justice. It is far less likely we will ever change our behavior if we hold to the belief that what we do only helps or harms ourselves. This exercise needs to be processed in depth in order to expand or at least plant the idea of how our behavior impacts others. The client is first asked to identify how he/she perceives his/her acting out behaviors have negatively impacted other people and himself/herself. Next, the client is encouraged to gather input from parents, friends, and so forth, to further assess the impact of his/her behaviors. The perspectives of others are important. It is suggested that in order to keep the momentum rolling, the client should mail the exercise to the other individuals with a note of explanation and a return stamped envelope to the person selected by the client. Lastly, the section on action to take to restore the damaged relationship is left open as opposed to offering options in order to see what the client might come up with. However, suggestions can be supplied by the therapist if the client is unable to come up with any constructive ideas.

MY BEHAVIOR AND ITS FULL IMPACT

All behavior has an effect on ourselves and others. Identify in the following, as honestly as you can, how your acting out or rebellious behaviors have caused problems for yourself and other people, as well.

1. Identify your behaviors that have caused problems for other people and yourself.

    A. _____

    B. _____

2. Rate the degree to which you feel your behavior has affected each of the following people, and then briefly explain your rating.

    MYSELF

Not at all	A little	Some	Quite a lot	A lot

    Explanation: _____

    _____

    VICTIM (if there is one)

Not at all	A little	Some	Quite a lot	A lot

    Explanation: _____

    _____

    PARENTS

Not at all	A little	Some	Quite a lot	A lot

    Explanation: _____

    _____

    FAMILY

Not at all	A little	Some	Quite a lot	A lot

    Explanation: _____

    _____

FRIENDS

Not at all	A little	Some	Quite a lot	A lot

Explanation: _____

_____

NEIGHBORHOOD/COMMUNITY INDIVIDUAL

Not at all	A little	Some	Quite a lot	A lot

Explanation: _____

_____

3. Now choose either a teacher, youth pastor, probation officer, or grandparent to rate the same areas and have him/her complete the following section. Ask him/her to briefly explain his/her ratings.

YOU

Not at all	A little	Some	Quite a lot	A lot

Explanation: _____

_____

VICTIM (if there is one)

Not at all	A little	Some	Quite a lot	A lot

Explanation: _____

_____

PARENTS

Not at all	A little	Some	Quite a lot	A lot

Explanation: _____

_____

FAMILY

Not at all	A little	Some	Quite a lot	A lot

Explanation: _____

_____

FRIENDS

Not at all	A little	Some	Quite a lot	A lot

Explanation: _____

_____

NEIGHBORHOOD/COMMUNITY INDIVIDUAL

Not at all	A little	Some	Quite a lot	A lot

Explanation: _____

_____

4. Look over your ratings and explanations and the ratings and explanations of the person you chose. Identify in the following space what you find that is new or surprising to you.

_____

_____

_____

5. Now note the level you see your behavior affecting others and the community where you live.

Not at all	A little	Some	Quite a lot	A lot

6. When your behaviors have had a harmful, hurtful impact on others, it is important to look at things you can do to begin the process of restoring the relationship with those who have been affected most by your behavior. In addition to apologizing (i.e., talk can be cheap unless it is backed by actions), what could you do to help mend these damaged relationships?

Victim (if there is one): _____

Parents: _____

Family: _____

Friends: _____

Community: _____

PATTERNS OF STEALING

GOALS OF THE EXERCISE

1. Identify frequency, duration, and severity of stealing behavior.
2. Assess factors or core issues contributing to the problem with stealing.
3. Develop and utilize effective coping strategies to resist the urge to steal.
4. Eliminate all acts of stealing.

ADDITIONAL PROBLEMS FOR WHICH THIS EXERCISE MAY BE MOST USEFUL

- Anger Management
- Attention-Deficit/Hyperactivity Disorder (ADHD)
- Negative Peer Influences
- Oppositional Defiant

SUGGESTIONS FOR PROCESSING THIS EXERCISE WITH THE CLIENT

It is recommended that the client complete this questionnaire in the beginning stage of treatment. The parents are welcome to help the client answer the various questions. The client's responses will help provide useful diagnostic information about the frequency, duration, and severity of his/her problem with stealing. It is further hoped that the exercise will help identify the external factors or underlying dynamics contributing to the problem. After reviewing the responses in the follow-up therapy session, the therapist can assist the client in developing effective coping strategies to resist the urge to steal.

PATTERNS OF STEALING

Please answer the questions or respond to the following items. Your parents may help you in completing this assignment. Your responses will help you and your therapist learn more about your problem with stealing.

1. At what age did you first steal an item? _____ years old

2. What did you first steal and from where or whom?

   _____

   _____

3. Approximately how often did you steal before the age of 10?

   ___ None   ____ 1–5 times   _____ 6–10 times

   ___ 11–15 times   ____ 16–20 times   _____ over 20 times

4. Approximately how often did you steal between the ages of 10 and 12?

   ___ None   ____ 1–5 times   _____ 6–10 times

   ___ 11–15 times   ____ 16–20 times   _____ over 20 times

5. Approximately how many times have you stolen something after turning 13 years old?

   ___ None   ____ 1–5 times   _____ 6–10 times

   ___ 11–15 times   ____ 16–20 times   _____ over 20 times

6. Please check the individuals or places from whom you have stolen in the past. (Check all that apply.)

   ____ Parents

   ____ Siblings

   ____ Friends

   ____ Peers at schools

   ____ Neighbors

   ____ Unknown people in community

   ____ School

   ____ Neighbor's home

_____ Car/vehicle

_____ Small store

_____ Large retail store

_____ Other (please identify)

_____

_____

7. Have you ever used force or threatened someone when stealing? _____ yes _____ no

8. What type of objects or items have you stolen? (Check all that apply.)

_____ Money

_____ Food/snacks

_____ Clothing

_____ Sporting goods

_____ Bike

_____ Car/vehicle

_____ School/art supplies

_____ Entertainment goods/appliances (e.g., TV, radio, stereo equipment, video games, MP3 player)

_____ Technology devices (e.g., computer equipment, palm pilot)

_____ Other (please identify)

_____

9. What percentage of the time have you stolen when someone else was with you?

_____ 0–20%　　_____ 20–40%　　_____ 40–60%　　_____ 60–80%　　_____ 80–100%

10. What have been the main reasons why you have stolen things in the past? (Please check all that apply.)

_____ Desire to have material good/item (i.e., "I wanted it")

_____ Selfishness

_____ Did not think of consequences

_____ Did not think how it would affect others

_____ Anger

_____ Desire to get revenge or get back at someone

_____ Desire to be accepted by peers

_____ Pressured by peers to steal

_____ Pressured or encouraged by parents/family members to steal

_____ Feelings of loneliness or being unwanted

____ Feel deprived of other basic needs

____ Other (please identify)

_____

11. Please explain further some of the stressful events or factors that have contributed to your problem with stealing.

_____

_____

_____

_____

12. What has been the longest period of time you have gone without stealing? (Please identify how long you went without stealing and at what age.)

_____

_____

13. What positive life events or people have helped you to resist the urge to steal?

_____

_____

_____

_____

BAD THOUGHTS LEAD TO DEPRESSED FEELINGS

GOALS OF THE EXERCISE

1. Verbalize an understanding of the relationship between distorted thinking and negative emotions.
2. Learn key concepts regarding types of distorted thinking.
3. Apply key concepts regarding distorted thinking to own experience.
4. Replace negative, distorted thoughts with positive, realistic thoughts that mediate recovery from depression.

ADDITIONAL PROBLEMS FOR WHICH THIS EXERCISE MAY BE MOST USEFUL

- Anxiety
- Eating Disorder
- Grief/Loss Unresolved
- Low Self-Esteem
- Social Phobia/Shyness
- Suicidal Ideation

SUGGESTIONS FOR PROCESSING THIS EXERCISE WITH THE CLIENT

The concepts of cognitive therapy can be difficult to explain to a client in the abstract. This assignment defines and gives adolescent life examples for each of the common types of distorted thinking. The content of this assignment leans heavily on the work of cognitive/behavior therapists such as Beck, Burns, and Lazurus. You may have to use this assignment as the stepping stone for educating the client on the importance of controlling and changing thoughts. Help him/her find examples of distorted thinking from his/her own life experience as it has been revealed to you in previous or current sessions. Then assist in generating positive replacement thoughts for the negative thoughts. After this tutoring, send the client home with the assignment again to try to identify and replace negative thoughts.

BAD THOUGHTS LEAD TO DEPRESSED FEELINGS

We used to believe that it was depression that made people think negatively, but psychologists and psychiatrists have discovered that most people who struggle with depressed feelings first had negative, pessimistic, distorted thoughts that produced those depressed feelings. People often have completely different reactions to the same situation. For example, John and Jack both heard their basketball coach say, "Every one of you guys has to work harder on defense. You're just standing flat-footed when you are guarding your man!" John thinks, "The coach is trying to help us win. I better step up my energy on defense." But Jack thinks, "He's blaming me for our losing this game. I feel responsible for our team's failure. Coach is going to bench me soon because he thinks I'm a loser." Then Jack goes out on the basketball court and feels depressed and dejected, making more defensive errors because his mind is not on guarding the opponent. As you can see, bad thoughts lead to depressed feelings.

1. Study the list of the types of negative thinking patterns that have been identified and defined and that are common to people who suffer from depression, anxiety, and low self-esteem.

DISTORTED THINKING

Type	Definition	Example
Black or white	Viewing situations, people, or self as entirely bad or entirely good—nothing in between.	Paul made an error while playing on the school's basketball team. He began thinking, "I'm a total failure for letting everyone down. Nobody will like me. Everyone will hate me."
Exaggerating	Making self-critical or other-critical statements that include terms like *never, nothing, everything,* or *always.*	Sharon was not asked on a date for the junior prom. She thought, "I'm never going to be asked on a date again. Nobody cares about me. Boys will always ignore me."
Filtering	Ignoring the positive things that occur to and around self but focusing on and accentuating the negative.	Kate had her hair cut short and styled differently. After receiving several compliments from friends and family, one person was mildly critical. Kate thought, "I knew I shouldn't have gotten it cut short. I look like a freak. People are laughing at me."

Type	Definition	Example
Discounting	Rejecting positive experiences as not being important or meaningful.	Tyler was complimented by his teacher for his interesting artistic drawing. He thought, "Anybody could have drawn that. She doesn't know anything about drawing. I don't have any special ability."
Catastrophizing	Blowing expected consequences out of proportion in a negative direction.	Betsy did not make the cheerleading squad after working hard at tryouts. She thought, "My life is over. I'll never have any friends or any fun. People will look down on me."
Judging	Being critical of self or others with a heavy emphasis on the use of *should have, ought to, must, have to,* and *should not have.*	John finally got up enough courage to call a girl from school that he liked. In spite of the fact that they had a lively conversation for 20 minutes, John told his friend, "I shouldn't have laughed so much. I have to be more relaxed or she'll think I'm a jerk."
Mind reading	Making negative assumptions regarding other people's thoughts and motives.	Aaron had a problem with acne. When he did not get the clothing sales job he wanted, he thought, "I know it's because the manager thinks I look bad. He said the position had been filled but I know better."
Forecasting	Predicting events will turn out badly.	Kelly finished taking an important test. She immediately predicted that she had failed. "I'll never get into college because I blew it here," she thought.
Feelings are facts	Because you feel a certain way, reality is seen as fitting that feeling.	Jim did not have plans for activity with any friends for the weekend. He felt lonely and inferior. He thought, "No one likes me. I have a terrible personality."
Labeling	Calling self or others a bad name when displeased with a behavior.	Brent had an argument with his parents about not cleaning his bedroom. He thought, "My folks are dictators. They are always telling me what I have to do."

Type	Definition	Example
Self-blaming	Holding self responsible for an outcome that was not completely under one's control.	Lateesha's parents separated after many months of arguing. She thought, "My parents argue so much because of me. If I acted better they wouldn't have to separate."

2. Now that you know 11 common types of distorted thinking, apply this information to your own way of thinking. List at least three examples of your own thoughts that lead you to feeling depressed and anxious. First, describe the event that prompted you to feel depressed and then describe the thoughts that promoted the bad feelings.

What Happened?   **Negative Thoughts You Had**

A. _____   _____

_____   _____

_____   _____

_____   _____

B. _____   _____

_____   _____

_____   _____

_____   _____

C. _____   _____

_____   _____

_____   _____

_____   _____

_____   _____

D. _____   _____

_____   _____

_____   _____

_____   _____

3. It is important to try to replace negative, distorted thoughts with positive, more realistic thoughts that can help you to feel more happy. Go back to each of your examples listed in 2 and write positive thoughts that you could have used to make you feel better.

A. _____   _____
   _____   _____
   _____   _____
   _____   _____
   _____   _____

B. _____   _____
   _____   _____
   _____   _____
   _____   _____
   _____   _____

C. _____   _____
   _____   _____
   _____   _____
   _____   _____
   _____   _____

D. _____   _____
   _____   _____
   _____   _____
   _____   _____
   _____   _____

4. Bring this list to your therapist and be alert to your negative thoughts. Throw them out of your mind and replace them with positive thinking. You'll feel better, really!

SURFACE BEHAVIOR/INNER FEELINGS

GOALS OF THE EXERCISE

1. Recognize that self-defeating, acting-out behavior is triggered by emotional pain.
2. Identify own feelings of hurt and sadness that have led to acting out.
3. Describe own acting-out behavior.
4. Identify trusted resource people with whom feelings can be shared.

ADDITIONAL PROBLEMS FOR WHICH THIS EXERCISE MAY BE MOST USEFUL

- Chemical Dependence
- Conduct Disorder/Delinquency
- Oppositional Defiant
- Runaway
- Suicidal Ideation

SUGGESTIONS FOR PROCESSING THIS EXERCISE WITH THE CLIENT

Adolescents often camouflage their depressed feelings in a cloak of anger or irritability. This exercise, designed for clients 10 to 16 years old, helps the client recognize this common dynamic by asking him/her to analyze a character in a story who covers his pain of rejection and lack of nurturing with self-defeating anger. The client may need help making the transition from recognizing this dynamic in the story character and seeing it in himself/herself. Process the questions with the client in a session if additional help is needed to bring this insight home.

SURFACE BEHAVIOR/INNER FEELINGS

Sometimes the feelings you show on the outside may not be an accurate reflection of the struggle that is going on inside. You may show anger when you really feel depressed. You may show a lack of interest in friends, schoolwork, and family when you actually feel rejected, hopeless, and helpless. Your behavior may be getting you in trouble because the feelings under the surface are all jumbled up, confusing, and painful. If you could just share your feelings and sort them out, life would be easier.

1. Read this story of a confused boy named Jack who showed one feeling, anger, on the surface when he felt so many different emotions on the inside.

Sadness Looks Like Anger

"Shut up and leave me alone!" shouted Jack to Mrs. Lewis, his sixth grade teacher. "I'm sick of you always bugging me about keeping my head up and having to listen to you. It's none of your business if I put my head down. I'm not bothering anyone. Nobody cares about what I do anyway," he snarled. Mrs. Lewis was shocked by Jack's disrespectful outburst toward her. He usually was polite and cooperative but lately he was withdrawn and his mind seemed to be on something other than schoolwork. Because of his angry refusal to obey her, she had to send him to the principal's office to discuss his lack of respect for authority.

Jack rose out of his seat in the classroom slowly and shuffled toward the door to the hall. Other students whispered and moved restlessly in their seats. They hadn't seen Jack act like this before. Jack kept his head and eyes toward the floor as he made his way down the aisle of desks and out the door to the hallway leading to the principal's office.

Jack was feeling sad and angry at the same time. Lately, he often felt confused; he would come close to tears but then force them back in anger. He was not sure why he had lashed out at Mrs. Lewis, either. She had always been kind and fair to him. But he felt so tired lately and not interested in school as much as he used to be. He even felt that the other kids didn't like him as much or include him as often as they used to.

As he turned the corner and headed down the long corridor leading to the front entrance of Hillbrook Middle School, he thought about the principal having to call his mother at work to discuss this incident. Jack didn't want his mother to know about his problems. She had enough to deal with herself since the divorce between her and Dad a year ago. She had to switch to full-time work at the hospital cafeteria where she served food to employees and visitors until 6 P.M. every night. She also worked every other Saturday to help pay the bills. Jack hated it that she was gone so much and hated it even more that he had to go to the latchkey daycare program after school every day because she didn't get home until 6:20

P.M. She was always so tired that she often fell asleep on the couch watching a video with him at night.

Now Jack could see the principal's office door as he rounded the last corner. Mr. Clarkson was a big man who spoke in a firm, deep voice that forced you to pay attention to every word. Jack entered the office slowly and sheepishly said to the secretary, "Mrs. Lewis sent me to see Mr. Clarkson." He was embarrassed but also felt somewhat numb and sad. "Have a seat by his door, young man," replied the secretary.

Jack sat down outside Mr. Clarkson's office and stared off into space with his face pointed toward the window, though he wasn't seeing anything outside. He was thinking about yesterday when Dad was supposed to come and pick him up and take him over to Grandma's for supper. "I'll be there at three o'clock tomorrow to get you," Dad had said on the phone on Saturday. Jack had called him to ask why he had not come to see him for 5 weeks in a row. "Been working a lot of hours and had to spend some time with Nancy," Dad explained. Nancy was his new girlfriend, who Jack did not like because she ordered Dad around so much and acted like Jack was an interference in their relationship.

On Sunday, as three o'clock approached, Jack was lying in his bedroom where he spent most of his time alone. He had a sick feeling in his stomach as 3:15 came and went. Then it was 3:30, and no Dad. When 4:00 arrived, Jack had begun to cry in spite of his angry efforts to fight back the tears. He sobbed into his pillow for a few minutes and then took a deep breath and tried to think of what he could have done to make Dad not want to be with him. His eyes burned and his heart pounded because he felt sad and angry at the same time. He began to think about running away. Perhaps he would go to his mother's parents' place in Chicago, 150 miles away.

Just then his thoughts of yesterday were interrupted when Mr. Clarkson opened his office door. "Jack, I'm surprised to see you at my office," Mr. Clarkson said with kindness and concern. "Something must be very wrong in your life to cause you to be sent to my office. Come on in and let's talk about it." As Jack rose to enter the principal's office, tears came to his eyes as his sadness replaced his anger.

2. Answer the following questions.

   A. What was Jack really feeling inside when he showed anger toward Mrs. Lewis?

   _____

   _____

   _____

   _____

   B. Why was Jack feeling sad?

   _____

   _____

   _____

   _____

C. What are the causes for your own sadness and hurt?

_____

_____

_____

_____

D. Tell about a time when you showed one feeling when you actually felt something different inside.

_____

_____

_____

_____

E. Who can you trust enough to tell your *real* feelings to?

_____

_____

_____

_____

F. Sometimes we do things that hurt ourselves and get ourselves into trouble (such as disobey rules, take drugs, run away, fight with someone) when we are actually feeling hurt and sad. Write down an example of a time or times when you have done this:

_____

_____

_____

_____

_____

_____

_____

_____

_____

_____

_____

THREE WAYS TO CHANGE THE WORLD

GOALS OF THE EXERCISE

1. Elevate mood by identifying steps that can be taken to cope with stress or to overcome life's problems.
2. Identify stressors or unmet needs that contribute to feelings of depression.
3. Express needs in the context of a supportive therapeutic relationship.
4. Establish rapport with the therapist in the beginning stages of therapy.

ADDITIONAL PROBLEMS FOR WHICH THIS EXERCISE MAY BE MOST USEFUL

- Anxiety
- Low Self-Esteem
- Physical/Emotional Abuse Victim
- Sexual Abuse Victim
- Suicidal Ideation

SUGGESTIONS FOR PROCESSING THIS EXERCISE WITH THE CLIENT

The Three Ways to Change the World game is an activity that can be used with adolescents with a variety of problems, but it has been included in this section on depression because of its potential for identifying unmet needs and core sources of the client's depression. In this activity, the client is requested to draw three separate pictures between therapy sessions that symbolize how he/she would like to change the world. Instruct the client to bring the drawings back to his/her next therapy session, along with the form containing his or her responses to several questions. The drawings and the client's responses to the questions will provide you with the opportunity to assess whether the desired changes are directly or indirectly related to his/her depression. If the desired changes are directly related to the client's problems, you can then help him/her develop coping strategies to manage stress or overcome problems. Furthermore, the drawings may reflect some of the client's unmet needs, which can facilitate a discussion on what steps he/she can take to meet his/her needs. This activity can also be helpful in identifying clear-cut therapy goals. It is recommended that this assignment be used in the beginning stages of therapy with clients who are over 10 years old.

THREE WAYS TO CHANGE THE WORLD

Have you ever dreamed of being an artist? If so, then this activity is just for you. You are invited to be an artist and create three separate drawings that show how you would like to change the world. Before you actually sit down to draw the pictures, spend a few minutes thinking about what it is you would like to express in your drawing. Find a quiet or relaxing place where you can reflect on how you'd like to change the world. Be yourself and express what is important to you, but also remember to have fun with this activity.

1. Just pretend for the sake of having fun that you have been granted the power to make any three changes in this world that you so desire. There are a number of ways that you could change the world. Perhaps you would like to produce a change in your world that directly affects you. On the other hand, you may like to see some change that would benefit another person, such as a family member, friend, peer, or teacher. Another option is to express a desire for change in your school, community, state, or country. Why, you may even wish to change something about the whole world.

2. There are only a couple of rules in this activity. First, at least two of your three desired changes must have something to do directly with your life. Second, we ask that you draw a picture of something that symbolizes or represents the desired change. Do not use any words in your drawings. The reason for this is so that your therapist can guess what you are trying to express in your drawing.

3. In the following space, list the three changes you would like to see happen in the world and your reasons for selecting each one of them. Please respond to the other questions that are appropriate to your desired change. Do not show this list to your therapist until he or she has attempted to guess what your desired changes are.

The first change I would like to see happen in the world is:

_____

_____

_____

_____

Reasons why I would like to see this change happen:

_____

_____

If this change is realistic or possible, what can I do to help bring about this change?

If this change is not likely to occur, what can I do to cope with this problem or issue?

Who can help me cope with this problem or issue?

The second change I would like to see happen in the world is:

Reasons why I would like to see this change happen:

If this change is realistic or possible, what can I do to help bring about this change?

If this change is not likely to occur, what can I do to cope with this problem or issue?

Who can help me cope with this problem or issue?

_____

_____

The third change I would like to see happen in the world is:

_____

_____

_____

_____

Reasons why I would like to see this change happen:

_____

_____

_____

_____

If this change is realistic or possible, what can I do to help bring about this change?

_____

_____

_____

_____

If this change is not likely to occur, what can I do to cope with this problem or issue?

_____

_____

_____

_____

Who can help me cope with this problem or issue?

_____

_____

UNMET EMOTIONAL NEEDS— IDENTIFICATION AND SATISFACTION

GOALS OF THE EXERCISE

1. Identify and specify unmet emotional needs.
2. Select someone with whom to share needs.
3. Identify self-help actions to meet emotional needs.
4. Make a commitment to share or begin self-help action.
5. Reflect on the consequences of action taken.

ADDITIONAL PROBLEMS FOR WHICH THIS EXERCISE MAY BE MOST USEFUL

- Eating Disorder
- Low Self-Esteem
- Runaway
- Social Phobia/Shyness
- Suicidal Ideation

SUGGESTIONS FOR PROCESSING THIS EXERCISE WITH THE CLIENT

Depressed clients need to identify specifically what is missing from their lives that leads to their feelings of sadness, hurt, frustration, loneliness, or hopelessness. This exercise helps clients focus on what their unmet emotional needs are. Furthermore, depression is most often accompanied by a sense of helplessness to do anything to improve their situation. The assignment challenges the client to think of people who can help meet his/her needs if they were shared. Additionally, the client is challenged to commit himself/herself to a self-help action plan. The therapist probably will have to guide the client in listing actions he/she could take to help improve the probability of getting his/her needs met.

UNMET EMOTIONAL NEEDS—
IDENTIFICATION AND SATISFACTION

All human beings have emotional needs that we want satisfied. When they are not satisfied, we feel sad, depressed, lonely, hurt, disappointed, or even worthless. At times, we are sad and we are not even sure why. This exercise is designed to help you identify and specify what needs of yours are unmet as well as to help you design a plan of action to get your needs met by sharing them with others and/or doing something constructive to help yourself take charge of the satisfaction of your own needs.

1. Review the list of common emotional needs and place a checkmark next to the ones that you feel are not met in your life. There are three blank lines for you to write in any unmet needs of yours that were left off the list.

Common Emotional Needs

____ 1. To feel loved unconditionally by at least a few people.

____ 2. To get recognition for accomplishments.

____ 3. To be touched, patted, and hugged affectionately.

____ 4. To be encouraged to do your best.

____ 5. To be listened to, understood, and heard.

____ 6. To feel supported when feeling hurt, weak, or vulnerable.

____ 7. To be praised and rewarded for your effort to do the right thing.

____ 8. To be treated with respect even if you disagree with someone.

____ 9. To be forgiven when you do something wrong.

____ 10. To feel accepted even with your faults or shortcomings.

____ 11. To be asked to join others in social gatherings.

____ 12. To be trusted and believed when telling your side of a story.

____ 13. To have friends you can trust.

____ 14. To have some talent or ability that gets you recognition and builds self-esteem.

____ 15. To feel accepted and loved by God.

____ 16. To be treated fairly, equally, and given an opportunity to succeed.

____ 17. To feel capable of competing adequately against others.

_____ 18. To feel your physical appearance is reasonably attractive.

_____ 19. To have someone believe in your capabilities.

_____ 20. To feel you fit in with a group of friends.

_____ 21. _____

_____ 22. _____

_____ 23. _____

2. Many times we have unmet needs that others are not aware of because we keep them to ourselves. When we do not share them, these unmet needs can cause disappointment, pain, and sadness. However, if we were to share these needs with close friends or family, we would often discover that these people would do whatever they could to help fill the void. It takes courage to be open about our needs because we want to appear self-sufficient, independent, and strong, but being honest with people that care about you is a sign of strength and trust. List the people who could help you get your needs met if you shared them with them. Write a target date on or before which you will share your needs.

Unmet Need	Someone to Share It With	Target Date of Sharing
_____	_____	_____
_____	_____	_____
_____	_____	_____
_____	_____	_____
_____	_____	_____
_____	_____	_____

3. At other times, we must take steps ourselves to get our needs met and not rely entirely on others to help us. Next to each unmet need, write one or two things you could do to help yourself move closer to getting your needs met. Perhaps your therapist can help you identify things you can do to help yourself. Write target dates for completing the steps you can take.

Unmet Need	Steps You Can Take	Target Dates
_____	A. _____	A. _____
	B. _____	B. _____
_____	A. _____	A. _____
	B. _____	B. _____
_____	A. _____	A. _____
	B. _____	B. _____
_____	A. _____	A. _____
	B. _____	B. _____

	A. _____	A. _____
_____	B. _____	B. _____
_____	A. _____	A. _____
	B. _____	B. _____

4. Write out the consequences of the action you have taken to share your unmet need with someone or to take steps to help yourself.

   _____

   _____

   _____

   _____

   _____

   _____

   _____

   _____

IDENTIFY A CHANGE RESULTING FROM PARENTS' DIVORCE

GOALS OF THE EXERCISE

1. Identify a difficult change from the parents' separation/divorce that has impacted both personal and family life.
2. Express thoughts and feelings about how the stressful change has impacted both family and self.
3. Identify effective coping strategies and/or people who can help cope with the stressful change.
4. Accept the parents' separation/divorce with consequent understanding and control of feelings and behavior.

ADDITIONAL PROBLEMS FOR WHICH THIS EXERCISE MAY BE MOST USEFUL

- Blended Family
- Depression
- Grief/Loss Unresolved

SUGGESTIONS FOR PROCESSING THIS EXERCISE WITH THE CLIENT

This assignment specifically examines what stressful change(s) have occurred as a result of the parents' separation/divorce. The client is asked to identify how the stressful change has impacted the family and himself/herself and given the opportunity to express his/her thoughts and feelings about the stressful change that has occurred. In processing the client's responses, the therapist should discuss whether the client would be willing to share his/her thoughts and feelings with the parent(s). Ultimately, the assignment seeks to help the client develop adaptive coping mechanisms to deal with the stressful or difficult change and identify other people who he/she can turn to for support or guidance. The therapist may want to consider giving this assignment more than once if additional stressful changes develop that have an impact on the family.

IDENTIFY A CHANGE RESULTING FROM PARENTS' DIVORCE

Families undergo many changes when a separation or divorce occurs. Some of these changes can be quite stressful and create hardships for all of the family members. For example, the family may have to move or the children may have to change schools. Likewise, many families going through a divorce find that they have less money to do the things they once were able to do. This assignment gives you the opportunity to share your thoughts and feelings about a stressful change that has occurred as a result of your parents' divorce. Please respond to the following questions to help you and your therapist better understand your thoughts and feelings about how this change has affected your family and you.

1. What has been the biggest or most difficult change that you have experienced as a result of your parents' divorce?

    _____
    _____
    _____
    _____

2. How has this change affected your parents and your brothers and sisters?

    _____
    _____
    _____
    _____

3. What are your thoughts and feelings about this stressful change?

    _____
    _____
    _____
    _____

4. How have you shown or expressed your feelings about this change?

    _____
    _____
    _____
    _____

5. Sometimes the change from the parents' divorce can seem unfair to the children. Have you ever felt that the change was unfair? If so, please describe how you feel the change has been unfair for you (or your brothers and sisters).

    _____

    _____

    _____

    _____

    _____

    _____

6. Looking back, how do you feel you have coped with this change?

    _____

    _____

    _____

    _____

7. If you have struggled to cope with this, what can your parents say or do to help you handle better the change?

    _____

    _____

    _____

    _____

8. What other individuals (either peers or adults) can help you cope with this change? Please list them in the following space.

    _____

    _____

    _____

    _____

9. How can these other people help you cope with the difficult change?

    _____

    _____

    _____

    _____

10. What can you do to help yourself cope better with this change?

    _____

    _____

    _____

    _____

INITIAL REACTION TO PARENTS' SEPARATION

GOALS OF THE EXERCISE

1. Identify the impact of parents' announcement that they are separating.
2. Facilitate expression of thoughts and feelings when first learning about parents' separation.
3. Express worries or concerns about parents' separation.
4. Learn to cope with parents' separation and prevent major regression in adaptive functioning.

ADDITIONAL PROBLEMS FOR WHICH THIS EXERCISE MAY BE MOST USEFUL

- Blended Family
- Grief/Loss Unresolved
- Parenting

SUGGESTIONS FOR PROCESSING THIS EXERCISE WITH THE CLIENT

This homework assignment is given to the client shortly after learning that his/her parents are separating or seeking divorce. The primary goal is to promote the client's expression of his/her thoughts, feelings, or concerns about the parents' separation. The client's responses to the questionnaire will also provide useful information about how he/she believes the separation will impact other family members and himself/herself. In processing the client's responses in the follow-up session, the therapist should assess whether the client feels ready to express his/her thoughts, feelings, and concerns with parents or siblings. If so, the client should be encouraged to express his/her thoughts and feelings in future family therapy sessions. It is hoped that the family members' discussion of how the separation has impacted the family will prevent a major regression in the client's overall adaptive functioning.

INITIAL REACTION TO PARENTS' SEPARATION

For many teenagers, it is painful to learn that their parents are getting a separation or are filing for divorce. The teenager may experience a number of different emotions. In order to better cope with this major change in the family, it is important that you express your thoughts and feelings and not stuff or bottle up these feelings or concerns. Please complete the following questions to help you and your therapist understand your thoughts, feelings, and concerns about your parents' recent separation.

1. How did you first find out that your parents were separating or seeking a divorce?

    _____

    _____

    _____

2. Some teenagers are quite surprised when they first learn that their parents are separating. However, other teenagers are not surprised and saw it coming for a long time. Were you surprised or not? Please explain.

    _____

    _____

    _____

    _____

3. How did you feel when you first learned of your parents' separation?

    _____

    _____

    _____

4. What did your mom say to you about the separation?

    _____

    _____

    _____

5. What did your dad say to you about the separation?

    _____

    _____

    _____

6. How did your brother(s) and/or sister(s) react to the news of separation?

   _____

   _____

   _____

7. What are your greatest worries or concerns about how your parents' separation will affect you?

   _____

   _____

   _____

8. How do you think your parents' separation/divorce will affect your school and social life?

   _____

   _____

   _____

9. What are your concerns or worries about how the separation will affect your brother(s) and/or sister(s)?

   _____

   _____

   _____

10. Many teenagers feel sad, angry, confused, and hurt about their parents' separation. However, in some cases, the teenager may actually be relieved that his/her parents are separating. Have you ever felt this way? Or, what possible good may come out of your parents' separation/divorce? Please explain.

   _____

   _____

   _____

   _____

11. What can your mom say or do to help you cope with the separation?

   _____

   _____

   _____

12. What can your dad say or do to help you cope with the separation?

   _____

   _____

   _____

FEARS BENEATH THE EATING DISORDER

GOALS OF THE EXERCISE

1. Identify the fears that exist under the surface of behavior.
2. Identify how those fears control behavior.
3. Accept and implement a plan of facing fears to reduce their influence on the behavior.

ADDITIONAL PROBLEMS FOR WHICH THIS EXERCISE MAY BE MOST USEFUL

*   None

SUGGESTIONS FOR PROCESSING THIS EXERCISE WITH THE CLIENT

A multitude of fears can exert a powerful influence on the client who has an eating disorder. This exercise is designed to help the client identify those fears, note how they impact his/her behavior, and commit to a plan of replacing the negative automatic thoughts associated with each fear. You will have to help the client become aware of how cognitive distortions precipitate fear and then suggest replacement thoughts that are realistic.

FEARS BENEATH THE EATING DISORDER

Anorexia and bulimia are behavioral problems that are based in fear. The fear may take many forms and can be caused by many distorted thoughts. For this exercise you are to try to identify the various fears that seem to control your eating behavior. You must then focus on the most powerful fears and understand how they are controlling your behavior. Finally, you must find ways to face your fears in order to overcome them.

1. Review the following list of fears and place a checkmark by those that you struggle with and those that influence your eating behavior. If the list is missing one or more of your fears, add them to the list at the bottom in the blank spaces provided.

   I have a fear of:

   ❑ Gaining weight

   ❑ Becoming obese

   ❑ Losing control of my eating and gorging myself

   ❑ Being a failure in many areas of my life

   ❑ Food not being available when I want it

   ❑ Becoming independent and living on my own

   ❑ Developing a sexually attractive body

   ❑ Not being perfect

   ❑ Being rejected by family and/or friends

   ❑ My sexual fantasies leading to impulsive sexual behavior

   ❑ Expressing my thoughts and feelings directly

   ❑ Speaking up for my rights

   ❑ Not having any worth apart from my appearance

   ❑ Becoming close and intimate with the opposite sex

   ❑ Someone else being in control of me

   ❑ _____

   ❑ _____

   ❑ _____

2. Now list the three most powerful fears in their order of strength.

    Fear Number One: _____

    Fear Number Two: _____

    Fear Number Three: _____

3. For each of the three fears listed in 2, write about how that fear influences your behavior. What impact does it have on your life? How might it affect your eating?

    Fear Number One: _____

    _____

    _____

    _____

    Fear Number Two: _____

    _____

    _____

    _____

    Fear Number Three: _____

    _____

    _____

    _____

Most irrational fears are triggered by distorted thoughts. First, people have thoughts about a situation and then these thoughts cause an emotional reaction. Therefore, the fears are reduced or eliminated if the negative thoughts can be changed to thoughts that are more realistic, hopeful, and positive.

4. For each of the fears listed in 2, identify the thoughts that you have that are associated with each fear. For example, if you fear gaining weight, one or more of the following negative thoughts could be triggering this fear:

    *   I'm already too fat.
    *   I'm going to become fat like my mother.
    *   I want to look skinny like a model.
    *   If I start to gain, I won't be able to stop.
    *   I look pretty when I'm thin.
    *   If I eat normally, I'll get fat.
    *   I can't eat like most people because I'll get fat.
    *   The only way I can stay fit is to constantly diet.
    *   It is not healthy to eat regular portions.

When thoughts like these are held onto, the fear of gaining weight grows.

Now write your thoughts that help to maintain or trigger each of your fears.

Fear Number One: _____

_____

_____

_____

Fear Number Two: _____

_____

_____

_____

Fear Number Three: _____

_____

_____

_____

To reduce these fears, you must replace the negative thoughts with positive, realistic thoughts. For our example of a fear of gaining weight, the following realistic thoughts could replace the negative thoughts:

- I'm not fat. In fact, I'm underweight.
- I need to gain some weight.
- I can control my weight gain so it is reasonable.
- Being too skinny is not healthy or attractive.
- I will look more attractive when I gain some weight.
- A fit body needs a normal amount of calories.
- Regular portions of food provide the necessary nutrition the body requires.

When thoughts like these are held onto, the fear of normal weight gain disappears.

5. Now write positive replacement thoughts for each fear that will reduce your irrational fear. Remember, thoughts are under your control and they cause your feelings.

Fear Number One: _____

_____

_____

_____

Fear Number Two: _____

_____

_____

_____

Fear Number Three: _____

_____

_____

_____

REALITY: FOOD INTAKE, WEIGHT, THOUGHTS, AND FEELINGS

GOALS OF THE EXERCISE

1. Break down denial regarding actual food intake, weight gain, and body size.
2. Identify the distorted thoughts that are associated with eating and the feelings such negative thoughts generate.
3. Reduce the incidence of dysfunctional behaviors used to control weight.
4. Make a concrete pledge to take responsibility for a steady weight gain to be achieved through healthy eating behaviors.

ADDITIONAL PROBLEMS FOR WHICH THIS EXERCISE MAY BE MOST USEFUL

• None

SUGGESTIONS FOR PROCESSING THIS EXERCISE WITH THE CLIENT

The distorted perception and denial that characterize the client with an eating disorder make it difficult to establish a basis for recovery. This exercise is designed to get the client to face the facts of what and how much has been eaten and how eating sets off a cognitive chain reaction that leads to irrational fear and dysfunctional weight control behaviors (e.g., vomiting, binging, excessive exercise, laxative abuse). You will have to educate the client regarding the relationship between cognitive distortions, negative emotions, and dysfunctional coping behaviors associated with eating. For example: Eating three crackers with cheese → "I am going to get fat. My tummy is bloated. I look like a fat pig." → Fear, low self-esteem, and negative body image → Strenuous exercise, forced vomiting, and/or laxative abuse.

After awareness of the destructive pattern is established, the client must be confronted with the personal responsibility to break the cycle and begin to eat normally to gain weight.

REALITY: FOOD INTAKE, WEIGHT, THOUGHTS, AND FEELINGS

When you are caught in the web of anorexia or bulimia, it is very easy to distort the reality of what and how much you have eaten, your actual body weight, and reasonable thoughts about food and body image. This journal form is designed to help you stay in touch with reality and not to exaggerate, promote denial, negatively forecast the future, or distort your thinking.

1. Keep a daily record of what foods you eat and the quantity. After each occasion of eating, write your thoughts about the food and yourself. Also, record your feelings connected to the food and yourself. Finally, in the last column, record the common, secret, dysfunctional coping behaviors you engaged in (such as overexercising, forced vomiting, food hoarding, laxative use, lying about eating). On a weekly basis record your weight.

WEEKLY REALITY JOURNAL Starting Weight: _____			
Food Consumed	**Thoughts**	**Feelings**	**Secret Behavior**
DAY 1 Breakfast:			
Lunch:			
Dinner:			
Snacks:			

Food Consumed	Thoughts	Feelings	Secret Behavior
DAY 2 Breakfast:			
Lunch:			
Dinner:			
Snacks:			
DAY 3 Breakfast:			
Lunch:			
Dinner:			
Snacks:			
DAY 4 Breakfast:			
Lunch:			
Dinner:			
Snacks:			

Food Consumed	Thoughts	Feelings	Secret Behavior
DAY 5 Breakfast:			
Lunch:			
Dinner:			
Snacks:			
DAY 6 Breakfast:			
Lunch:			
Dinner:			
Snacks:			
DAY 7 Breakfast:			
Lunch:			
Dinner:			
Snacks:			

2. Hopefully, you are becoming more realistic about the fact that you have not eaten normally, your body is in need of adequate nutrition and calories, and your weight and body size are below average. Denial must be broken and distorted thoughts must be recognized in order for you to get on the road to recovery and break the cycle of treating food as your enemy. The next step is to set goals for increasing weight gradually but steadily through increased food intake (and termination of the secret dysfunctional coping behaviors of excessive exercise, vomiting, lying, and so on). On the following form, record your pledge of a minimum weight gain per week based on healthy eating behavior:

PLEDGE

I, _____, set a goal of gaining _____ per week.
(Name of client)   (Weight amount)

I will eat meals on a regular schedule and eat normal portions of a balanced diet. I

will not engage in secret behaviors to control my weight or calorie intake.

Witness: _____   Signed:_____

Date: _____   Date: _____

CREATE A MEMORY ALBUM

GOALS OF THE EXERCISE

1. Tell the story of the loss through drawings or artwork.
2. Express feelings surrounding the loss of a significant person through the modality of art therapy.
3. Begin a healthy grieving process around the loss.
4. Establish a trusting relationship with the therapist or significant other(s) so grief can be shared in the context of a supportive environment.
5. Create a personal memory album that will serve as a keepsake and reminder of the relationship with the deceased person.

ADDITIONAL PROBLEMS FOR WHICH THIS EXERCISE MAY BE MOST USEFUL

• Anxiety
• Depression
• Low Self-Esteem

SUGGESTIONS FOR PROCESSING THIS EXERCISE WITH THE CLIENT

In this homework assignment, the client is asked to draw a series of pictures between therapy sessions that can be collected and made into a personal memory album. The client is given a list of suggested ideas for his or her own drawings. The client's drawings can be used as valuable therapeutic tools to facilitate a discussion about his/her feelings or grief experiences in the context of a supportive environment. After all the pictures have been completed and gathered together, they can be made into a personal memory album during one of the therapy sessions. The client may choose to include some actual photographs of the deceased person in the album. Likewise, he/she may want to add a letter to the deceased person (please see the following homework assignment entitled "Grief Letter"). This therapeutic intervention can become a valuable keepsake for the adolescent in later years.

CREATE A MEMORY ALBUM

This homework assignment gives you the opportunity to be an artist and create your own personal memory album of _____. You are asked to draw several pictures hav-
(Name of Person)
ing to do with your relationship with _____ and how you felt after he or she
(Name of Person)
died. You are asked to draw these pictures between therapy sessions and then to share them with your therapist in the following therapy sessions. These pictures will be collected and then made into your own personal memory album.

1. The purpose of this homework assignment is to help you share your feelings and experiences about your loss through pictures and artwork. After you have completed each picture and brought it back to the therapy session, you will discuss your draw-ings with the therapist. This will give you the opportunity to share your feelings and experiences with the therapist. Feel free to also share your pictures with other family members, friends, or peers.

2. Following is a list of suggested ideas or topics that you can draw about. Some of the pictures will allow you to identify what _____ was like before he/she
(Name of Person)
passed away. You may choose to draw pictures of what you enjoyed doing with _____ (name of person) in the past. You also have a choice of drawing
(Name of Person)
what your experiences have been like after _____ died. Please feel free to
(Name of Person)
draw other pictures that you feel are important. Give each picture a title when you have finished your drawing.

Suggested ideas for drawings:
    *   The entire family, including the deceased person, doing an activity together.
    *   Three activities that you enjoyed doing with the deceased person.
    *   A time when you felt proud of the deceased person or when he/she felt proud of you.
    *   A time when you felt especially sad or angry with the deceased person while he/she was living.
    *   How you felt when you first found out that the deceased person was seriously ill or dying.
    *   How you felt on the day that the person died.
    *   The funeral.
    *   Three activities that help you feel less sad about the loss.

GRIEF LETTER

GOALS OF THE EXERCISE

1. Begin a healthy grieving process around the loss of a significant other.
2. Identify and express feelings connected with the loss.
3. Create a supportive emotional environment in which to grieve the loss.
4. Start reinvesting time and energy into relationships with others and age-appropriate activities.

ADDITIONAL PROBLEMS FOR WHICH THIS EXERCISE MAY BE MOST USEFUL

- Anxiety
- Depression

SUGGESTIONS FOR PROCESSING THIS EXERCISE WITH THE CLIENT

Therapists have found letter-writing to be an effective intervention to assist the client in working through the grief process. In this assignment, the client is asked to first respond to a series of questions before actually writing the letter to the deceased person in order to help him/her organize his/her thoughts. The questions listed on the following pages are offered as guides to help write the letter. Some of the questions may not be relevant to your particular client. Encourage the client to express other thoughts and feelings that may be unique to his/her grieving process. After the client responds to the questions, he/she can then begin writing the actual letter. Instruct the client to bring the letter to the following therapy session for processing. Be sensitive to not assign this task to clients who dislike writing or have a learning disability in written expression.

GRIEF LETTER

Writing letters can be a way to help you identify and express your thoughts and feelings. This is especially true when you need to work through your feelings surrounding the death of an important person in your life. In this homework assignment, you are asked to write a letter to the deceased person to help you identify and express your own feelings about the significant loss in your life.

First, find a quiet or relaxing place where you can write the letter. This will help you to concentrate on writing down your own thoughts and feelings without being bothered by distractions. Perhaps you can write the letter in a quiet room in your house, go to the library, or you can go to a favorite outdoor place such as a park or beach.

After finding a quiet or relaxing place, please respond to the following questions. These questions will help you organize your thoughts and feelings before you begin to actually write the letter. You may find that some of these questions do not apply to you; therefore, you may leave those items blank. Space is also provided for you to express any additional thoughts or feelings that you may want to include in your letter. Feel free to write down whatever thoughts come into your mind at this stage in the assignment. You can decide later as to whether you want to include these thoughts in your final letter.

1. What thoughts and feelings did you experience around the time of the death or as soon as you learned of _____'s death?
   (Name of Person)

   _____

   _____

   _____

   _____

   _____

   _____

2. What are some of the positive things you miss about _____?
   (Name of Person)

   _____

   _____

   _____

   _____

   _____

3. What are some of the problems or disappointments that you had in your relationship with _____?
   (Name of Person)

   _____

   _____

   _____

4. It is not uncommon for some people to experience guilt or remorse about not having said or done something with a person before that person died. What, if anything, do you wish you could have said or done with _____ before he/she died?
   (Name of Person)

   _____

   _____

   _____

5. Do you experience any feelings that _____'s death was your fault? If so, please describe why you feel responsible.   (Name of Person)

   _____

   _____

   _____

6. Are you sorry about some of the things that happened between you and _____ _____? Describe.   (Name of Person)

   _____

   _____

   _____

7. Did _____ hurt you in some ways? Explain.
   (Name of Person)

   _____

   _____

   _____

8. How has the death affected your present life?

   _____

   _____

   _____

   _____

9. What are some of the important events that are occurring in your present life that you would life to share with _____?
   (Name of Person)

   _____

   _____

   _____

10. What dreams or goals do you have for yourself in the future because you knew
    _____?
    (Name of Person)

    _____

    _____

    _____

11. How would _____ feel about you today?
    (Name of Person)

    _____

    _____

    _____

12. What would _____ want you to do with your life now?
    (Name of Person)

    _____

    _____

    _____

13. Please use the following space to express any other thoughts or feelings that you
    would like to include in the letter.

    _____

    _____

    _____

    _____

    _____

    _____

14. Next, review your responses and begin to write the letter on a separate sheet of paper.
    Bring the completed letter to your next therapy session to go over with your thera-
    pist. After discussing the letter, please consider what you would like to do with the
    letter—do you want to destroy it or throw the letter away? Your therapist can help
    you answer these questions.

THREE WAYS TO CHANGE YOURSELF

GOALS OF THE EXERCISE

1. Elevate self-esteem.
2. Increase awareness of self and ways to change in order to improve self-image.
3. Identify steps that must be taken to produce positive changes in life.
4. Establish rapport with therapist in the beginning stages of therapy.

ADDITIONAL PROBLEMS FOR WHICH THIS EXERCISE MAY BE MOST USEFUL

- Anxiety
- Attention-Deficit/Hyperactivity Disorder (ADHD)
- Conduct Disorder/Delinquency
- Depression
- Eating Disorder

SUGGESTIONS FOR PROCESSING THIS EXERCISE WITH THE CLIENT

This activity can often be used as a sequel to the Three Wishes Game exercise. Like the Three Wishes Game, it is recommended that this activity be used in the beginning stages of therapy to help you establish rapport with the client. The Three Ways to Change Yourself activity can be used with adolescents who are exhibiting a variety of behavioral or emotional problems, but is included in this section because of its potential to increase the client's self-image. In this exercise, the client is asked to draw three separate pictures between therapy sessions that reflect three changes that he/she would like to make with him/herself. The client is instructed to bring the pictures back to the following therapy session to process with you. In discussing the drawings, assist the client in identifying ways that he/she can bring about positive changes in him/herself. The information gained from this exercise can also help the client and you establish clearly defined treatment goals.

THREE WAYS TO CHANGE YOURSELF

This activity can be a fun-filled way for your therapist to get to know you better. Here, you are invited to be a creative artist and draw pictures of three changes that you would like to make in yourself. Try to express what is really important to you, but also remember to relax and have fun when you are drawing your pictures.

Before you sit down to begin drawing the pictures, spend a few minutes thinking about the changes that you would most like to see happen in yourself or in your life. You can express your wish to change in a number of different ways. Some people want to develop a talent, skill, or interest in a certain area. For example, they may draw a picture of a ballet dancer, singer, or basketball player. Other people may choose to draw something that has to do with their personality. For instance, some people would like to see themselves control their temper, become more organized, or be less (or more) serious about life. Perhaps you would like to change how you get along with other people. Some people may choose to draw pictures that show that they have more friends, smile or laugh more often, or are friendlier and more caring. Finally, some people may express their wish to change something about their personal appearance.

There are only a couple of rules for this activity. First, think of three different changes that you would like to make in yourself. If you cannot think of at least three changes, then talk with someone you trust in order to develop some ideas. Second, don't use any written words in your drawings. This is because your therapist will attempt to guess what changes you would like to make after you bring your drawings back to the next therapy session. Your therapist will have three chances to guess what your desired changes are. If your therapist cannot guess what changes you would like to make in three tries, then, in baseball terms, your therapist has struck out. At that point, you can tell your therapist how you would like to change.

After you have given thought to the changes that you would like to make in yourself and listed them in the following spaces, please draw them on separate pieces of blank paper. Remember to bring the drawings to your next therapy session, along with your answers to the following questions.

1.   The first change I would like to make is:

   _____

   _____

   _____

   _____

2. Reasons why I would like to make this change are:

    _____

    _____

    _____

    _____

3. How will other people know that I have changed? What signs will I show them? How will my behavior be different?

    _____

    _____

    _____

    _____

4. The second change I would like to make is:

    _____

    _____

    _____

    _____

5. Reasons why I would like to make this change are:

    _____

    _____

    _____

    _____

6. How will other people know that I have made this second change? What signs will I show them? How will my behavior be different?

    _____

    _____

    _____

    _____

7. The third change I would like to make is:

    _____

    _____

    _____

    _____

8. Reasons why I would like to make this change are:

    _____

    _____

    _____

    _____

9. How will other people know that I have made this third change? What signs will I show them? How will my behavior be different?

    _____

    _____

    _____

    _____

Do not show this list to your therapist until he/she has attempted to guess what your desired changes are.

THREE WISHES GAME

GOALS OF THE EXERCISE

1. Increase ability to identify and express needs.
2. Identify steps that must be taken to meet needs.
3. Establish rapport with therapist in the beginning stages of therapy.

ADDITIONAL PROBLEMS FOR WHICH THIS EXERCISE MAY BE MOST USEFUL

- Anxiety
- Conduct Disorder/Delinquency
- Depression
- Oppositional Defiant

SUGGESTIONS FOR PROCESSING THIS EXERCISE WITH THE CLIENT

The Three Wishes Game is a fun-filled activity that you can use in the early stages of therapy to establish rapport with the client. This activity can be used with adolescents who are experiencing a variety of emotional or behavioral problems, but it has been included in this section on low self-esteem because of its potential to help improve the client's feelings about him/herself. In this exercise, the client is asked to draw three separate pictures between therapy sessions that reflect his/her own individual wishes. The client is instructed to bring the pictures to the following therapy session for processing.

Assess how realistic or attainable the client's wishes are. If the client has produced a picture that identifies his/her interests or potential talents, then he/she should be encouraged to take steps to develop those interests or talents. For example, if a 10-year-old child expresses a wish to be a basketball star or musician, then he/she should be encouraged to join a basketball team with same-aged peers or to take music lessons. On the other hand, do not be discouraged or consider the assignment a failure if the client draws a picture of a wish that is unattainable or is based solely on fantasy. At the very least, the exercise provides the client with the opportunity to express or identify his/her own individual needs. This game can also be incorporated into the therapy session.

THREE WISHES GAME

The Three Wishes Game is a fun-filled activity that can help your therapist get to know you better. Here, you have the opportunity to be an artist and draw pictures of your three most important wishes. Spend a few minutes thinking about what it is you would like to draw, but most of all, remember to relax, have fun, and be yourself.

1. Just pretend, for the sake of having fun, that you have been granted three wishes, and you can wish for anything in the whole world. Perhaps you would wish for a special item or material good(s). You may wish to go to someplace special on Earth or anywhere in the universe. Likewise, you may wish to accomplish some special feat by yourself or with another person. On the other hand, you can also choose to spend one or more of your wishes on someone else. You may make a wish for someone you really care about, such as a parent, sibling, grandparent, relative, friend, or someone in your school or on your team.

2. There are only two rules in this activity. First, you are allowed only three wishes. You cannot use one of your wishes to wish for more wishes. Second, you must draw a picture of something that represents each wish. You cannot use any written words in your drawings to express your wishes. This is because your therapist will attempt to guess what it is that you are actually wishing for after you bring your pictures to the next therapy session. Your therapist will have three chances to guess each one of your wishes. If your therapist cannot guess what each wish is, then you can tell your therapist what it is that you are wishing to come true.

3. List what your three wishes are and your reasons for selecting each one of them in the following space. Do not show this list to your therapist until he/she has attempted to guess each one of your wishes. Then draw each one of your wishes on a separate piece of paper.

   A. My first wish is for:

   _____

   _____

   _____

   _____

B. Reasons for this wish:

_____

_____

_____

_____

C. My second wish is for:

_____

_____

_____

_____

D. Reasons for this wish:

_____

_____

_____

_____

E. My third wish is for:

_____

_____

_____

_____

F. Reasons for this wish:

_____

_____

_____

_____

ACTION MINUS THOUGHT EQUALS PAINFUL CONSEQUENCES

GOALS OF THE EXERCISE

1. Identify impulsive behavior as distinct from more reasoned, thoughtful behavior.
2. Understand that impulsive behavior has costly negative consequences for self and others.
3. Review own behavior and see the impulsive actions and their negative consequences.
4. Think of more reasonable alternative replacement behaviors for those impulsive actions.

ADDITIONAL PROBLEMS FOR WHICH THIS EXERCISE MAY BE MOST USEFUL

- Attention-Deficit/Hyperactivity Disorder (ADHD)
- Chemical Dependence
- Conduct Disorder/Delinquency

SUGGESTIONS FOR PROCESSING THIS EXERCISE WITH CLIENT

Impulsive behaviors are much more easily recognized by others than by the clients with impulse control problems. They think their behavior is normal and typical. You must try to sensitize them to their pattern of acting before thinking of the consequences. Review this homework with them slowly, allowing time to process each scene they have described. They will want to quickly dismiss each item and move on to the next. That impulsive action is just the problem you are focusing on.

ACTION MINUS THOUGHT EQUALS PAINFUL CONSEQUENCES

This exercise is meant to help you think before you act so that you end up with better results.

Read the two behavior descriptions for each number and then circle the number of the one that shows a lack of proper control.

Which One Is Impulsive?

1. Buying the first CD that you think you might like.

1. Looking at all the CDs before selecting the best one.

2. Sitting quietly in class and listening to your teacher.

2. Standing up or talking while the teacher is talking.

3. Waiting your turn patiently at McDonalds.

3. Complaining loudly about waiting in line and trying to get ahead of others.

4. Grabbing the first piece of clothing to wear in the morning.

4. Selecting clothes that match and fit the situation.

5. Blurting out what you think is an answer to a question.

5. Thinking for a second or two before speaking.

6. Keeping some money for savings.

6. Spending any and all money as soon as you have it.

7. Waiting for a friend to stop talking before speaking.

7. Butting into a conversation between two friends, interrupting them.

8. Jumping to a new task before another task is finished.

8. Complete one task before starting another.

9. Start watching one TV program and then switch to another and another before any are over.

9. Watch a TV program until it is completed, then choose another.

10. When you are told you must stop while playing basketball with friends, get very angry and yell.

10. When told to stop during a basketball game with friends, stay calm and obey.

11. When a friend suggests doing something wrong or dangerous, think it over and say, "No way."

11. When a friend suggests doing something wrong or dangerous, be the first to jump up and say, "Yeah, let's do it!"

12. Promise your mom you will clean your room and then do it even though a friend calls you on the phone and invites you to come over.

12. Promise your mom you will clean your room and then forget about it when a friend calls to invite you over.

13. Ride your bike safely avoiding dangerous traffic and too difficult stunts.

13. Ride your bike fast in and out of traffic and do dangerous stunts.

14. When rollerblading, do jumps and twists before you have practiced thoroughly.

14. When rollerblading, gradually work your way up to difficult jumps.

Now, return to each of the preceding 14 scenes and write out what you think the *bad consequence* or result of the behavior of acting without first thinking about the consequences is for each one. (We did the first one for you.)

Impulsive Behavior Leads to Bad Consequences

1. You end up with several CDs that you really did not want after you hear others that you like better.

2. _____

3. _____

4. _____

5. _____

6. _____

7. _____

8. _____

9. _____

10. _____

11. _____
_____

12. _____
_____

13. _____
_____

14. _____
_____

Pick six out of the fourteen scenes described previously and write out a *similar scene from your own life* when *you* have been impulsive. Use names and places with which you are familiar.

My Impulsive Behaviors

1. _____
_____

2. _____
_____

3. _____
_____

4. _____
_____

5. _____
_____

6. _____
_____

Now describe the *bad results of your six impulsive actions.*

My Bad Consequences

1. _____
_____

2. _____
_____

3. _____

_____

4. _____

_____

5. _____

_____

6. _____

_____

Finally, look at your list of six impulsive actions and write out a more _calm, reasonable, considerate, polite, thoughtful way that you could have acted_ that would have brought better results.

Good Behavior Choices

1. _____

_____

2. _____

_____

3. _____

_____

4. _____

_____

5. _____

_____

6. _____

_____

CLEAR RULES, POSITIVE REINFORCEMENT, APPROPRIATE CONSEQUENCES

GOALS OF THE EXERCISE

1. Parents learn some basic tools of behavior modification.
2. Parents learn to write clear, behaviorally specific, positively directed rules.
3. Parents focus more on rule-keeping behavior and develop a repertoire of positive reinforcements for the adolescent.
4. Parents learn to confront rule-breaking in a calm, controlled, reasonable, behaviorally focused, respectful manner and develop a list of potential logical consequences.

ADDITIONAL PROBLEMS FOR WHICH THIS EXERCISE MAY BE MOST USEFUL

- Attention-Deficit/Hyperactivity Disorder (ADHD)
- Conduct Disorder/Delinquency
- Oppositional Defiant
- Peer/Sibling Conflict
- Runaway

SUGGESTIONS FOR PROCESSING THIS EXERCISE WITH THE CLIENT

Parents will find it difficult to express expectations in behaviorally specific language—so do therapists. We must patiently try to shape parents' behavior as we process the rules that they develop. Also, be careful to bring to light unspoken rules that are left unlisted but actually are very important for harmony in the household. Use counseling sessions to review lists and to model or role-play positive reinforcement of rule-keeping behavior. Watch out for consequences that are not "tied to the crime" and are too protracted.

CLEAR RULES, POSITIVE REINFORCEMENT, APPROPRIATE CONSEQUENCES

Rules are best kept when there are as few as possible; they are stated clearly and in a positive direction; obedience is recognized by reward; and disobedience is either ignored (if a minor violation) or met with a consequence that is swiftly administered, brief and not harsh, focuses on the offensive behavior and not on the adolescent, and is somehow related to the broken rule. This exercise is meant to get you to think about what your rules are for your adolescent and what the consequences for his/her obedience and disobedience are.

Think about, discuss, and then write out the three to five most important rules of the household for your adolescent. Try to write them concisely and clearly so there is no misunderstanding as to what is expected from the adolescent. Also, be sure to write them in observable terms and in a positive direction. For example:

EXAMPLE A

Bad Rule: Johnny must take his schoolwork more seriously and be more responsible about homework assignments.

Good Rule: Johnny must attend all his classes promptly and regularly, complete and hand in each assignment on time, keep the rules of the classroom, reserve at least one hour per night for quiet study, and obtain no grade below C–.

EXAMPLE B

Bad Rule: Johnny must not explode in anger whenever he is told he may not do some activity or must stop some activity he is doing.

Good Rule: When Johnny is told what he may or may not do, he must accept the parental or teacher limits with calm, obedient respect, carrying out the request within 30 seconds or less.

Three to Five Most Important Rules

1. _____

    _____

2. _____

    _____

3. _____

    _____

4. _____

_____

5. _____

_____

When rules are kept or reasonably obeyed, it is easiest to take this behavior for granted and overlook it. But when the goal is to build self-esteem, increase compliance, and reduce conflict with authority, then it is most advisable to focus positive attention on obedience or compliance. You must find ways to reward obedient behavior whenever and wherever it occurs. Rewards do not have to be elaborate or expensive. The reward can be as simple as "Thanks, I appreciate that," or an affectionate pat on the back. At times it may be appropriate to stop and give a little speech about how pleasant it is for everyone when rules are kept, respect is shown, and conflict is at a minimum. Finally, some rewards may be more concrete, such as a small gift, a favorite meal, a special outing, a privilege granted, or an appreciative note left on his/her pillow.

Now list ten ways that you could show positive recognition to your son/daughter for keeping the rules.

Ten Positive Reinforcements

1. _____
2. _____
3. _____
4. _____
5. _____
6. _____
7. _____
8. _____
9. _____
10. _____

Obviously, rules are not going to be kept 100% of the time by any adolescent. The difficult task of a parent is to decide how to respond to disobedience most effectively and reasonably. Two cardinal rules for punishment are: First, do not react when and if your anger is not well controlled; postpone action with an announcement of doing so. Second, keep your focus on the adolescent's behavior that is out of bounds and do not disparage, name-call, swear at, or belittle the adolescent; give consequences with an attitude of respect.

Also, consequences should be given as soon as reasonably possible after the disobedience—long delays before consequences reduce effectiveness significantly. Consequences should be brief and tied to the offensive behavior, if possible. Long and extended consequences breed resentment, cause hardship for the enforcers of the consequences, and are not any more effective than something more pointed and brief. Finally, be sure to be consistent in giving consequences; both parents have to work in tandem and misbehavior should not be overlooked one time and addressed the next.

Now list two possible consequences for each of the Three to Five Most Important Rules that you listed.

1a. _____

1b. _____

2a. _____

2b. _____

3a. _____

3b. _____

4a. _____

4b. _____

5a. _____

5b. _____

I AM A GOOD PERSON

GOALS OF THE EXERCISE

1. Increase genuine self-esteem through identification of positive character and personality traits.
2. Reduce braggadocio, self-disparagement, or self-destructive escape behaviors through the realistic identification of strengths and assets.
3. Decrease the feeling of inadequacy that underlies exaggerated claims of ability or social withdrawal and refusal to try new things.

ADDITIONAL PROBLEMS FOR WHICH THIS EXERCISE MAY BE MOST USEFUL

*   Chemical Dependence
*   Depression
*   Eating Disorder
*   Low Self-Esteem
*   Physical/Emotional Abuse Victim
*   Sexual Abuse Victim
*   Social Phobia/Shyness

SUGGESTIONS FOR PROCESSING THIS EXERCISE WITH THE CLIENT

Clients often have a distorted perception of themselves and the world that causes them to see only negative traits and remember only failures. For the manic patient, this underlying core of feeling inadequate is covered with a veneer of exaggerated confidence and willfulness. Genuine self-esteem must be built through realistic self-assessment bolstered by others' support.

I AM A GOOD PERSON

Often we are quick to mention our faults and overlook our good qualities. It is now time for you to pay special attention to what is *good* about you—focus on the aspects of your personality that make you *uniquely a good person*. It is time for you to look at yourself in an honest and realistic way. You should not try to be polite and deny your strengths, but also you should not have to exaggerate to make up for not feeling good enough to be accepted by others.

1. Find the words that apply to you in the following list of nice things people say about other good people. Circle all those that describe you.

Appreciative	Reliable	Friendly
Humble	Thoughtful	Wise
Creative	Warm	Thorough
Kind	Faithful	Independent
Sensitive	Articulate	Leader
Responsible	Open	Pleasant
Considerate	Communicative	Tolerant
Punctual	Spiritual	Energetic
Attractive	Loving	Includes others
Hard-working	Trustworthy	Physically fit
Intelligent	Reasonable	Conscientious
Sociable	Wide interests	Moral
Decision maker	Easy going	Humorous
Loyal	Mechanical	Talented
Ethical	Honest	Athletic
Musical	Organized	Artistic
Well-groomed	Well-dressed	Accepting
Insightful	Polite	Complimentary
Practical	Patient	Happy
Approachable	Good listener	Respectful
Obedient	Thrifty	Helpful

Other good things about me that are not on the list of choices are: _____

_____

2. Now give a copy of the form on the following page to two or three people that know you well (parent, friend, teacher, relative) and ask them to circle words that they believe describe you. Fill in their names and your name in the blank spaces.

3. Now write a list of your ten best qualities selected from the circled items on your list and the lists completed by others who circled items to describe you.

My Ten Best Qualities

A. _____

B. _____

C. _____

D. _____

E. _____

F. _____

G. _____

H. _____

I. _____

J. _____

4. Post your list of My Ten Best Qualities on a mirror in your home. Look yourself squarely in the eye as you say each of the words out loud at least one time a day for seven days in a row. At the end of the week, write a paragraph about how you feel about yourself in the following space.

_____

_____

_____

_____

_____

_____

_____

_____

_____

_____

_____

Dear _____,
(Person's name)

Because you know me very well, I would like you to tell me what you think are the best things about me. Please circle words that really describe _____.
(Your name)

Thank you very much for taking the time to do this for me.

Appreciative	Reliable	Friendly
Humble	Thoughtful	Wise
Creative	Warm	Thorough
Kind	Faithful	Independent
Sensitive	Articulate	Leader
Responsible	Open	Pleasant
Considerate	Communicative	Tolerant
Punctual	Spiritual	Energetic
Attractive	Loving	Includes others
Hard-working	Trustworthy	Physically fit
Intelligent	Reasonable	Conscientious
Sociable	Wide interests	Moral
Decision maker	Easy going	Humorous
Loyal	Mechanical	Talented
Ethical	Honest	Athletic
Musical	Organized	Artistic
Well-groomed	Well-dressed	Accepting
Insightful	Polite	Complimentary
Practical	Patient	Happy
Approachable	Good listener	Respectful
Obedient	Thrifty	Helpful

Other good things about me that are not on the list of choices are: _____

_____

_____

_____

_____

_____

COPING WITH A SIBLING'S HEALTH PROBLEMS

GOALS OF THE EXERCISE

1. Identify and express feelings about growing up or living with a sibling who suffers from a serious illness or has a chronic medical condition.
2. Identify family stressors and/or unmet needs that contribute to problems coping with sibling's serious or chronic health problem.
3. Develop positive coping strategies to help deal with the family stressors surrounding the sibling's serious or chronic health problem.
4. Assist in finding effective ways to meet important, unfulfilled needs.

ADDITIONAL PROBLEMS FOR WHICH THIS EXERCISE MAY BE MOST USEFUL

- Autism/Pervasive Developmental Disorder
- Mental Retardation
- Psychoticism

SUGGESTIONS FOR PROCESSING THIS EXERCISE WITH THE CLIENT

This exercise is designed to help the client identify and share his/her thoughts and feelings about what it has been like to grow up and live with a sibling who suffers from a serious or chronic health problem. The exercise will help to identify any family stressors and important unmet needs of the client. The client may very well need help sorting through his/her mixed emotions. In addition, the therapist should explore any resistance or reluctance that the client may have sharing his/her feelings or needs with the parents or other family members. The therapist can also talk with the client about whether he/she would be willing to share his/her feelings in future family therapy sessions.

COPING WITH A SIBLING'S HEALTH PROBLEMS

When a brother or sister suffers from a serious or long-term health problem, this can create stress not only for the child with the illness, but for the other family members, as well. Please complete the following survey to help your therapist gain a clearer understanding of how your sibling's serious health problem has affected your thoughts, feelings, and life in general.

1. What is your sibling's specific health problem?

    _____

    _____

2. Please review the following list and place a checkmark next to the factor(s) or thing(s) that upset you or cause you the most stress about your sibling's health problem.

    ____ Sadness/worry about sibling being sick or in pain

    ____ Sadness/worry about whether sibling will get better

    ____ Sadness/worry about whether sibling can live normal life

    ____ Mom and dad seem depressed or worried

    ____ Mom or dad seem irritable and stressed

    ____ Parent(s) spend long hours at hospital or away from home attending doctor appointments

    ____ Parent(s) work long hours to pay medical bills

    ____ Financial problems—family has less money to buy things or have fun

    ____ Feel ignored by parents

    ____ Parents fail to help with my problems or concerns

    ____ Parents spoil the sibling with health problems

    ____ Lack of quality time spent with parent(s)

    ____ Family has little fun or enjoyment

    ____ Have to help out by doing more chores

    ____ Have to babysit or take care of other sibling(s)

    ____ Unable to participate in sports or other school activities

    ____ Less time to spend with my friends

____ Unable to get homework done because of other responsibilities

____ Other (please identify)

_____

_____

3. What feelings do you have because of your sibling's health problems or condition? (Please check all that apply.)

____ Sadness

____ Devastated

____ Helpless

____ Hopeless

____ Confused

____ Lonely

____ Anxious/nervous

____ Worried

____ Fearful

____ Guilty

____ Angry

____ Frustrated

____ Jealous

____ Ignored

____ Unwanted

____ Acceptance

____ Love

____ Compassion

____ Other (please identify)

_____

_____

4. Please explain in further detail the reasons why you have the feelings you checked in question 3.

_____

_____

_____

_____

5. What message would you like to share with your parents about how your sibling's health problem has affected your life?

    _____

    _____

    _____

6. If you were free to say anything to your sibling with the serious health problem, what would you tell him/her?

    _____

    _____

    _____

7. What is an important need of yours that is not being met because of your sibling's health problem?

    _____

    _____

    _____

    _____

8. What (if anything) holds you back from sharing your thoughts and feelings with your parents or other family members?

    _____

    _____

    _____

    _____

9. What can your parents say or do to help reduce your stress or meet your important need(s)?

    _____

    _____

    _____

10. What could you do for yourself that would help you cope with your sibling's serious health problem?

    _____

    _____

    _____

    _____

EFFECTS OF PHYSICAL HANDICAP OR ILLNESS ON SELF-ESTEEM AND PEER RELATIONS

GOALS OF THE EXERCISE

1. Explore how physical handicap or serious illness impacts self-esteem and peer relationships.
2. Explore thoughts and feelings about how life has been affected by physical handicap or serious illness.
3. Develop greater acceptance of physical handicap or serious illness.
4. Identify personal strengths and interests that can be used to establish a healthy self-image and build meaningful relationships.

ADDITIONAL PROBLEMS FOR WHICH THIS EXERCISE MAY BE MOST USEFUL

- Attention-Deficit/Hyperactivity Disorder (ADHD)
- Psychoticism

SUGGESTIONS FOR PROCESSING THIS EXERCISE WITH THE CLIENT

In this assignment, the client is first asked to read a story about a physically challenged adolescent, Thomas, and then respond to the follow-up questions. It is hoped that in processing this assignment, the client will feel comfortable in sharing his/her thoughts and feelings about the effect that his/her physical condition or illness has had on his/her self-esteem and life in general. The client will also be given the opportunity to discuss how his/her physical condition or health problems have affected his/her peer relationships. The assignment will hopefully help the client identify personal strengths or interests that can help to build a positive self-image and gain greater peer acceptance. The therapist should be alert to any resistance or feelings of insecurity on the client's part that may keep him/her from reaching out to others.

EFFECTS OF PHYSICAL HANDICAP OR ILLNESS ON SELF-ESTEEM AND PEER RELATIONS

Please read the following short story and then answer the questions that follow.

Thomas sat in his wheelchair at the end of the court. It was the first big boys' basketball game of the year for Glenwood High School. They were playing their rival, Calvin High. Fans were filing into the gym. Occasionally, another student or teacher would stop by and talk to him for a brief moment. It sometimes bothered Thomas that other kids would only talk to him for a moment before going off to talk to someone else. It bothered him even more when other kids would talk either loudly or more slowly, thinking that because he had a physical handicap he must not be intelligent. Still, Thomas loved basketball and enjoyed watching the games. It gave him an opportunity to get out.

The excitement and noise level began to build as more students arrived. Thomas spotted Carl Boersen, the junior varsity basketball coach, walking up to him. Coach Boersen smiled and reached out to shake Thomas's hand. He said, "Hi, Thomas. I was wondering if you could help us out tonight. Amanda Jenson, one of our statisticians, had to go home early because she was sick. I'd appreciate it if you could help us keep track of some of the stats tonight like offensive and defensive rebounds and team turnovers." Thomas quickly asserted, "Sure, I'd love to help."

Thomas's heart began to pound. He was nervous about whether he would do a good job. Coach Boersen helped set him up at the end of the scorer's table next to Jenny Higgins, a starter on the girls' basketball team. Jenny's task was to keep track of the assists and points scored by the players on both teams. The game started and Thomas quickly focused on doing his job. He spoke very little to Jenny during the first quarter. As the game progressed, Thomas and Jenny found themselves double-checking with each other to make sure they credited the right player with an assist or rebound. At halftime, Thomas and Jenny began to discuss both teams' strategies. Jenny seemed surprised about how much Thomas knew about basketball. Thomas had learned a lot about basketball by watching pro and college games on weekend nights.

At the end of the game, Coach Boersen came over and thanked Thomas for helping out. Jenny chipped in and said, "Hey, Coach, Thomas did a great job. You should get him to help again." Coach Boersen smiled and said, "We could use you again, Thomas. In fact, we could sign you up as one of our team statisticians. The pay isn't good, but you'll get a good seat at every game." Thomas excitedly exclaimed, "I'd love to keep track of the stats!"

Thomas ended up helping to keep track of the stats for the rest of the season—both for the home and away games. He loved his job because it made him feel useful. Perhaps, best of all, he became good friends with Jenny. Jenny and he had a couple of classes together and she would often talk to him at lunch. Thomas enjoyed her sense of humor and she found him to be a good listener. By the time Thomas graduated the next year, he had made several other close friends.

1. How do your peers treat you because of your handicap or health problems?

   _____

   _____

   _____

   _____

2. How do you feel about the way your peers respond to your handicap or health problems?

   _____

   _____

   _____

   _____

3. In the story, Thomas is able to feel useful by keeping track of statistics at the basketball games. He also ended up making several friends. What are your strengths or interests? Please list them in the following space.

   _____

   _____

   _____

   _____

4. How can you use your strengths or interests to feel useful or establish new friendships?

   _____

   _____

   _____

   _____

5. What kind of activities would you like to become involved in at school or in the community?

   _____

   _____

   _____

   _____

6. What are your hopes and dreams for the future?

   _____

   _____

   _____

   _____

ACTIVITIES OF DAILY LIVING PROGRAM

GOALS OF THE EXERCISE

1. Function at an appropriate level of independence in the home setting.
2. Increase participation in family responsibilities.
3. Improve personal hygiene and self-help skills.
4. Increase parents' praise and positive reinforcement of client for assuming responsibilities and becoming more involved in activities at home.

ADDITIONAL PROBLEMS FOR WHICH THIS EXERCISE MAY BE MOST USEFUL

- Academic Underachievement
- Depression
- Oppositional Defiant

SUGGESTIONS FOR PROCESSING THIS EXERCISE WITH THE CLIENT

This intervention utilizes principles of positive reinforcement to reward the client for assuming basic activities of daily living at home. First, it is important to assess the client's overall intelligence, social/emotional maturity, and level of adaptive functioning before implementing the program. Obtain reports of any recent psychoeducational evaluations to gain insight into the client's level of functioning. Conduct or refer the client for a thorough psychoeducational evaluation if this has not been completed within the past three years. Knowledge of the client's level of capabilities will help you, the parents, and client select tasks that are appropriate for this program. After the assessment has been conducted, meet with the parents and client to identify specific activities or tasks of daily living that the client can assume on a regular or daily basis. Next, select the rewards that will be used to reinforce the client for completing the daily tasks. Include the client in the discussions about the specific tasks and rewards so that he/she feels like a part of the program. This program differs from the homework assignment, "You Belong Here," because it has been designed for clients who have been diagnosed with severe and moderate mental retardation. The program can also be used with clients with mild mental retardation who are resistant to performing basic activities of daily living.

ACTIVITIES OF DAILY LIVING PROGRAM
PARENTS' INSTRUCTIONS

This program seeks to increase your adolescent's level of responsibility and independence in the home by allowing the adolescent to assume basic activities of daily living. The program is designed to improve your adolescent's personal hygiene, increase his/her self-help skills, or help him/her become more responsible around the home.

1. First, meet with your therapist and son/daughter to develop a potential list of activities of daily living that your son/daughter can perform on a daily or regular basis. We strongly encourage your son/daughter to be included in many of the discussions about this program, particularly when it comes time to make any final decisions or explain the program to him/her. However, there may be times when you will need to talk privately with your therapist about the nature of the task or responsibility. In choosing the basic activities of daily living, it is important to consider your son/daughter's intellectual capabilities, social/emotional maturity, and overall level of adaptive functioning. Select tasks that your son/daughter can perform independently. Hopefully, your son/daughter can perform the tasks without a lot of supervision or monitoring, although some adolescents may need greater supervision or guidance in the beginning phases of the program. Likewise, some adolescents with severe limitations may need more supervision throughout the entire program. Talk with your therapist about how much supervision you will need to provide for your son/daughter.

   Expect your adolescent to perform three to five basic activities of daily living. Here again, the number of these basic activities or tasks can be adjusted to meet the needs of your adolescent. For some adolescents, you may want to begin the program by focusing on one specific task or activity. You can add other tasks or activities later as the adolescent becomes more proficient in performing the initial task.

   Following is a list of tasks or responsibilities that you may want to address in this program. This list is offered as a guide to help you select appropriate tasks. Feel free to select other tasks that you feel are more appropriate for your son/daughter.

   - Comb hair
   - Brush teeth
   - Wash hands or hair
   - Dust furniture
   - Take a bath

- Apply deodorant daily
- Shave
- Vacuum carpet
- Wash dishes
- Clean bedroom
- Pick up sticks in the yard
- Take out trash
- Apply makeup (for higher functioning adolescents)
- Dress self in preselected clothes
- Select own clothes appropriately and dress self
- Make bed
- Sweep the floor
- Load the dishwasher
- Set the table
- Get cereal in the morning
- Chew with mouth closed

2. Use a reward system to positively reinforce your son/daughter in assuming the activities of daily living. Rewards can help maintain your son/daughter's interest and motivation in fulfilling the tasks. Following is a list of tangible rewards that you can use to reinforce your son/daughter. Remember, the most powerful reinforcer or reward of all may be a spoken word of praise or an affectionate touch or hug. Praise your son/daughter often in addition to using more tangible rewards such as:

- Tokens that can be traded in to purchase larger prizes or privileges
- Money
- Snacks
- Extended bedtime
- Rent or go see a movie
- Read a book together
- One-on-one time with mother or father in an agreed-upon activity
- Allow adolescent to invite a friend over to the house
- Extra television time
- Extra time to play video games
- Outing to fast-food restaurant
- Outing to local park or nature center

3. Keep a record of how often your son/daughter successfully completes a task. Use the Activities of Daily Living sheet which follows to record when your son/daughter per-

forms the task. The Activities of Daily Living sheet will help remind you to reward your son/daughter. Post the Activities of Daily Living sheet in a visible place (such as the refrigerator or a bulletin board in the adolescent's room).

4. If your son/daughter is reading at a third grade level or above, have your son/daughter sign a formal contract to formalize the agreement. Use the Activities of Daily Living Contract form. Regardless of whether a formal contract is used, it is important to clearly spell out the terms of this program to your son/daughter in advance. Your son/daughter should be aware of how often he/she needs to perform his/her activities of daily living before he/she receives the reward. Post the contract in a visible place.

ACTIVITIES OF DAILY LIVING CONTRACT

If _____ performs the following task(s): _____
(Name of client)

_____

_____

_____

_____ per _____, then _____
(Frequency)   (Day or week)   (Name of client)

will receive the following reward:

_____

_____

_____

_____

_____   _____

Signature of Client   Signature of Parent

_____   _____

Signature of Parent   Signature of Teacher or Therapist

ACTIVITIES OF DAILY LIVING SHEET

Activity	DAY OF THE WEEK						
	Sun.	Mon.	Tues.	Weds.	Thurs.	Fri.	Sat.
1. _____							
2. _____							
3. _____							
4. _____							
5. _____							
6. _____							
7. _____							
8. _____							

Place a check (✓) mark in the appropriate box when the child performs the task on that specific date.

YOU BELONG HERE

GOALS OF THE EXERCISE

1. Promote feelings of acceptance and a sense of belonging in the family system, school setting, or community.
2. Increase responsibilities or involvement in activities at home, school, or community.
3. Assist parents in developing greater awareness of client's intellectual capabilities and level of adaptive functioning.
4. Increase parents' praise of client for assuming responsibilities and/or becoming involved in more activities at home, school, or community.

ADDITIONAL PROBLEMS FOR WHICH THIS EXERCISE MAY BE MOST USEFUL

- Academic/Underachievement
- Depression
- Low Self-Esteem

SUGGESTIONS FOR PROCESSING THIS EXERCISE WITH THE CLIENT

This assignment is aimed at working with clients who have been diagnosed with mild mental retardation (IQ scores 55 to 69) or borderline intellectual abilities (IQ scores 70 to 79). Meet with the client and parents to identify tasks or activities that the client can perform that will provide him/her with a sense of belonging. Carefully consider the client's intellectual capabilities, social/emotional maturity, and level of adaptive functioning before assigning a final task. Select tasks that are both challenging and interesting. At the same time, it is important to avoid placing unrealistic expectations on the client by assigning him/her tasks that clearly exceed his/her intellectual capabilities or level of adaptive functioning. Include the client in the discussions, as it is important that he/she be interested in or motivated to perform the task. Select a task that can be performed on a regular, full-time basis or choose a task that can be performed on a temporary or even one-time basis. This exercise provides you with the opportunity to assess whether the parents are being either overprotective of their son/daughter or unrealistic in their expectations of what he/she can accomplish.

YOU BELONG HERE
PARENTS' INSTRUCTIONS

We all have a need to feel accepted or experience a sense of belonging to at least one group. Many of us satisfy this need by using our strengths to perform tasks or activities that help us to gain acceptance and respect from others. The adolescent who is faced with intellectual limitations or has been labeled a *slow learner* has the same needs as others. Therefore, it is important that such adolescents be provided with opportunities to utilize their own individual strengths and engage in responsible behaviors that allow them to feel accepted. In this exercise, your adolescent will be assigned a task that will allow them to feel that they are making a contribution to their home, school, or community.

1. First, sit down with your therapist and son/daughter to brainstorm a potential list of activities that he/she can perform. Include your son/daughter in many of the discussions, particularly when it comes time to make any final decisions. However, there may be times when you will want to talk privately with your therapist about the nature of the task or responsibility. In selecting a task, it is important to consider your son/daughter's intellectual capabilities, social/emotional maturity, and level of adaptive functioning. After brainstorming, try to select a task that is both interesting and challenging for your son/daughter. Be careful not to pressure or coerce your son/daughter into performing any task that he or she is not interested in doing since this will not promote a sense of belonging. At the same time, it is important not to assign your son/daughter a task that exceeds his/her intellectual capability or level of functioning. If he/she selects a task that is unrealistic, it is important that your therapist and you discuss this issue with him/her. Listen to your son/daughter's desires or requests, but also assert your thoughts and concerns.

    The task can be assigned on a regular, full-time basis or can be performed on a temporary or even one-time basis. For some adolescents, it is best to select a variety of tasks that will help maintain their interest and motivation. You have the option of varying the tasks from day to day or week to week.

    The task or responsibility can be performed at home, school, or in the community. You may want to consider consulting with the school teachers, church officials, or community leaders before you decide on the final activity to be performed. Following is a list of tasks or responsibilities that you may want to review with your son/daughter before making a final decision. This list is offered as a guide to help in the selection of an appropriate task and may help generate other ideas that will match your son/daughter's interests or talents.

- Work alongside parent in preparing a special meal for the family
- Work alongside parent in performing a mechanical or construction task
- Assist parents with grocery shopping
- Bake a cake (with parental supervision)
- Wash car
- Go clothes shopping with money earned from allowance
- Learn how to sew or make blankets or clothes (e.g. hats, booties, socks) for young children or infants at a homeless agency
- Plant flowers, bushes, fruits, or vegetables in family garden
- Raise flag at school
- Give a simple announcement on the intercom at school
- Assist with setting up props at a school play
- Sing with choir at a school concert
- Participate in a community hunger walk or walk-a-thon
- Volunteer for assistant trainer or bat boy on school baseball team
- Sign up for sports team
- Sign up for swimming lessons
- Sign up for karate lessons
- Enter Special Olympics events
- Enter local road race or fun run
- Actively participate in church service (sing in choir, sign up as an altar boy, volunteer for community service work)

2. If these tasks do not seem appropriate for your son/daughter, then observe his/her behavior in the next week or in the time before your next therapy session. Record any positive, constructive, or responsible behaviors that he/she exhibits before the next therapy session on the following form. Observe your son/daughter's reaction to the positive or responsible behavior. Likewise, notice how others respond to his/her positive or responsible behavior.

   Bring the form into your next therapy session. Your therapist can review the form and help you decide on an appropriate task or activity for your son/daughter. This form can also be used throughout therapy to inform the therapist of any positive or responsible behaviors that your son/daughter has performed. The therapist can reinforce him/her for being responsible. This will help to boost his/her self-esteem.

RESPONSIBLE BEHAVIOR FORM

1. Describe the positive or responsible behavior by your son/daughter.

    _____

    _____

    _____

    _____

2. What frustrations or obstacles did your son/daughter encounter while engaging in the responsible behavior?

    _____

    _____

    _____

    _____

3. How did your son/daughter manage these frustrations?

    _____

    _____

    _____

    _____

4. How did other people respond to the positive or responsible behavior?

    _____

    _____

    _____

    _____

5. How did your son/daughter feel about his/her actions or behavior?

    _____

    _____

    _____

    _____

CHOICE OF FRIENDS SURVEY

GOALS OF THE EXERCISE

1. Explore nature of parent-adolescent conflict around the issue of choice of friends.
2. Assess parents' attitude and involvement with the client's choice of friends.
3. Reduce frequency and intensity of arguments surrounding the issue of choice of friends.
4. Assist parents in establishing healthy boundaries and providing appropriate parental guidance regarding the client's choice of friends.

ADDITIONAL PROBLEMS FOR WHICH THIS EXERCISE MAY BE MOST USEFUL

- Conduct Disorder/Delinquency
- Oppositional Defiant
- Parenting
- School Violence

SUGGESTIONS FOR PROCESSING THIS EXERCISE WITH THE CLIENT

This exercise is designed for the client who has found himself/herself in trouble at home, school, or in the community, in part, because of his/her susceptibility to negative peer group influences. The exercise contains separate questionnaires for both the parents and client to complete. The exercise explores the nature of the parent-client relationship around this issue. The parents' questionnaire examines how their upbringing or own experiences as an adolescent have shaped their approach with their son/daughter on this issue. On the client's questionnaire, the client is given the opportunity to share his/her thoughts and feelings about the parents' approach. Ultimately, it is hoped that the discussion of this assignment will help the parents establish healthy boundaries and provide appropriate parental controls around this issue.

The therapist may want to consider using this exercise in a therapy session. An interview format may be used. That is, the client may interview the parents using the parent form. Conversely, the parents may interview the client using the client questionnaire. The parents and client may want to ask other questions, as well, during their respective interviews.

CHOICE OF FRIENDS SURVEY
PARENT FORM

It is not unusual for parents to experience some anxiety and worry about their teenager's choice of friends. This issue can be a source of conflict and tension in the home. Please take time to answer the following questions to help you and your therapist gain a clearer picture of how your son or daughter's choice of friends has impacted your relationship. You will first be asked to answer some questions about your own upbringing and choice of friends when you were a teenager. It will be interesting to see if your own experience as a teenager has had any influence on your attitude about your son/daughter's choice of friends. Be prepared to share your responses in future therapy sessions.

1. How much ease or difficulty did you have in making and keeping friends as a teenager?

    _____
    _____
    _____
    _____

2. What type of peer group(s) did you socialize with during your teenage years?

    _____
    _____
    _____

3. How much conflict did you experience with your parents over your choice of friends as a teenager?

    _____
    _____
    _____
    _____

4. What type of comments did your parents commonly make about your friends? How did your parents accept and treat your friends when they came over to your house?

    _____
    _____
    _____
    _____

5. Looking back, how do you think your experience with your parents has affected your attitude about your own son or daughter's choice of friends?

_____

_____

_____

_____

6. What are your thoughts and feelings today about your son or daughter's choice of friends or peer group?

_____

_____

_____

_____

7. What is your greatest fear or worry about your son or daughter's choice of friends?

_____

_____

_____

_____

8. When your teenage child has a friend or socializes with peer(s) you do not like, what do you usually say to them and how do you say it?

_____

_____

_____

_____

9. How much control or influence do you think you have on your son or daughter's choice of friends?

_____

_____

_____

10. How much influence or say would you like to have with your son/daughter's choice of friends? Would you like to have more, less, or about the same? Please explain.

_____

_____

_____

_____

_____

CHOICE OF FRIENDS SURVEY
CLIENT FORM

It is not unusual for teenagers to experience some frustration with their parents over their choice of friends. This issue can be a source of arguments within the home. Please take some time to answer the following questions. Your answers will help you and your therapist better understand how you feel about your parents' approach to the issue of your choice of friends. Be prepared to share your answers in future therapy sessions.

1. What is your parents' attitude about your choice of friends?

   _____

   _____

   _____

   _____

2. What types of comments do your parents make about your friends?

   _____

   _____

   _____

   _____

3. How do your parents express their concerns about your choice of friends?

   _____

   _____

   _____

   _____

4. How do your parents treat your friends when they come over to the house?

   _____

   _____

   _____

   _____

5.   How would you like your parents to treat your friends?

_____

_____

_____

_____

6.   How much control or influence do you think your parents have with your choice of friends? For example, do you think your parents are too strict or try to have too much control? Or, are your parents too laid back and fail to provide enough guidance?

_____

_____

_____

_____

_____

7.   How much influence or say would you like your parents to have over your choice of friends? Would you like them to have less control? More? About the same? Please explain.

_____

_____

_____

_____

8.   When you have gotten into trouble along with your friends (or peers), what percentage of the blame on the average would you say *your parents* place on you or your friends? (Please check the appropriate space.)

_____ 100% my fault, 0% my friends' fault

_____ 75% my fault, 25% my friends' fault

_____ 50% my fault, 50% my friends' fault

_____ 25% my fault, 75% my friends' fault

_____ 0% my fault, 100% my friends' fault

9.   When you have gotten into trouble along with your friends (or peers), what percentage of the blame on the average would you say *you* place on you or your friends? (Please check the appropriate space.)

_____ 100% my fault, 0% my friends' fault

_____ 75% my fault, 25% my friends' fault

_____ 50% my fault, 50% my friends' fault

_____ 25% my fault, 75% my friends' fault

_____ 0% my fault, 100% my friends' fault

10. Why do you think your parents are so concerned about your choice of friends? What would you like to tell them about their concern?

_____

_____

_____

_____

_____

_____

_____

_____

_____

_____

I WANT TO BE LIKE . . .

GOALS OF THE EXERCISE

1. List positive role models and tell why they are admired or respected.
2. Encourage participation in positive peer group or extracurricular activities that are similar to those of identified role model.
3. Begin to build healthy self-image through participation in positive peer group or extracurricular activities.
4. Increase time spent in socialization with positive peer groups or close, trusted friends who can exert positive influence on behavior.

ADDITIONAL PROBLEMS FOR WHICH THIS EXERCISE MAY BE MOST USEFUL

- Anxiety
- Low Self-Esteem
- Sexual Identity Confusion
- Social Phobia/Shyness

SUGGESTIONS FOR PROCESSING THIS EXERCISE WITH THE CLIENT

In this assignment, the client is first asked to identify his/her positive role models and state the reasons why he/she admires or respects them. After identifying the positive role models, the client is encouraged to participate in prosocial or extracurricular activities that are similar to those of his/her identified positive role model. The client's participation in such activities will hopefully provide him/her with the opportunity to affiliate with positive peer groups. The therapist should be alert to any signs of resistance or underlying feelings of insecurity that the client may have about participating in these various activities or affiliating with other individual(s) from the positive peer groups. The reasons for the client's resistance and/or feelings of insecurity should be explored in greater depth. This assignment can be utilized with clients who are experiencing a variety of emotional or behavioral problems. It is included in this chapter because of its potential for encouraging the client to engage in more desirable or prosocial activities.

I WANT TO BE LIKE . . .

While growing up, it is important to have positive role models. Positive role models, through their words and actions, can teach us many valuable lessons about how to be successful in life. We can learn a lot from positive role models by listening to them and watching them in action. Many times, it is fun, exciting, and interesting to watch our role models in action. Sometimes, we make decisions about what we want to do or be in the future by modeling or following in the footsteps of the role model. Role models may also influence us to become involved in positive social or extracurricular activities that can keep us out of trouble. Participating in these activities can help us fit in and feel accepted by our peers.

In this assignment you are asked to list three positive role models that you admire or respect. Take a few minutes now to think about who you consider to be positive role models and choose three. Examine your reasons for selecting these people as positive role models. You can select role models who you know personally or have never met in your life. These people may be famous and well-known, or they may be individuals in your everyday life who you admire and respect.

After identifying the three positive role models, please respond to the following items or questions. Fill out a separate form for each role model *(Note: Your therapist will give you three copies of this form)*. Remember to bring the forms back to your next therapy session.

1. Identify the name of a positive role model: _____

2. What qualities or characteristics of this person do you admire or respect?

    _____

    _____

    _____

    _____

    _____

3. What helped this person become a positive role model in your eyes?

    _____

    _____

    _____

    _____

    _____

4. In what ways would you like to act or be like this positive role model?

    _____

    _____

    _____

    _____

5. What social or extracurricular activities can you become involved in that will help you to identify with or be like the positive role model?

    _____

    _____

    _____

    _____

6. What possibly keeps you from getting involved in these positive social or extracurricular activities?

    _____

    _____

    _____

    _____

7. Before your next therapy session, you are asked to take some chances or risks and engage in an activity that is similar to that of your positive role model. Please take a few minutes and write a few lines about how you felt while participating in this activity.

    _____

    _____

    _____

    _____

    _____

8. How did you relate to other peers while you were involved in this activity?

    _____

    _____

    _____

    _____

9. Would you be willing to participate in this activity again in the future? Please explain your reasons why you would or would not.

    _____

    _____

    _____

    _____

    _____

DECREASING WHAT YOU SAVE AND COLLECT

GOALS OF THE EXERCISE

1. Increase awareness and understanding of the obsessive-compulsive saving behavior.
2. Identify what is saved, collected, or can't be thrown away.
3. Identify the thoughts that prevent throwing or giving things away.
4. Complete one successful beginning experience of throwing or giving something away.

ADDITIONAL PROBLEMS FOR WHICH THIS EXERCISE MAY BE MOST USEFUL

- Anxiety
- Specific Phobia

SUGGESTIONS FOR PROCESSING THIS EXERCISE WITH THE CLIENT

An integral part of the processing of this exercise is for the therapist to build the therapeutic alliance by increasing understanding of the client's difficulty with discarding or throwing away useless items. Understanding will help the client make a commitment to take a step toward decreasing the obsessive-compulsive behavior. The processing needs to be very supportive and encouraging. The client may need assistance and support from either the therapist or parent to get rid of whatever is chosen. This could mean the therapist may need to do a session in the client's home in order for the goal to be achieved. All steps are significant and need to be followed by encouragement to do more.

DECREASING WHAT YOU SAVE AND COLLECT

Saving or collecting things and not being able to get rid of them often becomes a problem. It is a problem that usually starts small and grows. Our inability to get rid of things can be troubling. The purpose of this exercise is for you to explore the issue and to decide upon a first step to reduce the problem.

1. What are some things that you collect, save, or find yourself keeping because you can't throw or give them away? List each in the following space.

    A. _____

    B. _____

    C. _____

    D. _____

    E. _____

    F. _____

2. Where do you keep/store the things you collect, save, or cannot throw or give away?

    _____

    _____

    _____

3. Who is most aware of how much you accumulate things?

    _____

4. How concerned are you about the amount of things you collect, save, and have difficulty throwing away?

Not concerned	Some concern	Concerned	Quite concerned	Very concerned

5. What are the thoughts and feelings you have when you try to throw or give something away?

    A. _____

    _____

    B. _____

    _____

    C. _____

    _____

6. To begin to change, select an item that you feel you can be successful at throwing or giving away. Then establish a date to complete this by.

    Item: _____

    Completion date: _____

7. Who can you tell about your decision who would be helpful to you in accomplishing the previous task and/or hold you accountable for completing it?

    _____

8. After you have completed the task, answer the following questions with your therapist.

    A. What was it like for you to do this?

    _____

    _____

    _____

    _____

    B. How difficult was it for you? (Circle your response.)

    a. easy   b. quite easy   c. hard   d. very hard

    C. What were your feelings after you completed the task?

    _____

    _____

    _____

    _____

    D. What are the next two items that you will throw or give away?

    1) _____

    2) _____

REFOCUS ATTENTION AWAY FROM OBSESSIONS AND COMPULSIONS

GOALS OF THE EXERCISE

1. Identify the nature of the obsessions or compulsions.
2. Significantly reduce the frequency of obsessive thoughts and compulsive behavior.
3. Learn to refocus attention away from obsessions and compulsions by engaging in other positive or useful activities.

ADDITIONAL PROBLEMS FOR WHICH THIS EXERCISE MAY BE MOST USEFUL

- Anxiety
- Panic/Agoraphobia
- Specific Phobia

SUGGESTIONS FOR PROCESSING THIS EXERCISE WITH THE CLIENT

The purpose of this exercise is to train the client in the use of the therapeutic technique, refocusing, to help him/her reduce the frequency and severity of his/her obsessive thoughts and compulsive behaviors. The exercise actually has three parts. The first part requires the client to identify and list his/her specific obsessions or compulsions. Next, the client is asked to list 3–5 alternative behaviors that will help him/her refocus his/her attention away from the obsessions or compulsions by engaging in positive or useful activities. The therapist should train the client in the use of refocusing. To learn more about this technique, the therapist is encouraged to read *Brainlock: Free Yourself from Obsessive-Compulsive Behavior* (Schwartz 1996). After identifying the alternative behaviors, the client is required to practice the refocusing technique on at least three occasions before the next therapy session. The client is further encouraged to write about how successful he/she felt the refocusing technique was in managing the obsessions and/or compulsions.

Schwartz, J. M. (1996). *Brainlock: Free Yourself from Obsessive-Compulsive Behavior.* New York: HarperCollins Books.

REFOCUS ATTENTION AWAY FROM OBSESSIONS AND COMPULSIONS

The purpose of this assignment is to help your therapist gain a clearer picture of your specific obsessions or compulsions and teach you an effective therapeutic technique to manage these troubling thoughts or behaviors. The first step in learning how to manage or reduce these troubling thoughts, urges, or behaviors is to recognize when they are occurring. So, we will start by defining both obsessions and compulsions.

Obsessions are defined as recurrent, repeated, or persistent ideas, thoughts, impulses, or images that cause the person to experience much anxiety and distress. Compulsions are defined as repetitive behaviors or urges that the person feels driven to do or perform in response to the obsessive thoughts. The person realizes that the compulsive behaviors are excessive and unrealistic.

Part I—Identify Major Obsessions and Compulsions

This assignment begins with you first identifying your specific obsessions or compulsions. Please respond to the following questions.

1. What are your specific obsessions or repetitive thoughts, ideas, urges, or images? (Please check all that apply.)

    ____ Fear of germs

    ____ Fear of getting a dreadful disease or illness

    ____ Excessive worry about getting dirty or being unclean

    ____ Strong fear or worries about one's body

    ____ Feeling dirty or "gross" about having to perform activity related to going to the bathroom

    ____ Excessive concern about personal appearances

    ____ Superstitious fears

    ____ Strong, overwhelming urge to straighten out objects or arrange things in correct order

    ____ Excessive concern about moral issues or doing what is right or wrong

    ____ Troubling or disturbing religious thoughts

____ Frequent and troubling thoughts of violence or aggression

____ Fear or thoughts of hurting others

____ Images of violence in mind

____ Strong fear of causing a tragedy or catastrophe to occur

____ Troubling or uncomfortable sexual thoughts

____ Other (please identify)

_____

_____

_____

2. Please review the following list and identify your specific compulsions or repetitive behaviors.

____ Excessive washing compulsion (e.g., frequent hand washing, showering, bathing, tooth-brushing)

____ Excessive cleaning of household objects

____ Strong need for order or need to arrange objects in certain order (e.g., stack coins on dresser in exact order each day, hang clothes in certain order in closet)

____ Hoarding or saving compulsion (e.g., saving useless items)

____ Need to keep doing something until one gets it "just right"

____ Repeating routine activities over and over for no logical reason

____ Repeating questions over and over

____ Re-reading or rewriting words or phrases

____ Asking over and over again for reassurance

____ Strong need or urge to confess wrongdoing or "sins" to other person(s)

____ Mental rituals such as reciting silent prayers to make a bad thought go away

____ Repeated checking to see if door is locked

____ Repeated checking to see if appliances are turned off

____ Checking to make certain that no one has been harmed (e.g., driving around the block to make sure no one has been run over)

____ Checking and rechecking for mistakes (e.g., repeatedly balancing the checkbook)

____ Checking one's body over and over for disease, illnesses, or blemishes

____ Counting compulsion (e.g., counting signs on highway)

____ Compulsive behaviors based on superstitious beliefs (e.g., having certain bedtime rituals to "ward off" evil, need to avoid stepping on cracks in the sidewalk)

____ Excessive list making

____ Strong need to touch, tap, or rub certain objects repeatedly

____ Other (please identify)

_____

_____

_____

Part II—Refocusing

Now that you have identified your specific obsessions or compulsions, the question becomes, "What can I do about them?" Refocusing is a therapeutic technique that has proven to be effective in managing and reducing the frequency of the obsessions or compulsions. Refocusing simply calls for the person to turn their thoughts or attention away from the obsession or compulsion by doing something else that is positive and more useful (e.g., reading a book, doing a chore, singing a song, calling a friend). Take a few minutes to think about what positive or useful activities you can do to take your attention away from your obsession or compulsions. Please list 3–5 alternative behaviors in the following space.

1) _____

_____

2) _____

_____

3) _____

_____

4) _____

_____

5) _____

_____

Research has shown that it is helpful to have a support person or coach who can help turn your attention away from the troubling thoughts, ideas, or urges. Name at least three people who can help turn your attention away from the obsessions or compulsions.

1) _____

2) _____

3) _____

Part III—Practice Refocusing

The final stage of the exercise requires you to practice the refocusing technique. Choose at least one of your alternative behaviors listed and practice it at least three times before the next therapy session. Please write about your experiences when you practiced the refocusing technique. You can answer these questions to help write about your experiences: How successful was the alternative behavior in turning your attention away from your obsessions or compulsions? Would you continue to use this same alternative behavior to resist the obsessions or compulsions, or would you try another alternative behavior in its place? Did you find your coach or support person(s) helpful in turning your attention from the obsessions or compulsions? Please record any other information or details that you think are important for your therapist to know. Use additional paper if needed.

_____

_____

_____

_____

_____

_____

_____

_____

_____

_____

_____

_____

_____

_____

FILING A COMPLAINT

GOALS OF THE EXERCISE

1. Decrease the number of complaints about life and other people.
2. Increase the focus and specificity of identified complaints.
3. Identify the difference between a complaint and a request.
4. Develop the ability to request things from others in a manner of mutual respect.

ADDITIONAL PROBLEMS FOR WHICH THIS EXERCISE MAY BE MOST USEFUL

- Attention-Deficit/Hyperactivity Disorder (ADHD)
- Conduct Disorder/Delinquency
- Peer/Sibling Conflict
- Runaway

SUGGESTIONS FOR PROCESSING THIS EXERCISE WITH THE CLIENT

Those who are oppositional defiant or have that tendency often have a long litany of gripes and complaints. Nearly always, the complaints are wide open and nonspecific, making them difficult to pin down and quite impossible to resolve. In order to interrupt this pattern, it is essential to focus the client on one complaint and work with him/her to make that complaint as specific and clear as possible; with this comes the possibility of some type of solution or resolution. The client should be deterred from voicing another issue until he/she has reasonably settled the first. Once the client has done this, he/she can present the complaint to parents in a family session or be encouraged to try the process again with another complaint. After the client has worked through two or more complaints, he/she should be encouraged or challenged to try changing another complaint to a request. When the client completes the request form, he/she needs to present the request to the person who can fulfill it. Afterward, the experience can be processed and the results compared to that of complaining.

FILING A COMPLAINT

It's natural to sometimes become irritated when you're part of a social group or family. In order to resolve such conflicts, it's important to focus on one complaint at a time. Use these forms to help you specify what you do not like and then how you want things to change.

1. Using your experience in your family, with a group, or with a friend, complete the following form that specifically describes what irritates you about the situation or person.

COMPLAINT FORM

Name of person making the complaint: _____

Date: _____ Location at time of incident: _____

Nature of complaint (include names and be clear, specific, and detailed in describing the event or situation involved in the complaint):

_____
_____
_____
_____
_____
_____

How often has something like this occurred?

____ All the time ____ Most of the time ____ Sometimes ____ Once in a while ____ Rarely

How would you like to see this situation improved? (Be specific.)

_____
_____
_____
_____
_____
_____

Date: _____

Signature: _____

---

2. Having completed the Complaint Form, try to put the complaint you had in the form of a request for change. This may be difficult, but give it a try.

SPECIAL REQUEST FORM

Date of request: _____ Person making request: _____

Nature of request (be positive, specific, and as detailed as possible in order to assure the request will be accurately filled):

_____

_____

_____

_____

_____

_____

_____

Additional Comments:

_____

_____

_____

Signature: _____

---

3. Now that you have completed each of the two forms, which form do you prefer?

_____

_____

_____

4. Why do you prefer the one you chose over the other?

_____

_____

_____

5. Which of the two forms do you think would be more likely to get you what you want?

_____

_____

_____

6. File your Complaint and Request forms with your therapist.

IF I COULD RUN MY FAMILY

GOALS OF THE EXERCISE

1. Identify the changes desired in the family system in terms of rules.
2. Develop an awareness of what it is like to be in charge and responsible.
3. Reduce opposition by understanding what it is like to be in charge.

ADDITIONAL PROBLEMS FOR WHICH THIS EXERCISE MAY BE MOST USEFUL

- Peer/Sibling Conflict
- Runaway
- Sexual Abuse Victim

SUGGESTIONS FOR PROCESSING THIS EXERCISE WITH THE CLIENT

Being in charge or calling the shots can seem like a wonderful thing and even a dream come true. But one of the things you lose by taking charge is your power to resist, oppose, and defy. Being in charge greatly restricts these options especially if you want to be effective. Adolescents who have strong oppositional defiant tendencies are good at making others—especially parents—feel inadequate and ineffective. This exercise turns the tables by putting the oppositional person in charge. It offers you the opportunity to introject the reality of what it is like for the client to take responsibility for leadership and then try to get others to cooperate with him/her. A good follow-up assignment is to have the client organize and lead his/her choice of a family activity.

IF I COULD RUN MY FAMILY

We all dream that we could call the shots, be the boss in our homes. It can be fun to sit back and imagine how things would be if this were the way it was. Here is your chance to be just that: the boss.

Answer the following questions:

1.   If I could run my family, the first thing I would change would be:

_____

_____

_____

2.   Why would you change what you described in question 1?

_____

_____

_____

_____

_____

3.   What are the things you would keep the same?

_____

_____

_____

_____

_____

4.   List several of the rules you would have for the family.

_____

_____

_____

_____

_____

5. Would there be consequences for breaking the rules? What would those consequences be?

_____

_____

_____

_____

_____

6. List all the things that you would like about being in charge.

_____

_____

_____

_____

_____

7. What are the things you would not like about being in charge?

_____

_____

_____

_____

_____

8. How would you like parents and siblings to treat you? How could they disagree with you?

_____

_____

_____

_____

_____

9. Is there any one thing that you would not allow? Why?

_____

_____

_____

_____

10. What are the things you would do to keep peace within the family and to encourage each member to treat each other respectfully?

_____

_____

_____

_____

_____

11. If your brothers or sisters said, "I hate you," "You're so mean," "You're stupid," "Other kids do it," "I'm not going to do it because I'm not your slave," how would you handle these situations?

_____

_____

_____

_____

_____

_____

12. Being in charge would be (check one):

_____ A breeze, no problem   _____ Lot of problems

_____ A few problems   _____ A nightmare

_____ Sometimes good, sometimes bad

13. Would there be a way for you to quit the job if you got tired or did not like how things were going? How would that happen and who would you like to see take charge?

_____

_____

_____

_____

14. In the end, do you think your family members will love you or be more annoyed with you for the way you did the job? Give two reasons for your choice.

_____

_____

_____

_____

15. How do you think your parents do at being in charge, making decisions, and keeping the peace?

    _____

    _____

    _____

    _____

SWITCHING FROM DEFENSE TO OFFENSE

GOALS OF THE EXERCISE

1. Identify the adolescent's behaviors that are most problematic for parents.
2. Increase parents' focus on interventions for adolescent's specific, targeted problem behaviors.
3. Develop parental consistency in intervening with and giving consequences for undesirable behaviors when they occur.
4. Develop specific positive reinforcements that parents can give for cooperative behavior or negative consequences they can give for oppositional defiant behaviors.

ADDITIONAL PROBLEMS FOR WHICH THIS EXERCISE MAY BE MOST USEFUL

- Attention-Deficit/Hyperactivity Disorder (ADHD)
- Conduct Disorder/Delinquency
- Mania/Hypomania
- Peer/Sibling Conflict

SUGGESTIONS FOR PROCESSING THIS EXERCISE WITH THE CLIENT

Oppositional defiant adolescents are masters at manipulation, making parents feel inadequate and constantly on the defensive. To change this, parents must be focused on modifying their adolescent's specific, targeted, problematic behaviors in a consistent, nonreactive manner. They will need focus, guidance, and encouragement to stick to this goal. Review parents' interventions and assist them by using modeling and role-playing of more effective interventions. Remember to emphasize consistency and positive reinforcement for desired behaviors.

SWITCHING FROM DEFENSE TO OFFENSE
PARENTS' INSTRUCTIONS

As you have been working with an oppositional defiant adolescent, you know how quickly you are put on the defensive. Once there, you seem to never get the ball back and subsequently feel like you always lose. To start to change this pattern, you must move to the offense where you can gain control of the game and be an effective parent. Like any offense, you need a game plan, which is specific, focused, and consistent, and then success comes through effectively implementing that plan.

Identify Problematic Behaviors

1. List *as specifically as possible* several of the problematic behaviors of your adolescent:

    _____

    _____

    _____

    _____

    _____

    _____

    _____

    _____

    _____

    _____

2. Now go back over the list and select three of the behaviors that are the most problematic. (It is necessary to limit our focus in order to maximize our effectiveness.)

    A. _____

    B. _____

    C. _____

Describe Desired Positive Behaviors

For each of the behaviors you selected, describe the desired or expected behavior you would like to see from your adolescent. Make the expectation as specific and as realistic as possible.

Example:

Problem: Always argues then refuses to do any reasonable request or task.

Expected/Desired Behavior: Comply with request in a reasonable amount of time with minimal resistance.

Problem	Expected/Desired Behavior
1. _____	_____
2. _____	_____
3. _____	_____

Identify Rewards for Positive Behaviors

It is necessary to reward or reinforce the positive behavior when it is done by the adolescent in a reasonable way. This is crucial if you want to see more of that behavior. Remember, the rewards do not have to be big things. (See example.) List at least three rewards for the desired behaviors you described in the previous step.

Reward examples:

1. Thank you for doing that.

2. You sure did a nice job of cleaning up.

Desired behavior: _____

Reward 1: _____

Reward 2: _____

Reward 3: _____

Desired behavior: _____

Reward 1: _____

Reward 2: _____

Reward 3: _____

Desired behavior: _____

Reward 1: _____

Reward 2: _____

Reward 3: _____

Identify Punishments for Problem Behaviors

Now develop two or three negative consequences for each of the problem behaviors. Keep in mind that consequences are most effective when they are logical and tied as closely as possible with the behavior/offense. Also, it is best if punishments are brief in nature.

Example: Not allowed to go anywhere or have anyone over until the request/task is done.

Problem behavior: _____

Punishment 1: _____

Punishment 2: _____

Punishment 3: _____

Problem behavior: _____

Punishment 1: _____

Punishment 2: _____

Punishment 3: _____

Problem behavior: _____

Punishment 1: _____

Punishment 2: _____

Punishment 3: _____

Rewards or punishments should be administered in a prompt manner as near as possible to the achievement or misbehavior. It will take attention and focus to do this consistently.

Plan Ahead to Avoid Problems

To increase your effectiveness, it is helpful to anticipate and plan for possible misbehavior. This will better prepare you to intervene in a timely manner and on your terms and make you less likely to overreact. For each of the three problem behaviors, develop a strategy for trying to make the positive behavior occur and avoid the problem behavior.

Example: Let the adolescent know ahead of time that you plan to ask him/her to do something this afternoon.

1. _____
_____

2. _____
_____

3. _____
_____

PANIC ATTACK RATING FORM

GOALS OF THE EXERCISE

1. Reduce the frequency and intensity of panic attacks to a significant degree.
2. Develop effective coping strategies to manage panic attacks.
3. Develop insight into the factors contributing to the onset of panic attacks.
4. Provide feedback to the therapist regarding the effectiveness of coping strategies in managing panic attacks.

ADDITIONAL PROBLEMS FOR WHICH THIS EXERCISE MAY BE MOST USEFUL

- Anxiety
- Social Phobia/Shyness

SUGGESTIONS FOR PROCESSING THIS EXERCISE WITH THE CLIENT

In this homework assignment, the client is asked to complete a rating form and respond to several questions after he/she experiences a panic attack. We recommend that you first consider referring the client for a medication evaluation and train him/her in the use of various coping strategies before asking the client to complete the rating form. Teach such coping strategies as progressive relaxation, positive self-talk, cognitive restructuring, and diversion. On the form, the client is asked to rate the intensity of his/her anxiety, identify the precipitating events or factors contributing to the onset of the panic attack, and identify how other family members or significant others respond to his/her panic attacks. The client's response to this last question may help the therapist understand how other family members or significant others may react to reinforce or maintain the client's symptoms. The client is also asked how well he/she feels the coping strategies are helping to manage the panic attacks.

PANIC ATTACK RATING FORM

Panic attacks can seem frightening when a person is in the midst of one. The intense anxiety combined with other symptoms such as shortness of breath, pounding heart, dizziness, sweating, nausea, trembling, and shaking can cause the person to feel like he/she is not in control. It may help to know that you are not alone. Many people suffer from panic attacks. The good news is that panic attacks can be treated successfully. So, do not despair or give up hope! There are strategies that you can use to manage your anxiety.

In this homework assignment, you are asked to complete a rating form or questionnaire each time you experience a panic attack. However, before you are given the Panic Attack Rating Form, your therapist will talk with you about how you can manage your anxiety. Your therapist may refer you to your physician or psychiatrist for a medication evaluation. If you are placed on medication, then it is important that you keep a close watch on how well the medication is helping to manage your anxiety. Your therapist will also provide training on different coping strategies, such as relaxation, deep breathing, positive self-talk, diversion, behavior substitution, and challenging your irrational thoughts. Research has proven these strategies to be helpful in decreasing anxiety.

We encourage you to remember that all people experience some anxiety from time to time. Anxiety is a normal part of life. In line with this thinking, we encourage you to try to accept your anxiety when you feel a panic attack is coming on. It may sound odd, but try to accept your anxiety and "go with it." Relax and breathe deeply and slowly. Don't fight it! Fighting or resisting the anxiety only serves to create more anxiety and tension.

Next, watch and rate your anxiety during the panic attack. Rate your anxiety on a scale from 0 to 100. Notice that the intensity of your anxiety will go up and down. Your anxiety will not stay at a high level forever. Your anxiety attack will pass.

Try to act as normally as possible. Perform many of the activities that you typically do in your everyday life. You may need to slow down, but act as if you aren't having a panic attack. Remember to take slow, deep breaths. Some people find it helpful to listen to relaxing music. Walk around the house or neighborhood. Play cards or a game. Shoot some baskets. Clean your room (your mother will love that one).

If your anxiety persists, then just keep repeating these steps. Remember, the anxiety will pass. Your body will not allow you to have a panic attack forever.

After the anxiety attack has passed, compliment yourself on getting through it. Reflect on the positive steps that you have taken to manage your anxiety. Do not set a goal of never having another anxiety attack. Rather, remind yourself that you have the skills to manage your anxiety. Feel confident in knowing that if you do have another anxiety attack, you will know what to do.

PANIC ATTACK RATING FORM

Anxiety Scale

0	10	20	30	40	50	60	70	80	90	100

None   Mild   Moderate   High   Severe

- Please rate the overall level of your anxiety during the panic attack: _____
- What was the highest point of your panic attack? _____
- Approximately, how long did your panic attack last? _____
- What problems or stressful events were you experiencing shortly *before* your panic attack?

  _____

  _____

  _____

- What anxious or negative thoughts were you experiencing shortly *before* the panic attack?

  _____

  _____

  _____

- How did your family members, friends, or peers react *during and after* your panic attack?

  _____

  _____

- What strategies did you use to deal with your anxiety?

  _____

  _____

  _____

- How helpful were the strategies in managing your anxiety?

  _____

  _____

  _____

- What would you do differently, in the future, if you have another panic attack?

  _____

  _____

  _____

PANIC SURVEY

GOALS OF THE EXERCISE

1. Identify nature and frequency of panic attacks.
2. Explore situations, stressors, or events that can precipitate panic attacks.
3. Develop coping strategies to manage panic attacks more effectively.

ADDITIONAL PROBLEMS FOR WHICH THIS EXERCISE MAY BE MOST USEFUL

- Anxiety
- Posttraumatic Stress Disorder (PTSD)
- Social Phobia/Shyness
- Specific Phobia

SUGGESTIONS FOR PROCESSING THIS EXERCISE WITH THE CLIENT

This assignment is to be utilized in the early stages of treatment. In fact, the therapist may want to consider mailing the survey out before the initial session. The client's responses can help provide diagnostic information about whether he/she has a panic disorder. The assignment will also help the client identify the common signs of his/her panic attacks. The client's responses will indicate whether the panic attacks often seem to "come out of the blue" or whether they arise in certain situations. The client is also asked to identify what strategies or interventions have or have not proven to be effective in managing the panic attacks. After reviewing the client's survey, the therapist can then teach the client coping strategies to effectively manage the panic attacks.

PANIC SURVEY

Please complete the following survey to help your therapist gain a better understanding of your panic attacks.

1. What physical or bodily symptoms of a panic attack do you experience? (Please place a checkmark next to the appropriate space.)

    ____ Increased heart rate   ____ Sweating

    ____ Shortness of breath/rapid breathing/hyperventilating   ____ Dizzy/lightheaded

    ____ Nausea

    ____ Chest pain/pressure   ____ Hot flashes

    ____ Choking/suffocating feeling   ____ Tingling sensation in feet, arms, or legs

    ____ Trembling/shaking

2. What psychological or emotional signs of a panic attack do you experience? (Place a checkmark next to the appropriate space.)

    ____ Intense anxiety   ____ Feeling trapped

    ____ Fear or terror   ____ Feeling out of control

    ____ Thoughts that I am having a heart attack   ____ Depersonalization or feelings that things do not seem real

    ____ Fear of dying   ____ Fear of "going crazy"

3. How often do you experience the panic attacks? (For example, if you have on the average of three panic attacks weekly, then fill in the spaces as follows: __3__ times per __week__.)

    ____ times per ____ day ____ week ____ month ____ year

4. Do the panic attacks often seem to come "out of the blue?"

    ____ yes   ____ no

5. On the other hand, some people experience the panic attacks in certain situations. In what situations do you commonly experience the panic attacks? (Place check the appropriate spaces.)

____ Going out in public

____ Large, crowded settings (e.g., mall, sporting events)

____ Going home

____ Going to school or at school

____ Before taking a test

____ Before participating in a sporting event or concert

____ Going to a new place

____ Social events/peer gatherings

____ Driving

____ Talking to person of opposite sex

____ Other (please identify)

_____

_____

6. What strategies or interventions have helped you to manage or deal with the panic attacks? Review the following list and place a checkmark next to the strategies that have helped.

____ Deep breathing

____ Relaxation techniques

____ Accept anxiety/don't fight it

____ Distract myself

____ Listen to music

____ Clean/do schoolwork

____ Take a walk

____ Exercise

____ Perform physical activity

____ Talk to parent or friend

____ Write in journal

____ Other (please identify)

_____

_____

7. What strategies have not helped, or what things make the panic attacks worse?

_____

_____

_____

_____

Please bring your survey to your next session. Your therapist will review your answers and help you to identify coping strategies that can help you, in turn, manage the panic attacks.

EVALUATING THE STRENGTH OF YOUR PARENTING TEAM

GOALS OF THE EXERCISE

1. Parents identify strengths in order to build or increase confidence in parenting.
2. Parents identify any areas that could be strengthened.
3. Parents evaluate the distribution of parenting load and make any needed adjustments.
4. Parents resolve any conflicts or differences that have decreased effectiveness of the parenting team.

ADDITIONAL PROBLEMS FOR WHICH THIS EXERCISE MAY BE MOST USEFUL

- Attention-Deficit/Hyperactivity Disorder (ADHD)
- Autism/Pervasive Developmental Disorder

SUGGESTIONS FOR PROCESSING THIS EXERCISE WITH THE CLIENT

Parenting is an area that people enter with little, if any, training. While being a single parent is certainly easier in terms of not having to work things out with anyone else, the downside is that it leaves you in the trenches 24/7/365 and often feeling alone and overwhelmed. This exercise can be completed by one parent if only one is involved in the counseling process, or both individually if both are involved. The processing is best directed at identifying areas of strengths, cooperation, and continuity, and also at locating areas that need strengthening or conflict resolution. In addition it is suggested that special focus be placed on how the parenting load is divided. Adjustments made here can greatly effect the energy, attitude, and overall functioning of the parental team.

EVALUATING THE STRENGTH OF
YOUR PARENTING TEAM

1. List in the following space the areas of strength that you see in your parental team.

    _____

    _____

    _____

2. What do you see as your partner's main parenting strength?

    _____

3. What do you believe is your main parenting strength?

    _____

4. How evenly are the tasks of parenting divided between you and your partner? (Estimate percentage of 100.)

    You _____%   Partner _____%

5. How comfortable are you with this division?

Very satisfied	Quite satisfied	Okay (or Unsure)	Dissatisfied	Very dissatisfied

6. What percent of time do each of you spend in the roles of "black hat/white hat" or "good cop/bad cop?" (Estimate percentage of 100.)

    Partner: Good cop _____%   Bad cop _____%

    Yourself: Good cop _____%   Bad cop _____%

7. Rate the overall strength of your parental team:

Very weak	Weak	Average, 50/50	Strong	Very strong

8. Now rate yourselves as a team in each of the following areas:

    Consistency between us:

Rarely	Inconsistent	Average, 50/50	Consistent	Very consistent

Involvement with our child:

Very little	A little	Some	Involved	Very involved

Discipline of our child:

Very permissive	Lenient	Moderate/open	Quite strict	Strict

Guidance provided to our child:

Very little	A little	Some	Quite a bit	A lot

Supporting the other parent:

Not at all	A little	Some	Most of the time	Totally

9. What are one or two differences that you and your partner have had regarding parenting?

   A. _____

   B. _____

10. What is one area of your own parenting that could use strengthening?

    _____

11. Identify two things you could do to help strengthen this area.

    A. _____

    B. _____

12. Name two things your partner could do to help/support you in your parenting efforts.

    A. _____

    B. _____

ONE-ON-ONE

GOALS OF THE EXERCISE

1. Increase time spent with same-sex parent.
2. Facilitate a closer relationship with same-sex parent.
3. Increase involvement of detached parental figure.

ADDITIONAL PROBLEMS FOR WHICH THIS EXERCISE MAY BE MOST USEFUL

*   Conduct Disorder/Delinquency
*   Depression
*   Low Self-Esteem
*   Oppositional Defiant

SUGGESTIONS FOR PROCESSING THIS EXERCISE WITH THE CLIENT

This exercise can be utilized with clients who are experiencing a variety of emotional and/or behavioral problems. It is specifically designed for the client who has established a distant or estranged relationship with his/her same-sex parent. In this assignment, the client and the same-sex parent are instructed to spend more time together to help develop a closer relationship. The development of a closer relationship will hopefully help to elevate the client's mood, improve his/her self-esteem, and reduce the frequency and severity of angry outbursts or oppositional behaviors. The client and the same-sex parent are told to engage in three activities for a minimum of 1 hour before the next therapy session. The frequency and duration of the three activities can be modified, depending on the needs of the client, same-sex parent, or other family members. The activity can be either active or sedentary. If the client and same-sex parent have difficulty reaching an agreement on what activities to perform, then the client should have the greater say in making the final decision (unless the activity is costly). Instruct the client and same-sex parent to respond to several process questions after each activity. The response to these questions can help provide useful information on the nature of the parent-child relationship.

ONE-ON-ONE

In this assignment you are asked to spend one-on-one time together with the parent of your same sex on three separate 1-hour occasions before your next therapy session. The goal of this assignment is to help you establish a closer relationship and spend meaningful time with your same-sex parent. Your activities with the same-sex parent can be active ones that require a lot of energy or can be peaceful and quiet.

1. First, sit down with your parent and decide what activities you would like to do or what outings you would like to go on. Look at the calendar and plan in advance when you will spend time together. Hopefully, you can both agree on three mutual activities or outings, but if you cannot reach an agreement, then you may make the final decision. (*Note: Your parent has the right to limit the cost of the activity or outing.*) There are a number of activities that you can do together. The following is a list of ideas that may help you decide what to do:

   • Bike ride or roller-blade
   • Go fishing
   • Play basketball at local park or in driveway
   • Swim
   • Hike in woods
   • Go to the movies
   • Watch sporting event on TV
   • Watch a favorite video together
   • Spend one-on-one time talking about the parent's childhood experiences
   • Prepare a meal together
   • Bake cookies or a cake
   • Sew
   • Change oil in car
   • Build shelves in garage or closet
   • Go sledding
   • Visit a local museum
   • Go to a car show

- Go shopping
- Decorate house for holiday
- Visit another relative together

2. After you have finished each activity, please sit down with your parent and respond to the items or questions on the One-on-One Activity Form, which is on the following page. The therapist will give you three separate copies. Bring the responses to your next therapy session.

ONE-ON-ONE ACTIVITY FORM

1. Briefly describe the activity or outing.

   _____

   _____

   _____

   _____

2. What did you like about this activity or outing?

   _____

   _____

   _____

   _____

3. What did you dislike about this activity or outing?

   _____

   _____

   _____

   _____

4. How did you get along with your parent during the activity or outing?

   _____

   _____

   _____

   _____

5. Would you be interested in doing this activity in the future? Please explain your reasons for why you would or would not like to do this activity in the future.

   _____

   _____

   _____

   _____

   _____

6. What activities would you like to do with your same-sex parent in the future?

   _____

   _____

   _____

   _____

   _____

TRANSITIONING FROM PARENTING A CHILD TO PARENTING A TEEN

GOALS OF THE EXERCISE

1. Parents identify fears, worries, and concerns around parenting a teen.
2. Parents identify origins of fears, worries, and concerns.
3. Parents become aware of key areas where transitions in parenting will be needed.
4. Parents develop ideas of how to make transitions in key parenting areas.

ADDITIONAL PROBLEMS FOR WHICH THIS EXERCISE MAY BE MOST USEFUL

*   Attention-Deficit/Hyperactivity Disorder (ADHD)
*   Autism/Pervasive Developmental Disorder
*   Blended Family
*   Oppositional Defiant

SUGGESTIONS FOR PROCESSING THIS EXERCISE WITH THE CLIENT

Transition times are times of shifts and changes, which bring with them varying levels of anxiety and worry. For parents who have a child entering adolescence, this is such a time. This exercise has a past, present, and future perspective. The parents are asked to examine their own adolescent years to assess how their past experiences with their own parents may affect how they parent their own child who is now moving into or through the teen years. The processing of their own past experiences will hopefully help to decrease their level of anxiety in the present. The processing should emphasize as well as normalize the adolescent period as being one of turbulence and searching. By discussing and planning on how to deal with various issues that may arise during the teen years, the parents will feel better prepared and less anxious about facing these issues.

TRANSITIONING FROM PARENTING A CHILD TO PARENTING A TEEN

Moving into and through adolescence is a transition time for both parents and children. Identifying your concerns and feelings can be helpful. This exercise will also help you make some plans for the changes that your child is experiencing. The questions that follow can help get this started.

1. Identify your primary worries, anxieties, and/or fears about your child becoming a teen.

   _____

   _____

   _____

2. How would you describe your own teen years? (circle all that apply)

Wild/crazy	Rebellious	Quiet (underground)
Emotional	Moderate (up/down)	Turbulent
Moody	Continual crisis	Low-key/low conflict
Tense	Enjoyable/fun	Carefree

3. Describe your relationship with your parents during these years and identify the major conflicts you experienced with them.

   _____

   _____

   _____

   _____

4. Overall, my parents coped with me and my siblings' teen years:

   |_____|_____|_____|_____|
   Not at all   Poorly   Okay   Well   Very well

5. One thing I would have liked my parents to have done differently or better during my teen years was:

   _____

   _____

   _____

6. When it came to shifting from parenting a child to parenting a teen, my parents overall did:

Poor	Fair	Okay	Good	Great

7. Identify a shift you saw or experienced your parents make in their parenting. Be specific.

_____

_____

_____

8. Now, in looking at your present transition, identify the parenting changes or shifts you need to make in the following areas during your child's teen years.

A. Discipline: _____

_____

B. Responsibility: _____

_____

C. Privileges/Freedoms: _____

_____

D. Friends/Social Life: _____

_____

E. Money: _____

_____

9. How might you handle these specific issues that may arise:

A. Alcohol and drugs:

_____

_____

_____

B. Sex:

_____

_____

_____

10. What do you foresee as an area of particular concern for your child during these years and how might you approach and handle the issue?

_____

_____

_____

11. Looking at your approaches in questions 8, 9, and 10, it is often helpful to have support and feedback from others who are experienced and are a step removed from those involved. Who could provide this for you?

    ____ Older adult who has been through it

    ____ Teacher

    ____ Friend

    ____ Pastor/Youth Pastor

    ____ Counselor

    ____ Your own parent

    ____ Other: _____

12. Two important transitions to make in moving from parenting a child to parenting a teen are moving from dictating to negotiating and from lecturing to discussing. How ready are you to make these transitions?

    A. From dictating to negotiating:

    _____

    _____

    _____

    _____

    B. From lecturing to discussing:

    _____

    _____

    _____

    _____

CLONING THE PERFECT SIBLING

GOALS OF THE EXERCISE

1. Identify verbally and in writing a fantasy of a perfect sibling.
2. Develop a realistic perception of how siblings really are.
3. Begin to develop an understanding and appreciation of differences.
4. Identify sameness and perfection as boring and uninteresting.

ADDITIONAL PROBLEMS FOR WHICH THIS EXERCISE MAY BE MOST USEFUL

• Attention-Deficit/Hyperactivity Disorder (ADHD)
• Oppositional Defiant
• Runaway

SUGGESTIONS FOR PROCESSING THIS EXERCISE WITH THE CLIENT

Having a perfect sibling is a daydream each of us has had as an adolescent (perhaps one we have not yet given up). The assignment is designed to be on a light tone to move away from complaints, defenses, and justifications. It is meant to be fun and to promote dialogue. Also, the opportunity will occur to plant the seed of reality that, even if the daydream came true, there is a downside to everything being just as the client desires or everything being just like the client. Then further work can be approached on tolerating differences and favoritism.

CLONING THE PERFECT SIBLING

All of us have a dream of what the perfect brother or sister would be like. We would like you to give thought to your fantasy of a perfect brother or sister. Then identify the specific qualities of that person.

Clone your perfect brother or sister by answering the following questions.

1. Would my perfect sibling be a brother or a sister? _____

2. Would he/she be older or younger than me? _____

3. What age would this brother/sister be? _____

4. Why do I want him/her to be that particular age?

    _____

    _____

    _____

    _____

5. What things would the two of us do together?

    _____

    _____

    _____

    _____

    _____

6. Name three things he/she would never do to bug me.

    A. _____

    B. _____

    C. _____

7. How would my parent(s) treat him/her?

    _____

    _____

    _____

_____

_____

8. Would there be any ways my parents would treat him/her different from how they treat me? What would those ways be?

_____

_____

_____

_____

_____

9. If the two of us did argue or fight, what do I think the fight or argument would be about?

_____

_____

_____

_____

_____

10. What things would my parents have to do to keep this perfect situation going?

_____

_____

_____

_____

_____

11. What things can my parents do to spoil this situation?

_____

_____

_____

_____

_____

12. Are there things I could do to keep this going? What would those things be?

_____

_____

_____

_____

_____

13. What are some things I would need to do to be the perfect sibling to my brother or sister? (Name at least three things.)

    A. _____

    _____

    B. _____

    _____

    C. _____

    _____

    D. _____

    _____

    E. _____

    _____

14. Now, since it is not possible for me to be perfect, my brother or sister must put up with my quirks. What quirks do I have that others live with?

    _____

    _____

    _____

    _____

    _____

    _____

15. Sometimes our quirks are what really make us unique, our own person, an individual. Life is more enjoyable and interesting when there is variety in our daily living and in the people we live with. What are the unique characteristics that I could not only tolerate but actually enjoy in my brother and/or sister?

    _____

    _____

    _____

    _____

    _____

    _____

JOSEPH, "HIS AMAZING TECHNICOLOR COAT," AND MORE

GOALS OF THE EXERCISE

1. Accept the reality of parental favorites and sibling conflict.
2. Increase awareness of own part in contributing to the conflict.
3. Identify specific things that could be done to help reduce the conflict.
4. Accept the possibility of the resolution of the conflict.

ADDITIONAL PROBLEMS FOR WHICH THIS EXERCISE MAY BE MOST USEFUL

- Low Self-Esteem
- Physical/Emotional Abuse Victim
- Runaway

SUGGESTIONS FOR PROCESSING THIS EXERCISE WITH THE CLIENT

Two things that are very difficult for us to accept are that most parents have favorite children and that there is sibling conflict in all families. To know and to accept this as a normal occurrence, if it is not too extreme, normalizes it and can make it easier to deal with. The Old Testament of the Bible has three stories (Cain and Abel, Jacob and Esau, and Joseph) that are great examples of this conflict and how it can have bad results or be resolved to good ends. Stories stay with us and help us look at our own situations and, perhaps, see different possibilities. It could be beneficial to have the client review his/her responses with both you and the parents.

JOSEPH, "HIS AMAZING TECHNICOLOR COAT," AND MORE

Surprising to most of us, sibling and peer conflicts are almost as old as time. Even in Jesus's time, his disciples argued over who would sit at his right hand in heaven, but that's far from where these conflicts started. Cain and Abel, Jacob and Esau, as well as Joseph and his brothers are older examples of siblings who had big conflicts. Let's take a look at the story of Joseph to see what the conflicts were, what happened as a result of the conflicts, and if the siblings were able to work them out. The story can be found in the Bible in Genesis, Chapter 37 through Chapter 50 or, in a shorter version, in some book of Bible stories.

Carefully read the story and think about it, then answer the following questions.

1. What were the conflicts between Joseph and his brothers?

_____

_____

_____

_____

_____

_____

2. Can you identify the causes of these conflicts?

_____

_____

_____

_____

_____

_____

3. In this story, do you identify more with Joseph or his brothers? Give a brief explanation for your choice.

_____

_____

_____

4. What are your thoughts about parents like Joseph's dad, Jacob, who have favorite children?

    _____

    _____

    _____

    _____

    _____

    _____

5. Do you think (circle one) **All   Most   Some   A few   None**   of parents have favorites?

6. Your dad's favorite child is _____

    Your mother's favorite child is _____

    What do you think makes each of them your parent's favorite?

    _____

    _____

    _____

7. From the following list, can you identify feelings that Joseph's brothers had about him being the favorite? (Circle as many as you think may fit.)

Angry	Happy	Unloved
Sad	Hurt	Second best
Relief	Lonely	It was no big deal
Envious	Left out	Unwanted
Ignored	Lucky	Nice for him

8. If you are not a parent's favorite (in your opinion), which of the preceding feelings have you felt? (List at least three.)

    A. _____   B. _____   C. _____

9. How do you think you would feel if your brother or sister shared his/her dream where you and the rest of the family were bowing down to him/her?

    _____

    _____

    _____

    _____

    _____

    _____

10. Joseph's brothers made a plan to get rid of Joseph. What do you think of their plan and its results? Have you ever made plans in your head to harm or get rid of a brother or sister? What was your plan?

_____

_____

_____

_____

11. After the plan worked, what feelings do you think Joseph's brothers might have had? (Circle the feelings.)

Angry	Upset	Guilty
Worried	Overjoyed	Sad
Glad	Nervous	Lonely

12. It was a long time before Joseph saw his brothers again. In the following list, check what you think might have gone through his mind in those many years.

____ Maybe I shouldn't have bragged so much.

____ Why did they do that to me?

____ Just wait till I can get my hands on them. I'll . . .

____ Boy, they were sure ticked with me!

____ Acting so special really upset them.

13. What did you think of how they became friends again? Could you have done that if you were Joseph?

_____

_____

_____

_____

14. Since it was possible for Joseph to make peace with his brothers, how might you possibly resolve things with your brothers or sisters?

_____

_____

_____

_____

_____

_____

NEGOTIATING A PEACE TREATY

GOALS OF THE EXERCISE

1. Increase a general understanding of issues that cause conflict and what it might take to resolve them.
2. Identify specific personal issues that cause conflict and possible resolutions.
3. Identify barriers to reaching a state of peace.
4. Develop an understanding of the need to give and take in relationships in order to make them work.

ADDITIONAL PROBLEMS FOR WHICH THIS EXERCISE MAY BE MOST USEFUL

*   Attention-Deficit/Hyperactivity Disorder (ADHD)
*   Conduct Disorder/Delinquency
*   Oppositional Defiant
*   Runaway

SUGGESTIONS FOR PROCESSING THIS EXERCISE WITH THE CLIENT

As in most serious emotional conflicts, people get locked into a position from which they either willingly or unknowingly have difficulty shifting away from. This exercise is designed to look for cracks, little openings, and possibilities for further dialogue. When processing, suggest possible alternatives, different views, and possibilities. Hold out the ultimate hope of the client feeling better by reaching a settlement of the interpersonal conflict.

NEGOTIATING A PEACE TREATY

Most disagreements, wars, and so forth between countries are worked out and settled by a peace treaty. The process of reaching that point is the result of hours of talking to work things out, with perhaps both sides getting a little and giving a little. It starts with exploring the possibilities of both parties getting together. To understand what they are thinking and wanting, papers similar to this questionnaire are filled out and exchanged between the people who will attempt to work out the peace treaty.

As a beginning for you, answer the following questions.

1. Clearly state reasons for the disagreement or war you have with your brother or sister or peer.

   _____

   _____

   _____

   _____

2. What are the specific things he/she has done to you that caused the disagreement/war?

   A. _____

   B. _____

   C. _____

   D. _____

3. What is one thing he/she could start doing now to show you that he/she is serious about trying to get along?

   _____

   _____

4. Is there one thing you could begin to do now to show you are serious about making things better between you?

   _____

   _____

5. Name one specific thing that would have to change in order for you to make peace.

   _____

   _____

6. List other things that would need to change or stop for you to make peace with your sibling/s or peers.

    _____

    _____

    _____

    _____

7. To get what we want, we often have to give, at least a little: What do you think you need to do or give up to make peace a possibility? (Write down only those things you are really prepared to do or give up.)

    _____

    _____

    _____

8. Others can often be helpful in making a peace treaty truly work. Are there some specific things your parents could do to help make your agreement to peace successful?

    _____

    _____

    _____

9. What should your parents not do, in your opinion, because these things would only make the conflict between you and your sibling worse?

    _____

    _____

    _____

    _____

10. If one or both of you in the conflict fail to live up to what is agreed upon for making peace, what do you feel needs to be done?

    _____

    _____

    _____

    _____

11. As you have started to think about the possibility of making peace, how hopeful are you of this working out?

No chance	Doubtful	Maybe	Likely	Very sure

Now that you have completed this questionnaire, share it with your therapist and explore the possibilities, based on your answers here, of you and the other party meeting with a third party to try to negotiate a peace treaty.

LETTER OF EMPOWERMENT

GOALS OF THE EXERCISE

1. Tell the story of the physical abuse by writing a letter.
2. Identify and express feelings connected to the physical abuse in the context of a supportive, therapeutic environment.
3. Recognize and verbalize how physical abuse has impacted life.
4. Decrease feelings of shame and guilt by affirming the perpetrator as being responsible for the abuse.

ADDITIONAL PROBLEMS FOR WHICH THIS EXERCISE MAY BE MOST USEFUL

- Conduct Disorder/Delinquency
- Depression
- Oppositional Defiant
- Sexual Abuse Victim

SUGGESTIONS FOR PROCESSING THIS EXERCISE WITH THE CLIENT

In this assignment, the client is instructed to write a letter to the perpetrator in order to allow the client to express his/her feelings connected to the physical abuse. It is also hoped that the client will gain a sense of empowerment through writing the letter. First, the client is asked to respond to a series of questions before actually writing the letter to help him/her organize his/her thoughts. The questions listed on the following pages are offered as guides to help write the letter. Some of the questions may not be relevant to your particular client. Encourage the client to express other thoughts and feelings that may be unique to his/her traumatic experience. After the client responds to the questions, he/she can then begin to write the letter. Instruct the client to bring the letter to the following therapy session to process with you. This assignment is also appropriate for adolescents who may not have been actual victims of physical abuse, but may have witnessed other family members being victimized. Be sensitive to not assign this task to clients who dislike writing or have a learning disability in written expression.

LETTER OF EMPOWERMENT

Physical abuse produces a lot of pain and hurt, both physically and emotionally. It is very important for the person who has suffered the pain and hurt of physical abuse to be able to express his/her thoughts and feelings. In this assignment, you are asked to write a letter to the perpetrator or person who hurt you. Writing the letter not only gives you the opportunity to share your thoughts and feelings, but also the chance to tell how the physical abuse has affected your life. Bring the letter to your next therapy session so your therapist can discuss the letter with you and better understand your thoughts, feelings, and experiences. Your therapist will also talk with you about what you want to do with the letter.

First, find a quiet or relaxing place where you can write the letter. This will help you to concentrate on writing down your own thoughts and feelings without being distracted or interrupted.

After finding a quiet or relaxing place, please respond to the following questions. These questions will help you organize your thoughts and feelings before you actually begin to write the letter to the perpetrator. These questions are offered as a guide to help you write your letter. You may find that some of the questions may not apply to you. Therefore, you may leave those items blank. Space is also provided for you to express any additional thoughts or feelings that you may want to include in your letter. Feel free to write down whatever thoughts or feelings that come into your mind at this stage of the assignment. You can decide later as to whether you want to include these thoughts in your final letter.

1. What events occurred shortly before the physical abuse?

_____

_____

_____

_____

_____

2. When did the physical abuse occur and with whom? At what times or in what places?

_____

_____

_____

_____

_____

3. What thoughts and feelings did you experience toward _____ during the abuse?
    (Name of perpetrator)

    _____

    _____

    _____

    _____

4. What thoughts and feelings did you experience toward _____ after the abuse?
    (Name of perpetrator)

    _____

    _____

    _____

    _____

5. How did the physical abuse make you feel about yourself?

    _____

    _____

    _____

    _____

6. How has the physical abuse affected your life?

    _____

    _____

    _____

    _____

7. Have you experienced any shame or guilt about the physical abuse? If so, please explain.

    _____

    _____

    _____

    _____

8. If you were free to say anything to _____, what would you say
    to him/her?
    (Name of perpetrator)

    _____

    _____

    _____

    _____

    _____

9. How do you feel toward _____ today?
    (Name of perpetrator)

    _____

    _____

    _____

    _____

10. What is your relationship like with _____ today?
    (Name of perpetrator)

    _____

    _____

    _____

    _____

Please use the following space to express any other thoughts or feelings that you would
like to include in the letter.

_____

_____

_____

_____

_____

_____

11. Next, review your responses and begin to write your letter on a separate piece of paper.
    Remember, this is your letter, so share the thoughts and feelings that are important
    to you. Bring the completed letter to your next therapy session to go over with your
    therapist. After discussing the letter, please consider what you would like to do with
    the letter—do you want to destroy it or throw the letter away? Would you like to save
    the letter? Would you like to share the letter? Your therapist can help you answer
    these questions.

MY THOUGHTS AND FEELINGS

GOALS FOR THE EXERCISE

1. Increase ability to identify and verbally express thoughts, feelings, and needs.
2. Help establish rapport with therapist in the beginning stages of therapy.
3. Gain insight into family dynamics or the quality of relationships with family members or significant others.
4. Express feelings about family members or individual(s) associated with the physical abuse.

ADDITIONAL PROBLEMS FOR WHICH THIS EXERCISE MAY BE MOST USEFUL

*   Low Self-Esteem
*   Oppositional Defiant
*   Runaway
*   Sexual Abuse Victim

SUGGESTIONS FOR PROCESSING THIS EXERCISE WITH THE CLIENT

In this exercise, the client is instructed to fill out a form that is similar in format to an incomplete sentences blank. It is recommended that this exercise be used in the beginning stages of therapy to help you establish rapport with the client and to allow the client to begin to express his/her thoughts, feelings, or needs. The fill-in-the-blanks form can be used with adolescents who are experiencing a variety of emotional or behavioral problems. It has been included in this section for physical abuse victims because of its potential to help the client express his/her feelings about the individual(s) associated with the physical abuse. Use the exercise as a homework assignment or as an intervention in a therapy session. The significance of the responses on the form will vary. Some clients may produce responses of little therapeutic value, while other clients will produce very meaningful responses.

MY THOUGHTS AND FEELINGS

In this exercise, you are asked to complete several statements to express your true thoughts and feelings. There are no right or wrong answers, only your answers. Have fun while filling out the form, but also be serious.

Please complete the following statements. Please try to do all of them:

1. The best day of my life was when _____

_____

_____

2. The worst day of my life was when _____

_____

_____

3. I felt very proud of myself when _____

_____

_____

4. I felt very embarrassed when _____

_____

_____

5. The one thing I wish I could do all over again is _____

_____

_____

6. If I were stranded on a deserted island, the person(s) I would most like to have with me is/are _____

_____

_____

7. If I were stranded on a deserted island, the person(s) I would least like with me is/are

_____

_____

_____

8. The place I would most like to go to in the world is _____.
   (Name of place)

   _____

   _____

   _____

9. If I could send my mother/_____ anywhere in the world, I would
   (Name of adult female)
   send her to _____ because _____
   (Name of place)

   _____

   _____

   _____

10. If I could send my father/_____ anywhere in the world, I would send
    (Name of adult male)
    him to _____ because _____
    (Name of place)

    _____

    _____

    _____

11. If I could send _____ anywhere in the world, I would send him/her
    (Name of sibling or peer)
    to_____ because _____
    (Name of place)

    _____

    _____

    _____

12. I think I am most like the following animal: _____ because

    _____

    _____

13. I think my mother/_____ is most like the following animal:
    (Name of adult female)
    _____ because _____

    _____

    _____

14. I think my father/_____ is most like the following animal:
    (Name of adult male)
    _____ because _____

    _____

    _____

15. I think _____ is most like the following animal:
    (Name of sibling or peer)
    _____ because _____

    _____

    _____

16. If I were free to say anything to my mother/_____, I would tell
    (Name of adult female)
    her:

    _____

    _____

17. If I were free to say anything to my father/_____, I would tell
    (Name of adult male)
    him:

    _____

    _____

18. If I were free to say anything to _____, I would tell him/her:
    (Name of sibling or peer)

    _____

    _____

19. I would like to change the following rule at home:

    _____

    _____

20. I would like to add the following rule at home:

    _____

    _____

21. During times that I was being abused, my feelings toward the abuser were _____

    _____

    _____

22. During times of the abuse, my feelings about myself were _____

    _____

    _____

23. My father _____

    _____

24. My mother _____

    _____

25. I wish _____

    _____

26. In the following space, answer the incomplete statement your therapist has made up,
    or make up your very own incomplete statement to answer:

    _____

    _____

    _____

TAKE THE FIRST STEP

GOALS OF THE EXERCISE

1. Identify and express feelings connected to the physical abuse, particularly around the time that the abuse was first reported.
2. Recognize and share how physical abuse has affected life.
3. Decrease feelings of shame and guilt by affirming that the perpetrator was responsible for the physical abuse.
4. Reduce the rage and aggressiveness that stems from feelings of helplessness related to physical abuse.

ADDITIONAL PROBLEMS FOR WHICH THIS EXERCISE MAY BE MOST USEFUL

- Conduct Disorder/Delinquency
- Depression
- Sexual Abuse Victim

SUGGESTIONS FOR PROCESSING THIS EXERCISE WITH THE CLIENT

The physical abuse experience often produces a variety of confusing and painful emotions that can seem overwhelming for the victim. This exercise seeks to help the client identify and express his/her feelings associated with the physical abuse, particularly around the time when the abuse was first reported. Reinforce the decision to report the physical abuse to the appropriate agency or police. Instruct the client to read the short story about a young man, Brad, who decides to report the physical abuse in order to end the violence that is occurring in his family. After reading the story, the client is asked to respond to a series of process questions. The process questions allow the client to compare and contrast his/her experience with that of the main character. Tell the client to bring his/her responses back to the next therapy session in order to process them. This story may produce some strong or painful emotions in the client. Review this story in advance. If you feel that the story is too emotionally arousing, then read the story in the session instead of assigning it as homework.

TAKE THE FIRST STEP

Physical abuse can produce a variety of painful emotions for the victim and other family members. It is not uncommon for an adolescent who has been physically abused to feel confused by the many changes in his/her emotions. The victim of physical abuse may find his/her emotions shifting rapidly from sadness to guilt, helplessness to anger, and betrayal to loneliness. It is very important for the victim of physical abuse to share his/her emotions with a trusted person in order to begin the healing process and allow him/her to get his/her life back on the right track.

Read the following story of a young man, Brad, who has experienced the hurt of physical abuse. As you read this story, you may find that some of your experiences are similar to Brad's in some ways but different in others, particularly around the time that the abuse was first reported.

Thirteen-year-old Brad lay awake at night in his bed, staring up at the ceiling. He tried to block out the shouts that were coming from downstairs, but that was hard to do. His younger brother, 7-year-old Christopher, was singing. Christopher often would sing when his parents began arguing. At first, Brad used to get irritated by Christopher's singing, but after a while he realized that this was Christopher's way of trying to block out his parents' arguments.

Brad could hear his father yelling at his mother about the washing machine, which was broken. In his mind, Brad was thinking that his father was probably blaming his mother for it being broken. Lately, his father was always yelling and blaming somebody for something that went wrong. Life had been hard for everyone in the family since his father was laid off from his job. It seemed to Brad that a lot of other little things were going wrong all at once in his family.

His father had very little patience. He would blow up over the smallest things. Brad would often try to deal with his father's angry and irritable moods by leaving the house, but this wasn't always possible. He could not leave at night, and that's when his father seemed to be the most angry.

Brad sometimes blamed himself for his father's bad temper. His father would become angry and tell him, "Quit being an idiot," when he made a mistake. Likewise, his father would become angry and swear at him when Brad became involved in an argument or fight with Christopher. Brad tried hard not to get into fights with Christopher, but sometimes when the tension was high in the house, it was very easy for Brad to yell at Christopher and take his frustrations out on him. Brad realized that he had very little patience himself with his younger brother.

Brad's frustration and anger about his home life was carrying over to school, as well. He was developing a reputation as a bully. Brad boasted of being "The Enforcer." He had become involved in six fights over the past month at school. He also was kicked off the bus for spitting at another student and swearing at the bus driver. Part of Brad liked to fight because it made him feel strong and powerful, especially when things were not going well at home. However, Brad also recognized that he was headed in the wrong direction if he continued to fight. Brad's principal and school teachers were trying to help him. They set it up so that he could talk to the school social worker, Mr. Perry, each week. Mr. Perry listened closely to Brad and tried to help him find better ways to express and control his anger. Sometimes, Mr. Perry would ask more personal questions, and Brad would become angry and refuse to talk to him. Brad wasn't ready to allow Mr. Perry to see the sadness, hurt, and fear that were underneath his anger.

Brad's thoughts now shifted back to what was going on at home. He stopped thinking about his problems at school because he heard a loud crash come from downstairs. Brad immediately got up and ran downstairs to the living room. He saw a lamp lying on the floor next to his mother. His mother was rubbing her shoulder and appeared to be in pain. His father looked up and noticed Brad standing at the bottom of the stairway. He yelled at Brad, "What are you doing out of bed? Get upstairs where you belong." Brad felt the anger swell up inside of him, but felt helpless to do anything about it. He turned around and ran upstairs to his bedroom.

Upon entering his bedroom, Brad flopped on his bed and buried his head in his pillow. He shouted into his pillow with a muffled cry, "I hate you! I hate you!" He was tired of watching his father hit his mother and younger brother. He was tired of getting hit himself over little things and having to make up excuses about the bruises on his body. He wished he could do something about it, but he felt so small.

Brad rolled over on his back and began to stare up at the ceiling again. A tear rolled down his cheek. Just then, Brad remembered a commercial he had seen on TV a few days ago where a basketball player was telling the audience to stop physical abuse by reporting it. Brad wondered who he could tell. He also worried about what would happen if he did tell. He could just imagine how angry his father would become. Yet, Brad also realized that he would just continue to be angry if something wasn't done. He made up his mind that he would tell his counselor, Mr. Perry, the next morning.

Brad woke up early the next morning and got dressed and ready with plenty of time. He walked to the bus stop and hardly talked to anyone once he got there. On the bus, he nervously wondered whether telling was the right thing to do. He took a deep breath when the bus arrived at school, but kept telling himself he had to do this. He walked into the counselor's office and asked to see Mr. Perry. He had to wait a few minutes before Mr. Perry was able to see him. Mr. Perry came out into the waiting area and recognized right away that Brad was upset. Inside his office, Mr. Perry asked Brad what was wrong. Brad's knees quivered as he began to talk about the events that had happened the night before in his home. Mr. Perry listened quietly. Brad shared other incidents where his father had lost control and hit Christopher or himself so hard that he left bruises. After Brad finished sharing his stories, Mr. Perry looked at Brad and said, "I admire your courage in being able to tell me about what's going on in your family." Mr. Perry said that it was his responsibility to report the abuse. Brad nodded his head in understanding. Mr. Perry added, "I know it must be frightening for you to hear that I have to report this abuse, but you've done the right thing. You've taken the right step toward ending the abuse in your home."

Mr. Perry made a phone call. A caseworker from Children's Protective Services came to school later that afternoon to talk with Brad. Brad, with Mr. Perry's support, was able to talk about his father's loss of control. The caseworker told Brad that she would speak with his parents at a time when he was at school so he wouldn't have to be home when his father first found out about the report. Brad liked that idea.

The case manager talked with Brad's father the next day. As expected, Brad's father was very upset and angry. He first denied losing control of his anger. The caseworker spoke privately with Brad's mother and Christopher. After listening to everyone, the caseworker told Brad's father that she believed he was having trouble controlling his temper during this stressful period. She recommended that he seek counseling for himself and his family. At first, Brad's father reluctantly agreed to go to counseling, but after he attended a few sessions, he was able to trust the therapist. He began to learn ways to control his anger more effectively. He also was able to talk about the stressful events that led up to his loss of control. Through counseling, Brad's father was better able to deal with his layoff and other stressors. He was able to cope with problems in the home without becoming violent. Looking back, Brad was glad that he took the big step and reported the abuse. Even though he was scared, his family was able to receive the services it needed. Brad is able to sleep much better at night, now that the abuse has stopped.

Please respond to the following questions that relate to you. Bring your responses to your next therapy session.

1. How were your experiences similar to Brad's?

   _____

   _____

   _____

   _____

2. How were your experiences different than Brad's?

   _____

   _____

   _____

   _____

3. What were your strongest feelings about the physical abuse?

   _____

   _____

   _____

   _____

4. In the story, Brad found himself getting into more fights with his peers and younger brother. How did the physical abuse affect your relationships with your other family members and peers?

   _____

   _____

   _____

   _____

5. How did the person who abused you respond when he/she learned that the abuse had been reported?

_____

_____

_____

_____

6. How did your other family members respond when the physical abuse was first reported?

_____

_____

_____

_____

7. What is your relationship like today with the person who abused you?

_____

_____

_____

_____

8. In the story, Brad's father seeks counseling, which proves to be helpful. What changes occurred in your family after the physical abuse was reported?

_____

_____

_____

_____

9. Was anyone in your family removed from the home? If so, please describe.

_____

_____

_____

_____

10. In the story, Brad was able to turn to his counselor, Mr. Perry, for support. Who can you turn to for support and understanding?

_____

_____

_____

_____

11. List three ways that you have found helpful in dealing with your physical abuse.

A. _____

_____

_____

B. _____

_____

_____

C. _____

_____

_____

EFFECTS OF CHRONIC OR LONG-TERM TRAUMA/STRESS

GOALS OF THE EXERCISE

1. Identify the nature of long-term stressful or traumatic event.
2. Assess the impact of the stressful or traumatic event on psychosocial adjustment.
3. Facilitate expression of emotions on how stressful event has impacted personal life.
4. Develop effective coping strategies to help reduce the frequency and severity of symptoms associated with the trauma.

ADDITIONAL PROBLEMS FOR WHICH THIS EXERCISE MAY BE MOST USEFUL

- Divorce Reaction
- Grief/Loss Unresolved
- Physical/Emotional Abuse Victim
- Sexual Abuse Victim

SUGGESTIONS FOR PROCESSING THIS EXERCISE WITH THE CLIENT

This exercise is designed for the client who is enduring a chronic or stressful long-term event. The client's responses will help to identify the nature of the stressful event or trauma and how it impacts his/her life. Through processing the responses in the follow-up therapy sessions, the client should be given the opportunity to express his/her thoughts and feelings about the stressful or traumatic event. After expressing his/her thoughts and feelings, the client can then be taught effective coping strategies to help decrease the frequency and severity of the symptoms or painful emotions connected to the stressful event. This assignment is not designed solely for clients who are experiencing PTSD symptoms. It can be utilized with clients who are experiencing chronic stress over a variety of issues (e.g., growing up in a chaotic or dysfunctional family, living in a violent neighborhood).

EFFECTS OF CHRONIC OR LONG-TERM TRAUMA/STRESS

Your help in completing the following questionnaire will allow your therapist to better understand how the long-term stressful or traumatic event has affected your life.

1. Please review the stressful events listed and place a checkmark next to the item that best describes your trauma or stress. If your stressful event is not listed, then please identify this event in the space beside Other.

    ____ Being victim of acts of violence

    ____ Witnessing acts of violence within the home

    ____ Suffering or witnessing acts of violence outside the home

    ____ Growing up in a dangerous or violent neighborhood

    ____ Growing up in a war-torn country

    ____ Emotional abuse/neglect

    ____ Sexual abuse

    ____ Living with parent who has drug/alcohol problem

    ____ Living with parent who suffers from depression or other serious emotional problem

    ____ Witnessing or overhearing heated arguments between parents over long period of time

    ____ Having to deal with parents who continue to argue and fight long after separation or divorce

    ____ Death of parent

    ____ Death of sibling

    ____ Absence of parent

    ____ Absence of parent serving in war-torn country or combat zone

    ____ Chronic/long-term illness

    ____ Chronic/long-term illness of parent/sibling

    ____ Other (please describe)

    _____

    _____

2. Please describe the nature of the long-term stressful or traumatic event in greater detail. (Please use extra paper if needed.)

    _____

    _____

    _____

    _____

3. What symptoms have you experienced as a result of the long-term stressful or traumatic event? (Please check all that apply.)

    ____ Nightmares

    ____ Flashbacks

    ____ Frequent bad memories

    ____ Depression

    ____ Suicidal thoughts

    ____ Anxiety

    ____ Panic attacks

    ____ Startle or frighten easily

    ____ Angry outbursts

    ____ Fighting or aggressive behavior

    ____ Guilt

    ____ Sleep problems

    ____ Appetite problems (overeating or not eating a lot)

    ____ Withdrawn and quiet

    ____ Unable to trust others

    ____ Other _____

    ____ Other _____

4. How often does the stressful or traumatic event occur or intrude into your life?

    ____ times: ____ daily ____ weekly ____ monthly ____ yearly

    (Please identify number of times per day, week, month, etc.)

5. How often do you experience the symptoms listed in question 3?

    ____ times: ____ daily ____ weekly ____ monthly ____ yearly

    (Please identify number of times per day, week, month, etc.)

6. What triggers or causes you to experience these symptoms?

    _____

7. What would you like to say to the other people (for example, parents, siblings, friends, neighbors) who have also been involved in or affected by the stressful or traumatic event?

    _____

    _____

    _____

8. What has helped you to cope with the stressful or traumatic event? What helps to decrease or limit how often you experience these symptoms?

    _____

    _____

9. Who has helped you to cope with the stressful or traumatic event? (Please list names of supportive or helpful people.)

    _____

    _____

IMPACT OF FRIGHTENING OR DANGEROUS EVENT

GOALS OF THE EXERCISE

1. Describe the nature of the frightening or dangerous event in some detail.
2. Identify the ways that the frightening or dangerous event has impacted the quality of life both for self and others.
3. Express feelings and identify symptoms associated with the frightening or dangerous event.
4. Develop effective coping strategies to help reduce the frequency and severity of symptoms connected to the frightening or dangerous event.

ADDITIONAL PROBLEMS FOR WHICH THIS EXERCISE MAY BE MOST USEFUL

- Anxiety
- Depression
- Social Phobia/Shyness
- Specific Phobia

SUGGESTIONS FOR PROCESSING THIS EXERCISE WITH THE CLIENT

This exercise is to be given to a client who has experienced an acute or one-time frightening or dangerous event. It is not designed for clients who have suffered or endured chronic and long-term abuse or danger. The client's responses will help to identify the nature of the frightening or dangerous event and how it has impacted his/her life and the lives of significant others involved in the incident. In addition, the client is given the opportunity to express his/her feelings about any individual(s) who he/she sees as being responsible for the frightening event. The client is further asked to identify the symptoms he/she has experienced since the event. The therapist may want to review the list of symptoms with the client to clarify the meaning of some of the symptoms. During the follow-up therapy session, the client should be given the chance to share his/her feelings in greater detail. The therapist can teach the client effective coping strategies to help decrease the frequency and severity of the symptoms associated with the frightening or dangerous event.

IMPACT OF FRIGHTENING OR DANGEROUS EVENT

Please fill out the following questionnaire to help your therapist better understand how the frightening or dangerous event has affected your life.

1. Please describe the nature of the frightening or dangerous event, giving as many details as possible (e.g., when did it occur, your age, the place of occurrence, who else was present or involved, important details of what happened). Use additional paper to further describe the event, if needed.

   _____

   _____

   _____

   _____

   _____

   _____

2. How did you feel while the frightening or dangerous event was taking place? (Please check all that apply.)

____ Terrified	____ Vulnerable
____ Anxious	____ Angry
____ Worried	____ Sad
____ Helpless	____ Small or weak
____ Numb	____ Other (please identify)
____ Shocked	_____
____ Disbelief	_____

3. What was the strongest emotion you felt? Please describe in greater detail why this was the strongest emotion.

   _____

   _____

   _____

   _____

   _____

4. How did the frightening or dangerous event negatively affect your life (physically, emotionally, or socially)?

    _____

    _____

    _____

    _____

    _____

5. How did the frightening or dangerous event negatively affect the other people (such as other family members or friends, bystanders) who were involved in the incident (physically, emotionally, or socially)?

    _____

    _____

    _____

    _____

6. (If applicable) What were the consequences of the incident for the person who you believe was responsible for the incident?

    _____

    _____

    _____

7. (If applicable) If you were free to say anything to the person who you believe was responsible for the incident, what would you say to them?

    _____

    _____

    _____

    _____

8. What symptoms have you experienced since the frightening event? (Please check all that apply.)

____ Nightmares

____ Flashbacks

____ Frequent, painful memories

____ Panic

____ Shaking/trembling

____ Sweating

____ Heart pounding

____ Trouble breathing

____ Startle easily

____ Fearful

____ Avoid talking about the event

____ Avoid place where incident occurred

____ Aggressive

____ Easily angered

____ Nervous, tense, or edgy

____ Depression

____ Suicidal thoughts

____ Guilt, shame

9. Many people who have experienced a frightening or dangerous event will re-experience symptoms when reminded of the event or exposed to certain situations. What causes you to re-experience these symptoms?

_____

_____

_____

_____

_____

10a. How have you attempted to cope with these symptoms? What has helped?

_____

_____

_____

_____

10b. On the other hand, what have you tried that has not worked? What makes the symptoms worse?

_____

_____

_____

_____

RECOGNIZING EARLY WARNING SIGNS

GOALS OF THE EXERCISE

1. Parents increase awareness of the early warning signs of psychotic symptoms.
2. Parents decrease/reduce defenses around recognizing the symptoms.
3. Parents develop a plan for timely and effective intervention.

ADDITIONAL PROBLEMS FOR WHICH THIS EXERCISE MAY BE MOST USEFUL

- Mania/Hypomania
- Suicidal Ideation

SUGGESTIONS FOR PROCESSING THIS EXERCISE WITH THE CLIENT

The primary focus in this exercise is to help the client's parents/caregivers detect the early warning signs of the client's psychotic episode so they can intervene sooner to minimize the severity and duration of the episode. By closely identifying the specific steps that need to be taken, the parents/caregivers can quickly intervene when future psychotic episodes occur. The plan should be shared with the client for his/her awareness. The client's input and approval (if appropriate) should be obtained, as well. In processing the exercise, the therapist should be attuned to the reasons the parents/caregivers may have ignored or failed to respond to the early warning signs in the past.

RECOGNIZING EARLY WARNING SIGNS

To help those who have experienced psychotic symptoms, it can be very helpful for people who are close to them to recognize the early signs and then make appropriate interventions to get the individual the help needed in order to minimize the episode. Take a moment to think about your child's last episode, and then place a checkmark by the signs that you saw sometime before the full episode occurred.

1. Place a checkmark by all the signs that you observed in your child a time before the episode broke.

    ____ More suspicious of others and things

    ____ Isolating more from friends and family

    ____ Verbalizing bizarre thoughts

    ____ Change in sleeping pattern

    ____ Grandiose talk

    ____ More trouble focusing thoughts

    ____ Difficulty completing tasks

    ____ Decreased or change in appetite (avoiding certain foods)

    ____ Increased sensitivity to smells, sounds, and so forth

    ____ Not caring as much about hygiene/grooming

    ____ Increased fearfulness

    ____ More on guard/vigilant

    ____ More resistant to taking medications

    ____ More edgy/irritable

2. How have you usually responded when you first recognized the warning signs checked in question 1?

    ____ Ignored them

    ____ Minimize (not that bad)

    ____ Avoid thinking about them

    ____ React with anger

    ____ Rationalization (create a reason for)

_____ Confront him/her

_____ Question him/her carefully

_____ Other (please identify)

_____

3. When we first see signs, it can be helpful to have our observations confirmed by others. Who of the following could help confirm your observations?

    _____ Spouse

    _____ Child's friend

    _____ Family member

    _____ Youth pastor

    _____ Teacher

    _____ Neighbor

4. How effective has the feedback from the other individuals been previously?

    _____ Very effective

    _____ Somewhat effective

    _____ Not effective at all

    Explain: _____

5. What are the two most prominent or frequent warning signs that you checked in question 1?

    A. _____

    B. _____

6. How frequently have you observed the behavior?

    _____ A little

    _____ Some

    _____ A lot

7. With signs identified and confirmed, it is important to make a plan for a timely intervention to hopefully minimize the time and extent of the episode. Complete the following plan to prepare yourself.

    A. Identify the person (1) who would be best to intervene:

    _____

    B. Identify the approach you see as being the best:

    _____ Calm reassurance   _____ Tearful sadness

    _____ Stern confrontation   _____ Anxious worry

    _____ Angry denial   _____ Reality presentation

8. Identify specifically what steps need to be taken (ask therapist for input if needed):

    A. _____

    B. _____

    C. _____

9. Identify the assurances that you can give to your child if they follow your advice (i.e., by doing what you believe they need, they will feel better):

    A. _____

    B. _____

    C. _____

Review this with your child's therapist for input and feedback.

AIRING YOUR GRIEVANCES

GOALS OF THE EXERCISE

1. Identify specifically what the issues are that upset or that cause conflict with parents.
2. Increase visibility and specifics of underlying issues.
3. Decrease fight or flight response to issues or feelings of anxiety.
4. Develop the ability to verbalize issues and explore options for resolving them rather than merely reacting to them.

ADDITIONAL PROBLEMS FOR WHICH THIS EXERCISE MAY BE MOST USEFUL

- Anxiety
- Chemical Dependence
- Physical/Emotional Abuse Victim
- Sexual Abuse Victim

SUGGESTIONS FOR PROCESSING THIS EXERCISE WITH THE CLIENT

Adolescents who run away are most often from guarded, closed family systems with a high level of dysfunction. In order to get past the client's defenses, it is best to normalize things as much as is realistic and possible. Having grievances is something nearly all people who are raised in families have. This approach is designed to get the client talking more about him/herself and what bugs him/her about parents and family. The process should reflect the possibility of resolution and alternatives to coping with the identified situations.

AIRING YOUR GRIEVANCES

Grievance: A complaint or protest based on a supposed circumstance.
The American Heritage Dictionary, 2nd College Edition

All of us who are employed, attend school, live in a family, or are married develop grievances from time to time. It seems this is the nature of human beings that live and work close together or are in close personal relationships with one another. But sometimes we find it difficult to share what bugs us with those with whom we feel close. But by keeping these things to ourselves, they often fester and come out in other behaviors. Airing our grievances is a way of preventing this and feeling better in a healthy way.

Based on your family experience, complete the following exercise. Remember, getting them out into the open air is a risk, but a healthy one. (No one, except your counselor, will see this paper unless you show it to him/her.)

1. List as specifically as you can all the grievances you have regarding your family and its members. (Remember list all; none are too small or picky.)

    _____

    _____

    _____

    _____

    _____

    _____

2. Now that you have completed the list, go back over each one and rate it according to the following scale: 1 (major grievance), 2 (moderate), 3 (minor).

3. Next select your top three grievances from the ones rated as major.

    A. _____

    B. _____

    C. _____

4. From your three top grievances, pick the one you would most like to see resolved. In the following space, describe the particular grievance in more detail, focusing on how often it occurs, under what circumstances, and what your response is to it (include your feelings and behavior).

    _____

    _____

    _____

    _____

    _____

    _____

    _____

5. Can you suggest one or two ways to resolve the grievance?

    _____

    _____

    _____

    _____

    _____

6. Identify anything you can think of that might get in the way of this grievance being resolved.

    _____

    _____

    _____

    _____

7. What is your feeling regarding the likelihood of the grievance being resolved? Rate it on the following scale.

No chance	Unlikely chance	Possible chance	Good chance	Great chance

Take this to your therapist for review and discuss the next step.

HOME BY ANOTHER NAME

GOALS OF THE EXERCISE

1. Increase verbalization about the family and the home environment.
2. Decrease the resistance and secrecy about family issues.
3. Identify and begin verbalization of feelings connected to the family, its members, and its rules.

ADDITIONAL PROBLEMS FOR WHICH THIS EXERCISE MAY BE MOST USEFUL

- Anxiety
- Chemical Dependence
- Depression
- Physical/Emotional Abuse Victim
- Sexual Abuse Victim
- Suicidal Ideation

SUGGESTIONS FOR PROCESSING THIS EXERCISE WITH THE CLIENT

Adolescents who are emotionally immature often react in physical ways to the anxiety/conflicts that they experience. Usually the actions and their consequences become a screen or cloud that hides, as well as complicates, the real issue(s). It is frightening for runaway clients to examine and think about what is happening around them and within them. After a level of initial trust is established in therapy, normalize the situation that everyone has a wide range of feelings about families; this can be a helpful tool in allowing the client to begin talking about the family without increasing his/her anxiety level too much. In processing this particular assignment, keep it on the lighter side and have as much fun with it as possible. Tell the client how you viewed your family during the time you were his/her age. Always keep in mind that this assignment's purpose is to get underneath the action/behavior to find a source or reason for the anxiety; bear in mind this is something the client cannot yet see, verbalize, or acknowledge.

HOME BY ANOTHER NAME

There are many different ways that all of us feel about families and homes. These feelings can change from one time to another. Use your imagination and try to describe your family/home as either a prison, youth home, or military school.

Answer the following questions on the lines provided.

1. Describe the physical environment of the place with a special focus on your quarters (that is, your bedroom).

    _____

    _____

    _____

    _____

2. What are the guards/attendants/teachers (parents) like?

    _____

    _____

    _____

3. List the various rules of the establishment and tell whether you like or dislike the rule.

    Rule   **Like/Dislike**

    _____   _____

    _____   _____

    _____   _____

    _____   _____

4. Name the privileges available to you, what you need to do to earn a privilege, and what behavior will result in a privilege being taken away.

    | | | **Behavior/Privilege** |
Privilege	**Earn**	**Taken Away**
_____	_____	_____
_____	_____	_____
_____	_____	_____
_____	_____	_____

5. What do your fellow inmates/residents/students (brothers or sisters) feel about where they are, and how do you relate to them?

     _____

     _____

     _____

6. Rate the living conditions (that is, food, clothing, recreational activities).

     _____

     _____

     _____

7. List the fears, concerns, and so forth you have about living in this place?

     _____

     _____

     _____

8. If a strike or revolt occurred, what would cause it?

     _____

     _____

     _____

9. Given an opportunity to change just one thing about the place, what would you change and why?

     _____

     _____

     _____

10. Do you think you view this place more as one of confinement or one of safety? Why?

     _____

     _____

     _____

     _____

11. Describe how you would see yourself getting out of this place.

     _____

     _____

     _____

     _____

UNDERCOVER ASSIGNMENT

GOALS OF THE EXERCISE

1. Increase awareness of how family really is and how it operates.
2. Identify things within the family system that upset or bother self.
3. Reduce reactivity to people and events within the family system that occur by increasing awareness and understanding of self and system he/she is a part of.

ADDITIONAL PROBLEMS FOR WHICH THIS EXERCISE MAY BE MOST USEFUL

- Chemical Dependence
- Depression
- Physical/Emotional Abuse Victim
- Sexual Abuse Victim

SUGGESTIONS FOR PROCESSING THIS EXERCISE WITH THE CLIENT

Running away is essentially a reaction, an escape from unpleasant or threatening home situations. Usually runaways are immature young people who feel rejected, unfairly treated, abused, and/or anxious. Running away is an impulsive act that subverts more effective problem solving. This assignment is aimed at bringing out the unpleasant and threatening issues that are present in the family. It encourages the client to look at the family in the thoughtful manner of an observer versus a participant. By identifying specific major inconsistencies and problems, it is hoped the therapist can move on to addressing the client's issues within the greater family system.

UNDERCOVER ASSIGNMENT

Being a spy or going undercover is an exciting activity. For the next week, your assignment is to go undercover in your family to carefully watch your family, parents, brothers, sisters, and the events that happen daily in your home. In order to do this successfully, you need to remove yourself from the daily cycle of action and reaction to events and be more of an observer of what happens, what people do or say, and how they interact with each other.

The following areas are a guide in terms of what to look for and a place to record your observations. **Warning:** Keep your notes out of sight. (To do so, you will have to record them in a private place.)

1. Record daily the atmosphere or mood of the family as the day begins using the following code weather conditions: **sunny & warm, partly sunny, partly cloudy, cloudy, windy & cold, hot & humid, foggy, rain, thunderstorms.** Then forecast what the rest of the day will be like.

	Condition	**Forecast**
1st day	_____	_____
2nd day	_____	_____
3rd day	_____	_____
4th day	_____	_____
5th day	_____	_____
6th day	_____	_____
7th day	_____	_____

2. Record your observation of each family member's ability to listen to another.

Member	**How They Listen**
_____	_____
_____	_____
_____	_____
_____	_____
_____	_____
_____	_____
_____	_____

3. Often what others say and what they do don't match. Record your observations of times where you see this.

    Say

    (What is said and who says it)

    Do

    (What person does that doesn't fit with what was said)

    _____   _____
    _____   _____
    _____   _____
    _____   _____
    _____   _____
    _____   _____

4. List things that are said or things that happen to upset specific members of the family or the entire family.

    _____
    _____
    _____
    _____
    _____
    _____
    _____
    _____

5. Observe and record feelings that family members most frequently show or express (such as **angry, worried, sad, lonely, hurt, depressed, guilty, embarrassed, frustrated,** or **excited**).

    Family Member   **Feelings**

    Father   _____

    Mother   _____

    Brother _____   _____

    Sister _____   _____

    Others _____   _____

6. Observe and record compliments, positive feedback, strokes, and helpful things members do for each other.

    Member   **Compliment, Feedback, Helpful Act**

    _____   _____

    _____   _____

    _____   _____

    _____   _____

    _____   _____

    _____   _____

To successfully conclude your mission, take these sheets to your therapist for debriefing.

MY PENT-UP ANGER AT SCHOOL

GOALS OF THE EXERCISE

1. Identify factors that led up to aggressive or violent behavior at school.
2. Explore underlying emotions that contributed to angry outbursts or violent behavior at school.
3. Cease pattern of repressing anger for long periods of time until hostile feelings are discharged in an aggressive or violent manner.
4. Develop positive coping mechanisms and more effective ways to express and control anger.

ADDITIONAL PROBLEMS FOR WHICH THIS EXERCISE MAY BE MOST USEFUL

- Anger Management
- Depression
- Peer/Sibling Conflict
- Social Phobia/Shyness

SUGGESTIONS FOR PROCESSING THIS EXERCISE WITH THE CLIENT

This assignment is designed for a client who has engaged in rare or isolated incidents of aggression and violence at school and who the therapist suspects has repressed or bottled up anger for extended periods of time. By completing the assignment, the client will be able to identify other emotions besides anger that he/she experienced prior to the incident. The client is asked to identify the maladaptive ways that he/she has dealt with anger or underlying emotions in the past and more adaptive ways to deal with his/her anger or painful emotions in the future rather than allowing these emotions to build up over time and then be discharged in an unhealthy manner.

MY PENT-UP ANGER AT SCHOOL

Please respond to the following items or questions to help your therapist understand what led up to you becoming aggressive or violent at school.

1. Please describe the incident at school where you lost control of your anger and became aggressive or violent (e.g., describe where and when the incident occurred, names of other individuals involved in the incident, important details that led up to your act of aggression, and consequences of your aggressive act for yourself and others). Use additional paper if necessary.

    _____

    _____

    _____

    _____

    _____

    _____

    _____

    _____

    _____

    _____

    _____

    _____

2. What were you angry about?

    _____

    _____

    _____

3. How long had your anger been building up?

    _____

    _____

    _____

4. How did you show or deal with your anger in the past before you blew up and became aggressive? (Please review the following list and check all that apply.)

____ Became quiet/withdrew	____ Criticized others
____ Kept feelings bottled up inside	____ Criticized self
____ Moody/irritable around others	____ Felt depressed
____ Sulked or moped around	____ Cried
____ Whined or complained	____ Felt anxious or worried
____ Became irritated over little things	____ Refused to do schoolwork
____ Took anger out on family members	____ Refused to cooperate with teachers' requests
____ Took anger out on smaller, weaker, or less popular peers	____ Cut or harmed self
____ Used drugs or alcohol	____ Other (please identify)
____ Tried to laugh off stress or hurt	_____

5. What other emotions have you often felt before you lost control of your anger? (Please check all that apply.)

____ Sadness	____ Hurt	____ Helpless
____ Anxiety	____ Rejected	____ Hopeless
____ Worry	____ Ignored	____ Disappointed
____ Fear	____ Lonely	____ Other _____

6. How confident or assured are you that you will not lose control of your anger and become aggressive at school in the future?

    _____

    _____

    _____

7. What are some more positive ways for you to deal with your anger or other painful emotions if they begin to build up again in the future? (*Note: Your therapist will also help you to identify other more effective ways to deal with your anger and emotions in future therapy sessions.*)

    _____

    _____

    _____

8. Who can you turn to for help or support at school if your anger or other emotions begin to build up?

    _____

    _____

    _____

SCHOOL VIOLENCE INCIDENT REPORT

GOALS OF THE EXERCISE

1. Identify contributing factors and sequence of events that led up to violent behavior at school.
2. Explore underlying emotions that contribute to violent behavior at school.
3. Express hurt and anger in nonviolent ways.
4. Eliminate all acts of violence at school.

ADDITIONAL PROBLEMS FOR WHICH THIS EXERCISE MAY BE MOST USEFUL

- Anger Management
- Depression
- Negative Peer Influences
- Oppositional Defiant

SUGGESTIONS FOR PROCESSING THIS EXERCISE WITH THE CLIENT

The client's responses to this questionnaire will provide insight into the factors or sequence of events that contributed to the client's threatening or violent behavior. The client is asked to identify the underlying emotions that he/she was experiencing prior to the violent incident. The assignment is designed to teach the client more adaptive ways to express and/or manage his/her anger other than behaving in a threatening or violent manner. It is acceptable for teachers or other school officials to help the client complete the questionnaire.

SCHOOL VIOLENCE INCIDENT REPORT

1. Date of incident: _____

    Approximate time: _____

    Class or setting: _____

2. Please describe the incident where you either threatened someone or became physically aggressive or violent.

    _____

    _____

    _____

3. What events led up to you threatening or physically harming the other individual(s)?

    _____

    _____

    _____

4. What had your mood and behavior been like within 24 hours of the incident? (Please check all that apply.)

    ____ Angry   ____ Disappointed

    ____ Irritated   ____ Flat, no emotion

    ____ Frustrated   ____ Anxious/nervous

    ____ Lonely   ____ Worried

    ____ Felt unwanted or rejected   ____ Fearful

    ____ Happy or content   ____ Guilt/shame

    ____ Elated   ____ Embarrassed

    ____ Hyperactive   ____ Other (please identify)

    ____ Depressed   _____

    ____ Quiet and withdrawn   _____

5. What thoughts did you experience before you made the threats or became violent?

    _____

    _____

    _____

6. What were the consequences of your behavior for the victim?

_____

_____

_____

7. How did other students react to your aggressive or violent behavior?

_____

_____

_____

8. How did the teachers or school officials react to your aggressive or violent behavior?

_____

_____

9. How did your parents react to your aggressive or violent behavior?

_____

_____

_____

10. What consequences did you receive from both home and school as a result of your aggressive or violent behavior?

_____

_____

_____

11. What other coping strategies could you use in the future to control your anger at school? (Please check all that apply.)

____ Walk away

____ Ignore teasing, mocking, or criticism

____ Talk calmly to other student(s) about the problem

____ Listen better to other student with whom I am angry

____ Find physical outlet to express anger (e.g., play sports, run)

____ Express anger by writing in journal

____ Express anger through artwork or drawings

____ Talk to friends or other peers about problem

____ Talk to counselor or teacher

____ Meet with other student involved in incident and school official to discuss problem

____ Other (please identify)

_____

12. If you could do it all over again, how would you express your feelings differently?

_____

_____

_____

GETTING STARTED

GOALS OF THE EXERCISE

1. Identify the need to become honest in order for treatment to be successful.
2. Develop a knowledge and understanding of the key terms involved in treatment.
3. Increase openness and disclosure about self and acts of sexual abuse.

ADDITIONAL PROBLEMS FOR WHICH THIS EXERCISE MAY BE MOST USEFUL

- Attention-Deficit/Hyperactivity Disorder (ADHD)
- Conduct Disorder/Delinquency
- Low Self-Esteem
- Physical/Emotional Abuse Victim
- Sexual Abuse Victim

SUGGESTIONS FOR PROCESSING THIS EXERCISE WITH THE CLIENT

Use this assignment after the third or fourth therapy session in order to allow some time for the client to become more comfortable with you. Whether the assignment is or is not done well, it still provides a good indicator of where the client is and just how strong his/her defenses are. Emphasize honesty and its positive effect on self-esteem. You can repeat the assignment if the client is too evasive in answering the questions. Also, you can repeat it later to measure how far the client has come in his/her treatment.

GETTING STARTED

When you become involved in treatment for a sexual-related offense, you need to become familiar with many new terms that have an impact on dealing with the issue. The following exercise is designed to familiarize you with some of these important terms.

1.   See how many of the following words you can match with the definitions. The number of letters for the appropriate word is provided to help you.

Grooming	Victim	Trigger
Boundary	Fantasies	Offender cycle
Denial	Empathy	Offender

A.   ___ ___ ___ ___ ___ ___

The person who has been abused or violated by another, either sexually, physically, or emotionally. (6 letters)

B.   ___ ___ ___ ___ ___ ___ ___

The quality of being understanding, sensitive, and aware of the feelings, thoughts, and experiences of other human beings. (7 letters)

C.   ___ ___ ___ ___ ___ ___

A defense used by people to avoid facing the reality of their behavior or life events. (6 letters)

D.   ___ ___ ___ ___ ___ ___ ___

A person, place, activity, or feeling that could create the urge to become involved in sexually inappropriate behavior. (7 letters)

E.   ___ ___ ___ ___ ___ ___ ___ ___

Where your personal space ends and another person's individual space begins. (8 letters)

F.   ___ ___ ___ ___ ___ ___ ___ ___

Name given to a person who sexually takes advantage of another person who is younger than him/her (whether or not the younger person is a participant). (8 letters)

G.   ___ ___ ___ ___ ___ ___ ___ ___   ___ ___ ___ ___ ___

A circuit of behaviors/actions that result in inappropriate sexual behavior. (13 letters, 2 words)

H. ___ ___ ___ ___ ___ ___ ___ ___

Behaviors/actions that have the specific purpose of preparing another for being taken advantage of sexually. (8 letters)

I. ___ ___ ___ ___ ___ ___ ___ ___ ___

Thoughts or daydreams that most often have sexual themes. (9 letters)

2. The next important step is to bring things out in the open. Sexual offenses are surrounded by secrecy and dishonesty. In order to begin your recovery, you need to reveal more of what you have kept secret. This is risky and takes courage, but in doing so, you increase the possibility of recovery. Answer the following questions as honestly and completely as you can.

A. Describe the sexual abuse incident that caused you to be ordered into treatment.

_____

_____

_____

_____

B. What were the thoughts and feelings you experienced when others discovered this incident?

_____

_____

_____

_____

C. What was the reaction of your parents when they were made aware of the incident?

_____

_____

_____

_____

D. Explain what made you think the sexual abuse would be okay to do?

_____

_____

_____

E. Was this the first time you ever did anything like this? Yes   No (circle one)
If not, for how long have you been involved in sexual activities?

_____

_____

_____

_____

F. List all the sexual activity you have been involved in:

Name (person/partner)	Type of Activity (What did you do?)	How Often It Occurred and for How Long?
_____	_____	_____
_____	_____	_____
_____	_____	_____
_____	_____	_____
_____	_____	_____
_____	_____	_____

G. Now rate on a scale of 1 to 10, with 1 being not at all honest and 10 being totally honest (I've told all), how honest you have been in your answers. Explain your rating.

_____

_____

_____

_____

H. Has anyone ever done anything that was sexually inappropriate to you? If yes, indicate who it was and what he/she did.

_____

_____

_____

_____

When you have completed your responses share them with your therapist. Remember, honesty and openness are your goals; however, getting to that point involves risk and pain. Try to be as open as you can to the therapist's questions as you go over your responses.

OPENING THE DOOR TO FORGIVENESS

GOALS OF THE EXERCISE

1. Increase awareness and understanding of the significance of forgiveness.
2. Identify whose forgiveness must be asked.
3. Decrease the fear or other blocks that may interfere with taking the step of asking for forgiveness from the sex-abuse victim.

ADDITIONAL PROBLEMS FOR WHICH THIS EXERCISE MAY BE MOST USEFUL

- Chemical Dependence
- Conduct Disorder/Delinquency
- Peer/Sibling Conflict
- Physical/Emotional Abuse Victim
- Sexual Abuse Victim

SUGGESTIONS FOR PROCESSING THIS EXERCISE WITH THE CLIENT

Working on the issue of forgiveness is one of the last phases of work in treatment for perpetrators. (Last step in relapse prevention.) Asking for or granting forgiveness is not easy at any age, but this concept may be more difficult for adolescents. In order for a perpetrator to have a good chance of recovery, this issue must be dealt with. This exercise is meant to stimulate thinking about forgiveness and to begin a dialogue about it. Questions need to be processed slowly in an effort to give time for disclosure. The client responses, questions, and disclosure should provide a good indicator of where he/she is in terms of moving toward writing letters to his/her victims or preparing for a session with a victim in order to verbally apologize and ask for forgiveness.

OPENING THE DOOR TO FORGIVENESS

Being able to ask for forgiveness and to forgive others are key parts of being an emotionally healthy, mature human being. They are also critical aspects of victims of sexual abuse becoming free again and perpetrators becoming healthy. The purpose of the following questions is to get you thinking about forgiveness and encourage you to begin that important process.

Defining Forgiveness

1. What does it mean to forgive someone?

   _____

   _____

   _____

   _____

2. Can you give a definition of forgiveness as you see it? After completing your definition, look *forgiveness* up in the dictionary and write the dictionary definition under yours. How do they compare? Differ?

   My definition: _____

   _____

   _____

   _____

   Dictionary definition: _____

   _____

   _____

   _____

   Comparison: _____

   _____

   _____

   _____

The Emotional Side of Forgiveness

1. If you were to ask someone to forgive you, which two of the following emotions do you think you would feel?

Depressed	Humbled	A loser	Relieved	Humiliated
Shameful	Sad	Remorseful	Low	Stupid

2. Give a brief explanation for choosing those two feelings.

    _____

    _____

    _____

3. Why do you think it is difficult for people to ask forgiveness from someone they have hurt or wronged?

    _____

    _____

4. Has anyone ever asked you to forgive them? If so, describe the situation and what the experience was like for you.

    _____

    _____

    _____

5. What would make you believe someone is serious and genuine when they ask to be forgiven?

    _____

    _____

6. What would indicate to you that they were not being genuine?

    _____

    _____

Seeking Forgiveness

1. Who do you need to ask to forgive you? In the following space, list their names as well as what specifically you need to ask their forgiveness for.

Name	Ask Forgiveness For
_____	_____
_____	_____
_____	_____
_____	_____

2. Now write a brief note asking for forgiveness from one of the people you listed. Be specific in regard to what you want them to forgive you for, and share the feelings you have that are connected to what happened. (This note will not be sent.)

    _____

    _____

    _____

    _____

    _____

    _____

3. Put a mark on the following line where you think you are presently in terms of being ready to ask that person to forgive you.

Impossible, I'll never do it	Unsure if I can	Thinking about it	Willing, but afraid	Know I need to and I'm ready

    Explain briefly why you placed the mark where you did.

    _____

    _____

    _____

    _____

Giving Forgiveness

1. Is there someone you need to forgive for whatever they have done to you? List who you need to forgive and what specifically you need to forgive them for.

Name	Forgive them for For
_____	_____
_____	_____
_____	_____
_____	_____

2. Now write a brief note giving forgiveness to one of the people you listed. Be specific in regard to what you are forgiving them for and share your feelings connected to what has happened. (This note will not be sent.)

    _____

    _____

    _____

    _____

    _____

    _____

3. Put a mark on the following line where you think you are presently in terms of being ready to give forgiveness to that person.

Impossible, I'll never do it	Unsure if I can	Thinking about it	Willing, but afraid	Know I need to and I'm ready

Explain briefly why you placed the mark where you did.

_____

_____

_____

_____

YOUR FEELINGS AND BEYOND

GOALS OF THE EXERCISE

1. Increase awareness and understanding of feelings.
2. Become able to identify feelings.
3. Develop the initial awareness to recognize the feelings of others.

ADDITIONAL PROBLEMS FOR WHICH THIS EXERCISE MAY BE MOST USEFUL

- Conduct Disorder/Delinquency
- Oppositional Defiant
- Peer/Sibling Conflict

SUGGESTIONS FOR PROCESSING THIS EXERCISE WITH THE CLIENT

None of us were born empathic. This quality needed to be developed in us through the guidance and encouragement of others, which usually begins to happen during childhood and adolescence. It is essential for those who are sexual perpetrators to begin to show some empathy, because if they do not, the risk of their reoffending is increased significantly. This assignment is designed to educate and act as an indicator of where a client is in terms of understanding his/her feelings and those of others. It can be assigned in sections, given as one piece, or repeated at intervals to see how the client is progressing. Processing should be done slowly to explore responses, to educate, and to encourage increased expression and deeper exploration of, first, the client's feelings and then, hopefully, the feelings of others.

YOUR FEELINGS AND BEYOND

The fact that we as human beings can feel such a wide range of emotions makes us unique among all living things. Feelings play a key role in our daily lives and, therefore, it is important for us to be able to recognize and understand how we feel as well as learn how to cope with all the possible feelings we experience daily. Being able to do that will make us emotionally healthy and mature. Since no one is just born being able to do this, it is important for us to learn how we can handle our feelings. The following exercise can help you begin to learn this sensitivity.

1. Choose one of the following weather conditions that best describes how you feel today:

    Partly cloudy   Heavy rains   Partly sunny with a chance of a shower
    Windy and cool   Warm and humid   Cloudy and cold
    Foggy   Sunny and hot   Snow and cold

    Now briefly explain what you have chosen.

    _____

    _____

    _____

2. Select a color that fits the mood you are in today. Then give a brief explanation for the choice you made.

    _____

    _____

    _____

3. Now give a forecast for either your feelings or mood for the next 4 to 5 days. Complete this by giving some supportive evidence for your forecast.

    _____

    _____

    _____

4. Write down all the facts that you know to be true about feelings (for instance, feelings are neither right nor wrong).

_____

_____

_____

_____

_____

5. List all of the possible feelings you can think of and then place an asterisk (*) next to those you feel/experience most often.

_____   _____   _____

_____   _____   _____

_____   _____   _____

_____   _____   _____

_____   _____   _____

_____   _____   _____

6. Complete the following feeling sentences:

I feel excited when _____

I feel depressed when _____

I feel worried when _____

I feel embarrassed when _____

I feel afraid when _____

I feel ashamed when _____

I feel lonely when _____

I feel happy when _____

6. List two things that would make you feel the following emotions. Then ask two other people what would make them feel angry, lonely, sad, or guilty and record their answers.

SELF   **OTHERS**

Angry   **Angry**

1. _____   Person 1 _____

2. _____   Person 2 _____

Loved   **Loved**

1. _____   Person 1 _____

2. _____   Person 2 _____

Sad | **Sad**

1. _____	Person 1 _____
2. _____	Person 2 _____

Guilty | **Guilty**

1. _____	Person 1 _____
2. _____	Person 2 _____

7. Now look back over your responses and those of the people you asked. What similarities or differences do you see?

_____

_____

_____

_____

In order to be fully human, we must move beyond just being able to recognize, understand, express, and cope with our own feelings. We must be able to recognize, understand, and be sensitive to the feelings of others. This compassion for and sensitivity to the feelings of others is called *empathy*. Empathy is not something any of us are born with, but it is something that must be developed within us if we are to become mature, healthy human beings. It also makes it possible for us to live together in a civilized way. To help you begin to be empathic, identify how the various people in the following stories might be feeling.

1. Mark's parents had always argued a lot, but now they were hardly talking to each other at all. This concerned Mark, so he asked his mom why Dad was coming home late and why they were not talking. His mother said it was nothing more than that she did not feel like talking to Dad.

    Mark felt the following feelings about his parents' behavior. (Circle three possibilities.)

Angry	Afraid	Hurt	Happy
Worried	Okay	Reassured	Irritated

Now list the feelings you chose and give a brief explanation of your choices.

Feeling | **Explanation**

1. _____   _____

_____   _____

_____   _____

2. _____   _____

_____   _____

_____   _____

3. _____   _____

  _____   _____

  _____   _____

2. Doug was slow at getting up for school and even slower at getting ready. His mom was on him to get moving, as she did not want him to be late on his first day at a new school. Doug told his mom he did not want to go. "Could I just start next week?" Doug's mom said that he really didn't need to be worked up or concerned about a new school since he had done just fine on his first days at other new schools; why would this day be any different?

  What do you think Doug was feeling about a new school and about what his mom said to him? (Circle three.)

Relieved	Worried	Afraid	Anxious
Excited	Angry	Unsure	Misunderstood
Depressed	Confident	Happy	Hopeful

Now list the feelings you chose and give a brief explanation for your choices.

Feeling   **Explanation**

1. _____   _____

  _____

  _____

2. _____   _____

  _____

  _____

3. _____   _____

  _____

  _____

LETTER OF FORGIVENESS

GOALS OF THE EXERCISE

1. Increase feelings of empowerment and self-worth.
2. Identify self as a survivor of sexual abuse.
3. Increase level of forgiveness toward the perpetrator and others associated with the sexual abuse.
4. Promote healing and letting go process and begin to feel free to establish trusting relationships and invest energy and enthusiasm into relationships and activities.

ADDITIONAL PROBLEMS FOR WHICH THIS EXERCISE MAY BE MOST USEFUL

- Depression
- Grief/Loss Unresolved
- Physical/Emotional Abuse Victim

SUGGESTIONS FOR PROCESSING THIS EXERCISE WITH THE CLIENT

In this exercise, the client is asked to write a letter of forgiveness to the perpetrator or significant other(s) associated with the sexual abuse. Use this exercise in the later stages of therapy after the client has already verbalized and worked through many of his/her feelings surrounding the abuse. This exercise is for clients whose life situations have stabilized and who are emotionally ready to offer forgiveness to the perpetrator or significant other(s). The client is first asked to respond to a series of questions to help organize his/her thoughts and feelings before writing the actual letter. The questions listed on the following pages are offered as guides to help write the letter. Some of the questions may not be relevant to a particular client. Encourage the client to express other thoughts and feelings that may be unique to his/her situation. After the client responds to the questions, he/she can then begin to write the actual letter. Instruct the client to bring the letter to the following therapy session for processing. Talk with the client about whether he/she wants to actually send the letter of forgiveness to the perpetrator or significant other(s). The letter can also be used to help the client prepare for a therapy session or a face-to-face meeting where he/she offers forgiveness and receives a formal apology from the perpetrator or significant other(s).

LETTER OF FORGIVENESS

In this exercise, you are asked to write a letter of forgiveness to the perpetrator or other important people connected with the sexual abuse. The fact that you have been given this assignment is an accomplishment in and of itself. It is a sign that you have already done a lot of hard work. You have been able to identify, verbalize, and work through many of your thoughts and feelings surrounding the sexual abuse. At this point, you are now much stronger emotionally and are ready to offer forgiveness to the perpetrator or significant other person(s) associated with the sexual abuse.

First, find a quiet or relaxing place where you can reflect and organize your thoughts before writing the actual letter. Finding a quiet or relaxing place will help you to concentrate better and avoid being distracted or interrupted. You may want to write down your thoughts and feelings in a quiet room in your house or go to the library. Some people find it helpful to go to a favorite place such as a park, beach, or scenic area.

Before you begin to write the actual letter, please respond to the following questions. These questions will help you organize your thoughts and feelings before you write the letter to the perpetrator or significant other person(s). These questions are offered as a guide to help you write your own personal letter. You may find that some of the questions do not apply to you; therefore, you may leave these items blank. Space is also provided for you to express any additional thoughts or feelings that you may want to include in your letter. Feel free to write down whatever thoughts or feelings that come into your mind as you respond to the questions. You can decide later as to whether you want to include those thoughts or feelings in your final letter.

1. How has the sexual abuse affected your life?

    _____

    _____

    _____

2. How do you feel about yourself at this point in your recovery?

    _____

    _____

    _____

    _____

3. What positive changes have you seen in yourself since the sexual abuse ended?

    _____

    _____

    _____

    _____

4. What changes have occurred in your family since the sexual abuse was reported?

    _____

    _____

    _____

    _____

5. What are your present feelings toward the perpetrator of your sexual abuse or significant other people?

    _____

    _____

    _____

    _____

6. What changes have occurred within you that now allow you to be able to forgive the perpetrator or significant other person(s)?

    _____

    _____

    _____

    _____

7. What, if anything, has the perpetrator or significant other person(s) said or done that has allowed you to feel forgiveness?

    _____

    _____

    _____

    _____

8. If the perpetrator or significant other has said or done nothing to promote your forgiveness, why are you choosing to practice forgiveness?

    _____

    _____

    _____

    _____

9. At the present time, what is your relationship like with the perpetrator?

_____

_____

_____

_____

10. What is your relationship like now with your other family members or significant other people?

_____

_____

_____

_____

11. What goals do you have for yourself in the near future?

_____

_____

_____

_____

12. Please use the space provided to express any other thoughts or feelings that you would like to include in your letter:

_____

_____

_____

_____

_____

_____

_____

_____

_____

_____

_____

_____

_____

_____

_____

_____

_____

Next, review your responses and begin to write your letter on a separate piece of paper. Remember, this is your letter, so share the thoughts and feelings that are important to you. Bring the completed letter back to your next therapy session to go over with your therapist. Your therapist will talk to you about what you want to do with the letter. You have several options to consider: Do you want to destroy or throw away the letter? If so, how? Would you like to save the letter? Would you like to share the letter with the perpetrator or significant other person(s)? Your therapist can help you answer these questions.

You may have written this letter to help you prepare to share your thoughts and feelings directly with the perpetrator or significant other(s) in a future therapy session or face-to-face meeting. Talk with your therapist about what you would verbally like to say to the perpetrator or significant other(s). Likewise, consider what you would like to hear from the perpetrator or significant other(s). Finally, you are to be commended and praised for the hard work that you have put forth in therapy.

MY STORY

GOALS OF THE EXERCISE

1. Tell the story of sexual abuse through the use of a journal.
2. Identify and express feelings connected to the sexual abuse.
3. Recognize how sexual abuse has affected life.
4. Begin the healing process by working through thoughts and feelings associated with the sexual abuse.
5. Decrease feelings of shame and guilt, and affirm self as not being responsible for the abuse.

ADDITIONAL PROBLEMS FOR WHICH THIS EXERCISE MAY BE MOST USEFUL

- Grief/Loss Unresolved
- Low Self-Esteem
- Physical/Emotional Abuse Victim

SUGGESTIONS FOR PROCESSING THIS EXERCISE WITH THE CLIENT

The client is instructed to keep a journal at home to help him/her express his/her feelings about the past sexual abuse. The journal can be utilized throughout therapy, but can be particularly helpful during the initial stages of therapy when you are attempting to join with the client and fully understand his/her experiences. The client is given a list of questions that he/she can respond to in order to help express his/her thoughts and feelings. Encourage the client to use the journal to express his/her story in his/her own words. Inform the client that he/she may find the journal particularly helpful around the time that he/she is experiencing strong or distressing emotions. Instruct the client to bring the journal notes to the therapy sessions for processing. The journal notes may also help prepare the client to perform other therapeutic tasks such as verbally confronting the perpetrator or sharing his/her thoughts and feelings about the sexual abuse with other key family members. The journal notes can also help the client prepare for a formal apology from the perpetrator. Be sensitive to any signs that the client blames him/herself for the sexual abuse. Seek to empower the client and affirm him/her as not being responsible for the abuse.

MY STORY

Sexual abuse can produce many confusing and strong emotions. Keeping a journal can help you identify, express, and work through your many thoughts and feelings about the sexual abuse. The journal gives you the opportunity to share your own story and tell how the abuse has affected your life. Bring the journal notes to your therapy session each week to help your therapist better understand your thoughts and feelings.

How people choose to write in a journal varies. Some people find it useful to set aside a certain time each day to write in a journal, such as when they wake up in the morning or before they go to bed. This option allows them to spend some personal time alone each day to record their thoughts and feelings. Other people prefer to write down their thoughts and feelings as they occur throughout the day.

1. Find a quiet or relaxing place to write down your thoughts and feelings. This will help you to concentrate and block out any distractions. Many people find it best to record their thoughts in a quiet room in the home, such as in the privacy of their own bedroom. Other people find it helpful to go to a favorite place such as a park, farm, or beach, to write their thoughts and feelings.

    Remember, this is your journal, and you have the option of writing in it in the time and place in which you feel most comfortable. Feel free to express your thoughts and feelings without worrying about being judged or criticized. Don't worry about spelling or grammar errors; just get your thoughts and feelings down on paper however you can.

2. Following is a list of questions or items that you may choose to respond to in your journal. Respond to those that you feel are appropriate to your experience.

    *   Describe some of the events leading up to the sexual abuse. Where did the sexual abuse occur and with whom? At what times or at what places?

    *   Where were other people in the family when the abuse occurred?

    *   What thoughts and feelings did you experience toward the perpetrator before the abuse?

    *   What thoughts and feelings did you experience toward the perpetrator during the actual sexual abuse?

    *   What thoughts and feelings did you experience toward the perpetrator after the sexual abuse occurred?

    *   How has the sexual abuse made you feel about yourself?

- What effect has the sexual abuse had on your life?

- How has the discovery of the sexual abuse affected your family members' lives?

- How have the other family members acted toward you since the sexual abuse came out in the open?

- Do you think someone besides you and the perpetrator was aware that the sexual abuse was occurring and did nothing about it? If so, who was it and why did he/she do nothing?

- How did other people find out about the sexual abuse?

- What was the reaction of others when they found out that you were abused?

- How did you feel about the reaction of others when they found out you were abused?

- What has been the most painful or difficult aspect about your sexual abuse experience?

- If you were free to say anything to the perpetrator, what would you say to him/her?

- Who do you hold responsible for the sexual abuse?

- Have you ever experienced any guilt about the sexual abuse? If so, please elaborate.

YOU ARE NOT ALONE

GOALS OF THE HOMEWORK

1. Identify and express feelings connected to the sexual abuse in the context of a supportive, therapeutic environment.
2. Recognize and share how sexual abuse has affected life.
3. Begin the healing process by working through thoughts and feelings associated with the sexual abuse.
4. Decrease feelings of shame and guilt, and affirm perpetrator as being responsible for sexual abuse.

ADDITIONAL PROBLEMS FOR WHICH THIS EXERCISE MAY BE MOST USEFUL

- Depression
- Grief/Loss Unresolved
- Physical/Emotional Abuse Victim

SUGGESTIONS FOR PROCESSING THIS EXERCISE WITH THE CLIENT

The sexual abuse experience often produces a myriad of confusing and ambivalent emotions for the victim. This exercise seeks to help the client identify and express his/her feelings associated with the sexual abuse. The client is instructed to read a short story about a girl, Jenny, who has experienced the pain of both sexual abuse and subsequent removal from her home. After reading the story, the client is asked to respond to a series of process questions. The process questions allow the client to compare and contrast his/her experience with that of the main character. Instruct the client to bring his/her answers back to the next therapy session for processing. Be alert to any signs that the client blames him/herself for the sexual abuse. In this event, the therapist should identify the perpetrator as being responsible for the sexual abuse and not the client.

YOU ARE NOT ALONE

Read the following story of a young girl, Jenny, who has experienced the hurt of sexual abuse, as well as the pain and loneliness of being removed from her home. As you read the story, you may find that some of your experiences are similar to Jenny's in some ways, but different in others. You may have experienced some similar life changes as Jenny, but, perhaps, your experiences have been much different. In either case, your therapist has assigned this exercise to give you the opportunity to express your own thoughts and feelings about your experiences.

Jenny sat quietly, staring out the window of her bedroom in her foster home. Her mind was taking her away again to a familiar and comfortable place. Jenny was daydreaming about visiting with her best friend, Alisha. She was remembering a time when Alisha and she got into a huge water fight with some of the neighborhood boys. A smile came across her face. Alisha was her very best friend. She could always count on Alisha to be there to listen and understand.

Jenny missed Alisha now. She was saddened by not being able to visit with her friend nearly every day like she used to before she was placed in the foster home. Jenny was removed from her home three months ago and was placed in the Jacksons' foster home. The Jacksons seemed like friendly people. They tried to be supportive and make her feel welcome and at home, but, no matter how hard they tried, Jenny still did not feel like it was her home.

Jenny longed to be with her mother and two brothers, yet, that thought also made her feel frightened. She was afraid of her stepfather, Joe, who had sexually abused her over a two-year time period. The sexual abuse usually occurred in her bedroom late at night or when her mother was out running errands. Jenny recalled feeling confused when the "bad touches" first began. Part of her liked the attention and affection she received from Joe, but at the same time, it also made her feel ashamed and dirty. As time went on, the bad touches just made her feel more helpless and trapped. When the sexual contact occurred, Jenny would try to escape the pain by allowing her mind to drift away to a more peaceful place—Alisha's house.

Jenny was warned by her stepfather not to tell anyone. She held on to the secret until the guilt and shame increased so much that she just had to share the hurt with someone else. She thought about telling her mother, but was afraid that her mother would become angry and not believe her. Alisha realized that something was wrong with Jenny, so Jenny eventually told her. Alisha said she had to tell someone who could help and went with Jenny to tell the school counselor about the sexual abuse. Jenny felt some relief in telling Alisha and the school counselor, but her worries increased when she found out that Children's Protective Services would have to be informed.

Children's Protective Services temporarily removed Jenny from her home. Her stepfather, Joe, strongly denied the charges that he had sexually abused Jenny. Jenny's older brother, Joshua, became very angry and called Jenny a liar. He said that she had been watching too many talk shows on TV. Her youngest brother, Brian, chose not to say anything. Perhaps, what hurt the most was that her mother did not know who to believe. Her mother felt caught in the middle, and in choosing not to choose sides, Jenny felt like her mother chose to side with Joe.

It seemed so strange to go into a new home. Jenny felt like she was being punished, because she was the one who had to leave. She missed her mother and two brothers. She missed visiting with Alisha every day after school. Jenny was able to visit with Alisha five or six times after she was placed in the foster home. However, she often wished that she could see her more, especially since Jenny was attending a new school and had to make new friends. Jenny was meeting with her counselor, Mrs. Wohlford, every week for counseling. Mrs. Wohlford helped her sort through her feelings and told Jenny that the sexual abuse was not her fault. She found the counseling sessions helpful. Still, Jenny needed a friend like Alisha to talk to on a regular basis.

A tear rolled down Jenny's face as she sat staring out the window of her bedroom, thinking about Alisha and being away from her family. She was awakened out of her daydream by a knock on her bedroom door. Jenny called out, "Come on in." Mrs. Jackson peeked her head in and said, "You've got a phone call from Alisha." Jenny ran downstairs to get the phone. She picked up the phone and smiled when she heard the friendly and familiar voice say, "Hi, Jenny, this is Alisha."

Please respond to the following questions that relate to you. Bring your responses back to your next therapy session.

1. How were your experiences similar to Jenny's?

_____

_____

_____

_____

_____

2. How were your experiences different than Jenny's?

_____

_____

_____

_____

_____

_____

_____

3. What are your strongest feelings about the sexual abuse?

_____

_____

_____
_____
_____

4. In the story, Jenny was hurt by the response of her mother and two brothers. How did your family members respond when they first learned about the sexual abuse?

_____
_____
_____
_____
_____
_____

5. How did the person who sexually abused you respond when he/she learned that the abuse had been reported?

_____
_____
_____
_____
_____
_____

6. What is your relationship like with your family members today?

_____
_____
_____
_____
_____
_____

7. What is your relationship like with the sexual abuser today?

_____
_____
_____
_____
_____
_____

8. If you were removed from your home, describe how you felt when you were first placed in another home or setting.

_____

_____

_____

_____

_____

_____

9. If another family member was removed from your home, describe how you felt when he/she had to leave the home.

_____

_____

_____

_____

_____

_____

10. In the story, Jenny is saddened about moving away from her best friend, Alisha. Alisha was a special friend to Jenny because she provided a lot of understanding and support. Who are the special people in your life who you have been able to count on for understanding, support, and to be there when you needed them?

_____

_____

_____

_____

_____

11. Jenny used daydreaming as a way to escape the pain of the actual sexual abuse and to deal with the sadness of being removed from her home. How have you dealt with the pain and hurt of your sexual abuse experience?

_____

_____

_____

_____

_____

_____

_____

List three ways that you have found helpful in dealing with your hurt or pain.

A. _____

_____

_____

_____

_____

B. _____

_____

_____

_____

_____

C. _____

_____

_____

_____

_____

CONNECTING SEXUAL BEHAVIOR WITH NEEDS

GOALS OF THE EXERCISE

1. Make a cognitive connection between sexual behavior and needs.
2. Identify specific needs and their level of importance.
3. Eliminate sexual acting out by meeting deeper, unfulfilled needs in a healthy manner.

ADDITIONAL PROBLEMS FOR WHICH THIS EXERCISE MAY BE MOST USEFUL

*   Low Self-Esteem
*   Negative Peer Influences
*   Sexual Abuse Perpetrator

SUGGESTIONS FOR PROCESSING THIS EXERCISE WITH THE CLIENT

Without question, it is important for each of us to recognize what our needs are and to have them met in order for us to maintain our emotional health. Of course, it is best when needs are met in socially appropriate ways that are not self-defeating. The processing of this assignment should center on identifying specific emotional needs and building a connection to how we get these needs met.

CONNECTING SEXUAL BEHAVIOR WITH NEEDS

Behavior and needs have a strong connection. All our behavior—whether good or bad, helpful or harmful—in some way meets needs we have. As we become better at recognizing what our needs are, we can then take steps to meet our needs in constructive, nonharmful ways. The following exercise will help you begin to make this connection between needs and behaviors.

1. Check the needs in the two following lists that are important to you:

   Emotional Needs

   ____ Attention

   ____ Be liked

   ____ Excitement

   ____ Affection

   ____ Be loved

   ____ Be listened to

   ____ Be taken seriously

   ____ Recognition

   ____ Other: _____

   Physical Needs

   ____ Clothing

   ____ Money

   ____ Car

   ____ Good grades

   ____ Nice house

   ____ Status/popularity

   ____ Physically attractive

   ____ Job/position

   ____ Other: _____

2. From the needs you have selected, choose two that are most important to you from each area. List each in the following space and briefly explain why it is important.

   Emotional

   A. Need: _____

      Explanation: _____

      _____

   B. Need: _____

      Explanation: _____

      _____

   Physical

   A. Need: _____

      Explanation: _____

B. Need: _____

    Explanation: _____

    _____

3. Now rate the degree to which your unhealthy sexual behavior has met either of the two emotional needs you identified in item 2.

    |_____|_____|_____|_____|
    Not at all   A little   Some   Mostly   Totally

4. Identify two negative consequences that have occurred as a result of your sexual behavior:

    A. _____

    B. _____

5. When you factor in the negative consequences of your sexual behavior with the emotional needs the sexual behavior meets, is it still worth it? (Please circle one of the following.)

    For the most part   Yes, without question

    Questionable   Good trade off

    Unsure   Not at all

6. The range of possible alternative behaviors that might meet your emotional needs is vast. Please identify one or two new healthy behaviors that would meet your emotional needs.

    A. _____

    B. _____

7. After reviewing your identified emotional needs, ask an adult (e.g., teacher, youth pastor, counselor) how they would recommend that you meet this need.

    _____

    _____

    _____

8. What would have to happen for you to stop the sexual behavior and begin to engage in a new behavior to meet your emotional need(s)?

    _____

    _____

    _____

    _____

    _____

LOOKING CLOSER AT MY SEXUAL BEHAVIOR

GOALS OF THE EXERCISE

1. Expand the awareness of own sexual behavior.
2. Obtain a more complete history of the sexual acting out behavior.
3. Identify feelings that underlie the sexual behavior.
4. Increase awareness of what need(s) are met through the sexual acting out behavior.

ADDITIONAL PROBLEMS FOR WHICH THIS EXERCISE MAY BE MOST USEFUL

- Conduct Disorder
- Negative Peer Influences
- Oppositional Defiant
- Sexual Abuse Victim

SUGGESTIONS FOR PROCESSING THIS EXERCISE WITH THE CLIENT

The main purpose of this exercise is to expand the client's awareness of the factors that contribute to his/her sexual acting out behaviors. It is hoped that the exercise will help the client identify the thoughts and feelings he/she experienced both before and after the sexual activity. The client is encouraged to reflect on what other need(s) the sexual activity meets. It is suggested that the exercise not be aggressively processed. Rather, it should be processed in a careful and deliberate manner. This will help the client examine for himself/herself the reasons for engaging in the sexual acting out behaviors. Even resistance to a question or nonresponses can be valuable for future focus as it reveals sensitive areas that need therapeutic intervention.

LOOKING CLOSER AT MY SEXUAL BEHAVIOR

Complete the following questions about your sexual behavior.

1. When did you first become involved in the sexual behavior? How old were you?

    _____

    _____

2. Describe briefly your first experience.

    _____

    _____

    _____

3. To what extent are alcohol and/or drugs used before, during, or after sexual behavior?

    _____ often   _____ sometimes   _____ rarely   _____ never

4. What is the level of pleasure you experience?

    |⌴_____|_____|_____|_____|
    None   A little   Some   Quite a bit   A lot

    Explain: _____

    _____

5. Describe briefly how things are going in the following areas:

    A. At home: _____

    B. At school: _____

    C. With parents: _____

    D. Parents getting along with each other: _____

    E. With friends: _____

6. Prior to involving myself in sexual behavior, I feel: (circle all that apply)

Anxious	Excited	Worried
Unsure	Nervous	Rebellious
Out of control	Depressed	Eager

7. After the sexual activity, I feel: (circle all that apply)

        Anxious   Excited   Worried

        Unsure   Nervous   Rebellious

        Out of control   Depressed   Eager

8. Prior to my becoming involved in sexual activities, I tell myself:

_____

_____

_____

9. Afterwards, I tell myself:

_____

_____

_____

10. What are two things that I like about the sexual behavior?

    A. _____

    B. _____

11. What are two things that I dislike or that concern me about my sexual behavior?

    A. _____

    B. _____

12. All our behavior, whether it be "good" or "bad," meets some need that we have. What *need* or *needs* does your sexual activity fulfill?

_____

_____

_____

13. How motivated or willing are you to change this behavior?

_____

_____

_____

14. What do you think would have to happen for you to change your sexual behavior?

_____

_____

_____

PARENTS' THOUGHTS AND FEELINGS ABOUT SON/DAUGHTER'S SEXUAL ORIENTATION

GOALS OF THE EXERCISE

1. Parents share their thoughts and feelings about the client's recent disclosure that he/she is or may be gay.
2. Parents express their emotions about their son/daughter's sexual orientation in a controlled manner.
3. Parents explore how the client's recent disclosure about his/her sexual orientation has impacted their relationship with him/her.
4. Parents identify what type of relationship they would like to have with their son/daughter in the future.
5. Parents maintain, establish, or rebuild a close relationship with their son/daughter who has decided he/she is gay.

ADDITIONAL PROBLEMS FOR WHICH THIS EXERCISE MAY BE MOST USEFUL

• None

SUGGESTIONS FOR PROCESSING THIS EXERCISE WITH THE CLIENT

This homework assignment is designed for the parents of the client who has recently disclosed that he/she is or may be gay. The parents are asked to respond to a series of questions that will help identify their thoughts and feelings about the client's sexual orientation. The parents are then asked to share their thoughts and feelings about the client's sexual orientation by writing a rough draft of a letter to him/her. The parents should be discouraged from sending this rough draft to their son/daughter without first having the opportunity to reflect on the contents of the letter and process their thoughts and feelings with the therapist. The parents can then be helped to decide whether they want to write a final letter to their son/daughter or express their thoughts and feelings in a face-to-face meeting. The parents should also be discouraged from expressing any potentially damaging remarks that will place a permanent strain on the parent-child relationship. The therapist should further explore with the parents what type of relationship they would like to have with the client in the future and identify the steps that they can take to maintain, establish, or rebuild a close relationship with their son/daughter.

PARENTS' THOUGHTS AND FEELINGS ABOUT SON/DAUGHTER'S SEXUAL ORIENTATION

When a son or daughter discloses that he/she is or may be gay, this can produce strong and, perhaps, confusing emotions for the parents. The parents may react with a variety of emotions such as anger, sadness, guilt, despair, fear, or worry. Sometimes the son or daughter's disclosure about their sexual orientation can place a strain on the parent-child relationship. Please answer the following questions to help provide insight into your thoughts and feelings about your son/daughter's recent disclosure that he/she is or may be gay.

1. When and how did you first learn that your son/daughter is or may be gay?

   _____

   _____

   _____

2. How did you feel when you first learned that your son/daughter is or may be gay?

   _____

   _____

3. What did you say or how did you react to your son/daughter?

   _____

   _____

   _____

4. What is your greatest fear or worry about your son/daughter's disclosure about his/her sexual orientation?

   _____

   _____

   _____

5. How has your son/daughter's disclosure about his/her sexual orientation affected your relationship with him/her at the present time?

    _____

    _____

    _____

    _____

    _____

6. From your point of view, how has your son/daughter's disclosure affected his/her relationships with other family members?

    _____

    _____

    _____

7. How has your son/daughter's disclosure affected your relationship with your spouse?

    _____

    _____

    _____

8. How open have you been in sharing this news with other family members and friends?

    _____

    _____

    _____

9. (If applicable) How have you responded to other family members' or friends' reactions to your son/daughter's disclosure?

    _____

    _____

    _____

10. How would you feel if your son/daughter brought his/her partner home in the future?

    _____

    _____

    _____

11. What kind of relationship would you like to have with your son/daughter in the future?

_____

_____

_____

12. What type of relationship do you foresee yourself having with your son/daughter 5 years from now? 10 years from now?

_____

_____

_____

_____

_____

_____

_____

13. What would you like to say to your son/daughter that you have not already said?

_____

_____

_____

_____

_____

OPTIONAL—Next, review your answers to the questions and write a rough draft of a letter to your son/daughter. Please feel free to express any thoughts and feelings that you may have about your son/daughter's sexual orientation in this rough draft. Do not share the rough draft with your son or daughter without first having taken the time to reflect on what you have said in the rough draft. Secondly, you are also strongly encouraged to process the contents in the rough draft with your therapist. The therapist can help you to decide whether you want to write a final letter and/or share your thoughts and feelings in a face-to-face meeting with your son/daughter.

UNSURE

GOALS OF THE EXERCISE

1. Identify and verbalize factors contributing to anxiety and confusion over sexual identity.
2. Reduce overall frequency and intensity of anxiety associated with sexual identity so that daily functioning is not impaired.
3. Share sexual desires, fantasies, and experiences in the context of a supportive, therapeutic environment.
4. Begin to resolve anxiety and confusion over sexual identity formation.

ADDITIONAL PROBLEMS FOR WHICH THIS EXERCISE MAY BE MOST USEFUL

- Anxiety
- Social Phobia/Shyness

SUGGESTIONS FOR PROCESSING THIS EXERCISE WITH THE CLIENT

This assignment is given to the client who is experiencing anxiety or confusion about his/her sexual identity and questioning whether he/she may be gay. The client is first asked to rate his/her overall level of anxiety and the amount of attraction he/she experiences to both males and females. The assignment will identify possible factors that contribute to the client's confusion over his/her sexual identity formation. The client is asked to identify what current factors are causing him/her to believe that he/she may possibly be gay. The client's responses will also identify any fears that he/she may have about possibly being gay. The therapist should be alert to issues of confidentiality and should assess how comfortable the client is in sharing his/her confusion over this issue with parents or caretakers. If the client is concerned about his/her parents possibly reading the responses, then steps should be taken to ensure that the responses are kept private and confidential. The therapist may want to consider using this assignment in the therapy session.

UNSURE

The teenage years can be a time of many important changes. The teenager changes physically, emotionally, and socially. Family and peer relationships often change, as well. Some of these changes feel good, while other changes may cause the teenager to feel anxious or confused. It is not uncommon for some teenagers to experience anxiety, worry, or confusion about their sexual identity. Some teenagers struggle with whether they may be gay. This assignment will help your therapist better understand your anxiety or confusion about this issue. Please respond to the following items.

1. Please rate your level of anxiety and confusion about your sexual identity on a scale from 0 to 10 (0 = none, 10 = extreme). Place a checkmark at the appropriate level.

0	1	2	3	4	5	6	7	8	9	10

None   Mild   Moderate   High   Extreme

2. Please rate your level of attraction to same-sex peers on a scale of 0 to 10 (0 = no attraction, 10 = very strong attraction).

0	1	2	3	4	5	6	7	8	9	10

No attraction   Mild attraction   Moderate attraction   High attraction   Very strong attraction

3. Please rate your level of attraction to opposite-sex peers on a scale of 0 to 10 (0 = no attraction, 10 = very strong attraction).

0	1	2	3	4	5	6	7	8	9	10

No attraction   Mild attraction   Moderate attraction   High attraction   Very strong attraction

4. When did you first have thoughts that you might be gay? What age were you?

_____

_____

_____

5. What life experiences have you had that lead you to believe that you may be gay?

    _____

    _____

    _____

    _____

6. Have you ever been sexually abused? ____ yes ____ no
    If yes, please explain.

    _____

    _____

    _____

    _____

7. Have you ever had any homosexual experiences? ____ yes ____ no
    If yes, please explain.

    _____

    _____

    _____

    _____

8. At the present time, what causes you to believe that you may be gay?

    _____

    _____

    _____

9. What is your greatest fear or worry about possibly being gay?

    _____

    _____

    _____

10. How do you think your parents or family members would react if they learned that you were gay?

    _____

    _____

    _____

    _____

11. How do you think your friends or peers would react if they were to learn that you were gay?

_____

_____

_____

_____

12. Who do you feel comfortable talking to about your sexual identity?

_____

_____

_____

GREETING PEERS

GOALS OF THE EXERCISE

1. Reduce social isolation and excessive shrinking away from others.
2. Increase frequency of social interactions with same-aged peers or acquaintances.
3. Develop basic social skills that will improve the quality of interpersonal relationships.
4. Begin to take steps toward building peer friendships.

ADDITIONAL PROBLEMS FOR WHICH THIS EXERCISE MAY BE MOST USEFUL

- Anxiety
- Depression
- Low Self-Esteem
- Panic/Agoraphobia

SUGGESTIONS FOR PROCESSING THIS EXERCISE WITH THE CLIENT

This homework assignment is designed for the extremely shy or reserved adolescent in the beginning stages of therapy. The anxious and shy client often withdraws or shrinks away from social contacts for fear that he/she will be met with criticism, disapproval, or rejection. The shy client avoids eye contact as well as the act of greeting others. In this assignment, the client is asked to initiate three social contacts per day. (The frequency of the social contacts per day or per week can be modified to meet the client's needs.) The client should be encouraged to maintain good eye contact and avoid looking away from others when greeting them. The client may also need to be coached in the therapy sessions as to how to greet others. Role-play a positive greeting (i.e., strong voice, good eye contact, smile) in advance. The client is further requested to rate his/her anxiety level during the social contacts. The rating scale can help you determine when the client feels comfortable enough to take on more challenging or complex social interactions.

GREETING PEERS

The purpose of this exercise is to help you feel more comfortable around your peers at school and in your neighborhood. You are to initiate three social contacts per day with peers or acquaintances (close or regular friends are excluded from this assignment). Remember to maintain good eye contact and avoid looking away when greeting others. Good eye contact lets others know that you are interested in talking to them. Greet the other person with some of the expressions (such as "good morning," "how are you today?") that were practiced in the therapy session. Don't forget to smile!

In this exercise, you are asked to record the names of three individuals with whom you initiated contact during the day. It is important that you record their names because this will help you to stay focused on performing the task. Put the assignment sheet in your notebook or place it in your desk so that you can easily record the names of the individuals you greeted. Hopefully, some of these simple greetings will lead to longer conversations, but that is not the primary goal of this assignment. The primary goal is for you to feel comfortable and less anxious as you give a simple greeting.

Use the following rating scale to identify your anxiety level during each social contact, and then write the number on the following pages in the blank space under the column marked Anxiety Level:

Anxiety Level

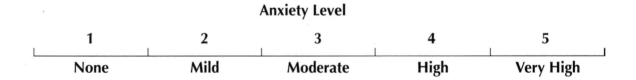

1	2	3	4	5
None	Mild	Moderate	High	Very High

Use the following sheets to record the names of the three peers with whom you initiated contact each day. Remember to rate your anxiety level for each contact. Please feel free to make any additional comments about your experiences or contacts, which can be discussed in therapy.

Please remember to bring the assignment sheets to your next appointment.

DAY 1

Person's Name   **Anxiety Level**

1. _____   _____

2. _____   _____

3. _____   _____

Comments: _____
_____
_____
_____
_____

DAY 2

Person's Name   **Anxiety Level**

1. _____   _____

2. _____   _____

3. _____   _____

Comments: _____
_____
_____
_____
_____

DAY 3

Person's Name   **Anxiety Level**

1. _____   _____

2. _____   _____

3. _____   _____

Comments: _____

_____

_____

_____

_____

DAY 4

Person's Name   **Anxiety Level**

1. _____   _____

2. _____   _____

3. _____   _____

Comments: _____

_____

_____

_____

_____

DAY 5

Person's Name   **Anxiety Level**

1. _____   _____

2. _____   _____

3. _____   _____

Comments: _____

_____

_____

_____

_____

DAY 6

Person's Name   **Anxiety Level**

1. _____   _____

2. _____   _____

3. _____   _____

Comments: _____

_____

_____

_____

_____

DAY 7

Person's Name   **Anxiety Level**

1. _____   _____

2. _____   _____

3. _____   _____

Comments: _____

_____

_____

_____

_____

REACH OUT AND CALL

GOALS OF THE EXERCISE

1. Increase frequency of social contacts with same-aged peers or acquaintances.
2. Decrease feelings of insecurity and anxiety when conversing with peers.
3. Develop basic conversation skills.
4. Take steps toward building peer friendships.

ADDITIONAL PROBLEMS FOR WHICH THIS EXERCISE MAY BE MOST USEFUL

- Anxiety
- Depression
- Panic/Agoraphobia

SUGGESTIONS FOR PROCESSING THIS EXERCISE WITH THE CLIENT

This homework assignment is aimed at working with shy preadolescent or adolescent clients. It is not uncommon for the preadolescent child or adolescent to spend an increased amount of time on the phone with peers. The shy individual, on the other hand, often avoids social contact, and this includes talking on the phone with his/her peers. In this assignment, the client is asked to engage in a very normal activity: making phone calls to three separate peers during the course of the week. The actual number of phone calls per week can be adjusted for each client. You may instruct the client to talk on the phone for a minimum period of time (e.g., 5 to 10 minutes). Use role-playing and behavioral rehearsal to help the client develop his/her basic conversation skills before this assignment is given. Encourage the client to think of a list of ideas to discuss in advance and to make positive statements about him/herself or the other person.

REACH OUT AND CALL

The goal of this assignment is to help you feel more comfortable and at ease while talking with some of your peers. You are asked to make phone calls to three separate peers or acquaintances during the week. In order to complete this assignment, you must be successful in getting through to the other person. You will not receive credit if you do not actually talk to the other person. The purpose of your phone call may be purely social (that is, just calling to talk) or you may want to call the other person for a specific purpose, such as obtaining information about a school or homework assignment. Remember to try and be warm in your initial greeting. You are also encouraged to make positive statements about the other person or yourself.

If you are a person who struggles with shyness or social anxiety, it can be very difficult to find interesting topics to talk about with your peers. Think of some topics in advance that you may discuss with your peers. You will likely feel less anxious and come across as more confident if you have in front of you a potential list of topics to discuss. This list can serve as a guide to help you converse more easily, but do not feel that you are bound to this list and have to talk about all of the different subjects. Be flexible and ready to discuss other interesting topics or events that may arise during the course of the conversation.

Following is a list of suggested topics that you may want to talk about with your peers in your phone conversations:

- School or homework assignments
- Past, present, or future school events
- Past, present, or future sporting events
- Common interests, hobbies, or extracurricular activities
- Daily experiences
- Weekend plans
- Movies or TV shows
- Favorite songs or musicians
- The opposite sex
- Fashion and makeup
- Family vacations
- Holiday events
- The weather
- Expectations and rules established by parents and teachers

Record the names, dates, and times of your three phone conversations per week. The recording of the names on this list will help you to stay focused on performing this task.

Put this assignment sheet in your notebook, by the phone, or in another accessible place. It is hoped that some of your phone calls will lead you to get together socially with some of your peers after school or on the weekend. However, this is not the primary purpose of this assignment at this time. Please feel free to make any comments about some of your phone conversations. The comment section may serve as a reminder of things you may want to discuss in the therapy sessions.

REACH OUT AND CALL

WEEK 1

Name   Date of Phone Call   Time

1. _____   _____   _____

2. _____   _____   _____

3. _____   _____   _____

Comments: _____

_____

_____

WEEK 2

Name   Date of Phone Call   Time

1. _____   _____   _____

2. _____   _____   _____

3. _____   _____   _____

Comments: _____

_____

_____

WEEK 3

Name	Date of Phone Call	Time
1. _____	_____	_____
2. _____	_____	_____
3. _____	_____	_____

Comments: _____

_____

_____

WEEK 4

Name	Date of Phone Call	Time
1. _____	_____	_____
2. _____	_____	_____
3. _____	_____	_____

Comments: _____

_____

_____

WEEK 5

Name	Date of Phone Call	Time
1. _____	_____	_____
2. _____	_____	_____
3. _____	_____	_____

Comments: _____

_____

_____

WEEK 6

Name   Date of Phone Call   Time

1. _____   _____   _____

2. _____   _____   _____

3. _____   _____   _____

Comments: _____

_____

_____

WEEK 7

Name   Date of Phone Call   Time

1. _____   _____   _____

2. _____   _____   _____

3. _____   _____   _____

Comments: _____

_____

_____

SHOW YOUR STRENGTHS

GOALS OF THE EXERCISE

1. Increase frequency of social contacts with same-aged peers or acquaintances.
2. Utilize strengths and interests to help take steps toward building peer friendships.
3. Reduce social isolation and excessive shrinking away from others.
4. Increase positive self-statements in social interactions.

ADDITIONAL PROBLEMS FOR WHICH THIS EXERCISE MAY BE MOST USEFUL

- Depression
- Low Self-Esteem
- Panic/Agoraphobia

SUGGESTIONS FOR PROCESSING THIS EXERCISE WITH THE CLIENT

The purpose of this exercise is to help the socially anxious or shy client to begin to establish peer friendships by utilizing his/her strengths and interests. First, meet with the client (and parents) to identify specific strengths and interests. Then, instruct the client to share his/her strengths or interests with three different peers before the next therapy session. Emphasize how the client will likely feel less anxious and insecure around peers when he/she utilizes his/her strengths or interests. Next, the client is required to respond to several process questions after each social contact. The responses to these questions will allow you to reinforce effort and/or offer suggestions to improve his/her social skills. Teach basic social skills (i.e., greeting others, maintaining good eye contact, smiling) using role-playing and behavioral rehearsal. Encourage the client to make positive statements about him/herself or the other peer(s).

SHOW YOUR STRENGTHS

The purpose of this exercise is to help you feel less anxious and more comfortable around your peers at school or in the neighborhood. It will also give you the opportunity to have fun and be yourself around your peers. That is important when it comes to making friends! You are asked to share your strengths or interests with three different people before your next therapy session. Sharing your strengths and interests will help you forget about your worries or nervousness when you interact with others. Remember to maintain good eye contact when you are talking to your peers. Be positive! Compliment your peers, and say something good about yourself. Don't forget to smile, laugh, and have fun.

1. The first step in this exercise is to meet with your therapist (and parents) to identify a list of your strengths and interests. This part of the exercise should take place in the therapy session. Identify at least five strengths, talents, or interests. (*Note: Your strengths and interests may not necessarily be the same.*)

Strengths and Interests

A. _____

B. _____

C. _____

D. _____

E. _____

F. _____

G. _____

H. _____

I. _____

J. _____

2. Share your strengths or interests with three different peers in the next week or before your next therapy session. Remember to use the skills that you have learned in your therapy sessions to feel more comfortable around your peers.

3. Please respond to the following items or questions after each occasion when you shared your strengths or interests. Fill out a separate form for each social contact. (*Note: Your therapist will give you three copies of this form.*) Remember to bring the forms back to your next therapy session.

    A. Identify name(s) of peer(s) with whom you shared your strengths or interests.

_____

_____

_____

_____

    B. What strength or interest did you share with your peer(s)?

_____

_____

_____

_____

    C. How did you feel about yourself when sharing your strength or interest?

_____

_____

_____

_____

    D. How did your peer(s) respond to you when you shared your strength or interest?

_____

_____

_____

_____

    E. What opportunities will you have to share this strength or interest in the future?

_____

_____

_____

_____

GRADUALLY FACING A PHOBIC FEAR

GOALS OF THE EXERCISE

1. Identify precisely what the feared object or situation is.
2. Describe the emotional, physiological, and behavioral impact that the fear object or situation has had.
3. Develop and implement a plan of systematically exposing self to the feared object or situation until fear is extinguished.

ADDITIONAL PROBLEMS FOR WHICH THIS EXERCISE MAY BE MOST USEFUL

- Academic/Underachievement
- Anxiety
- Social Phobia/Shyness

SUGGESTIONS FOR PROCESSING THIS EXERCISE WITH THE CLIENT

Systematic desensitization to a phobic object or situation has proven to be a very successful approach to extinguishing a fear response. This assignment focuses the client on the phobic stimulus and its effect on his/her life. Then, the client must develop a gradual hierarchy of exposure steps to the feared stimulus. You probably will have to be directly involved in constructing this hierarchy with the client. As preparation for beginning the in vivo exposure to the feared stimulus, it is recommended that you teach the client some behavioral and cognitive anxiety reduction skills such as deep breathing, progressive relaxation, positive imagery, confidence-building self-talk, and so on. Monitor and reinforce his/her implementation of these skills as the exposure program progresses. Urge the patient to increase exposure as anxiety diminishes to the current step.

GRADUALLY FACING A PHOBIC FEAR

Fears that are so strong that they control our behavior need to be faced and overcome. This exercise will help you do just that: Identify what your fear is; describe how if affects you; develop a plan to face it systematically; and, finally, actually take steps to face your fear and win.

1. It is important to clearly identify what you fear and how it affects you emotionally (for example, feel nervous and tense), behaviorally (such as avoid contact and/or don't talk about the feared stimulus), and physically (for instance, heart pounds, sweaty forehead and palms, stomachache, nausea). Describe what the feared object or situation is and then tell how it affects you.

Feared Object or Situation   **Reaction to Feared Object or Situation**

_____   Emotional reaction: _____

_____   _____

_____

_____   Behavioral reaction: _____

_____   _____

_____

_____   Physical reaction: _____

_____   _____

To overcome a fear, it must be faced in a gradual but systematic fashion. We call it *exposure*. When you practice exposure in the proper way, fear steadily diminishes until it does not control your behavior or affect you physically. The key to the process is to develop a plan for gradually increasing exposure to the feared object or situation. Once the plan is developed, you then expose yourself one step at a time to the feared object or situation. You do not take the next step in the gradual exposure plan until you are quite comfortable with the current level of exposure.

For example, say your fear is of sleeping alone in your bedroom at night with the lights off. You could design a plan as follows:

-   Step 1. In the bedroom with small lamp on and someone within 20 feet of your bedroom door.

- Step 2. In the bedroom with small lamp on, someone in the house and close enough to be called easily, if necessary.
- Step 3. In the bedroom with small lamp on, someone in the house.
- Step 4. In the bedroom with small nightlight on, someone in the house.
- Step 5. In the bedroom with small nightlight on, parents out for social evening.
- Step 6. In the bedroom with nightlight in the hall or bathroom, parents out for social evening.

Each next step is taken only after the fear is low or gone in the current step.

2. Now create a gradual exposure program to overcome your feared object or situation. The steps can increase the time you spend with the feared object or situation, increase your closeness to it, increase the size of the object, or a combination of these things. Use as many steps as you need. Your therapist is available to help you construct this plan, if necessary.

Step 1. _____

_____

_____

Step 2. _____

_____

_____

Step 3. _____

_____

_____

Step 4. _____

_____

_____

Step 5. _____

_____

_____

Step 6. _____

_____

_____

Now it's time for a gradual but steady exposure to your feared object or situation. Stay relaxed. Your therapist may teach you some deep breathing, muscle relaxation, and positive self-talk techniques that you can use to keep yourself relaxed. For each step you take, rate your degree of fear on a scale of 1 to 100, with 100 representing total panic, the sweats, and heart-pounding shakes. The rating of 1 represents total calm, complete confidence, peace of mind, looseness, and relaxed feeling. When your rating is reduced to 10 or lower on a consistent basis for the exposure to a particular step, then it's time to consider moving on to the next step.

Ratings for Exposures

Step 1. _____   _____

_____   _____

_____   _____

Step 2. _____   _____

_____   _____

_____   _____

Step 3. _____   _____

_____   _____

_____   _____

Step 4._____   _____

_____   _____

_____   _____

Step 5._____   _____

_____   _____

_____   _____

Step 6._____   _____

_____   _____

_____   _____

SCHOOL FEAR REDUCTION

GOALS OF THE EXERCISE

1. Utilize a systematic desensitization program to manage anxiety and gradually attend school for longer periods of time.
2. Reduce anxiety and expression of fears prior to leaving home and after arriving at school.
3. Decrease the frequency and intensity of temper outbursts, regressive behaviors, somatic complaints, and pleading before going to and after arriving at school.

ADDITIONAL PROBLEMS FOR WHICH THIS EXERCISE MAY BE MOST USEFUL

- Academic/Underachievement
- Anxiety
- Panic/Agoraphobia
- Social Phobia/Shyness

SUGGESTIONS FOR PROCESSING THIS EXERCISE WITH THE CLIENT

This exercise is designed for the school-phobic adolescent who is exhibiting very high levels of anxiety and has already missed a substantial amount of time from school. Meet with the client, parents, and school officials to develop a systematic desensitization plan that gradually allows the client to attend school for longer periods of time. The client incrementally works his/her way back to attending school on a full-time basis. The highly anxious and resistant client may begin attending school for 2 hours each day in the beginning phase of this program. (*Note: This time can be adjusted depending on the client's level of anxiety and degree of pathology.*) Once the client shows that he/she can attend school without exhibiting a significant amount of emotional distress, then the length of the school day is increased either in time (i.e., 45 minutes to 1 hour) or by the number of classes attended. Use a reward system to reinforce the client for attending school for increasingly longer periods of time. Expect more anxiety or resistance around the periods where the length of the school day increases. Teach the client coping strategies (i.e., positive self-talk, thought substitution, relaxation techniques) during the therapy sessions to help the client manage his/her anxiety and stress.

SCHOOL FEAR REDUCTION
PARENT/TEACHER INSTRUCTIONS

This systematic desensitization program is designed for the student who is experiencing a high level of anxiety and has already missed a substantial amount of time from school because of anxiety and fearfulness. In this program, the student is gradually expected to return to school on a full-time basis. Before beginning the program, it is imperative that the student, parent(s), teacher(s), and therapist all sit down together as a team to work out the specific details of this plan. The team will develop a schedule that gradually increases the time the student is expected to be in school each day or week. The student will spend increasingly longer periods of time at school as he/she becomes more confident and self-assured. Use a reward system to reinforce the student for attending school without exhibiting a lot of emotional distress.

1. The first order of business is for the team to come together to work out the specific details of this plan. The student should be informed that the goal of this program is for him/her to eventually attend school on a full-time basis. However, in recognition of a student's high level of anxiety and fearfulness, the team will structure the plan so that the student begins attending school on a part-time basis. It is suggested that the student begin attending school under this plan for a minimum of 2 hours. This time can be adjusted, depending on the student's level of anxiety and fearfulness. For example, a severely anxious adolescent may start this program by attending school for 1½ hours per day, whereas a less anxious adolescent may start the program by attending school for 3 hours a day. The student is strongly encouraged to use the coping strategies (such as positive self-talk, thought substitution, relaxation techniques) that he/she has practiced in therapy sessions.

2. The length of the school day is increased in increments when the student shows that he/she can attend school without exhibiting a significant amount of emotional distress. A significant amount of emotional distress can be demonstrated in any of the following ways:

    *   Excessive pleading and whining
    *   Refusing to get up and out of bed
    *   Numerous somatic complaints
    *   Crying

- Frequent verbalizations of unrealistic fears
- Temper outbursts (yelling, screaming, swearing)
- Refusal to enter school building or classroom
- Leaving classroom or school grounds
- Trembling and shaking
- Refusal to talk when appropriate

3. It is recommended that the student attend school 80 percent of the time (4 out of 5 days or 8 out of 10 days) without showing a significant amount of emotional distress before increasing the length of the school day. If the student successfully meets this criteria, then it is suggested that the expected time spent at school be increased by 45 minutes to an hour. For middle or high school students, the team may want to increase the time spent at school by one period. The steps of the program are then repeated before moving on to the next level.

4. Use a reward system. The student should be reinforced for attending school for the expected period of time without displaying significant distress. The student and other team members should identify the specific reward(s) to reinforce him/her for attending school. Use the following contract form as a means of formalizing the agreement with the student. Establish a new contract for each phase of the program. Place the contract in the student's notebook or post it in his/her room to remind him/her of the agreement. The team should consult with the student about appropriate rewards that can be used to reinforce school attendance. Following is a list of potential rewards:

- Extra time to spend watching television or playing video games
- One-on-one time with mother or father (e.g., attend a movie, exercise together, play a board game)
- Extended bedtime
- Extra time on telephone or computer
- Allow student to go over to a friend's house after school or invite a friend to sleep over at house
- Outing to favorite fast-food restaurant
- Money
- Snacks
- Tokens that can be cashed in for a larger reward or privilege at a later date
- Use of car (for teenagers who have driver's license)

SCHOOL ATTENDANCE CONTRACT

I, _____, agree to attend school for _____ per day, in a calm,
     (Name of student)   (Time)
cooperative manner, and without showing a significant amount of emotional distress.
A significant amount of emotional distress is defined as:

_____

_____

_____

_____

If _____ attends school for the agreed upon period of time and
      (Name of student)
without resistance, then he/she will receive the following reward:

_____

_____

In witness of this contract, we have signed our names on this date _____.

_____   _____

Signature of Student   Signature of Parent

_____   _____

Signature of Parent   Signature of Teacher or Therapist

NO SELF-HARM CONTRACT

GOALS OF THE EXERCISE

1. Develop an action plan to follow if suicidal thoughts or urges to harm self are experienced.
2. Establish support network of individuals and agencies that can be turned to when experiencing suicidal thoughts or urges to harm self.
3. Cease all suicidal thoughts and/or acts of self-harm, and return to highest previous level of daily functioning.
4. Reestablish a sense of hope for self and life in the future.

ADDITIONAL PROBLEMS FOR WHICH THIS EXERCISE MAY BE MOST USEFUL

- Depression
- Mania/Hypomania
- Sexual Abuse Victim

SUGGESTIONS FOR PROCESSING THIS EXERCISE WITH THE CLIENT

In this intervention, the client must sign a formal contract, whereby he/she agrees to contact specific individuals or agencies in the event that he/she experiences suicidal thoughts or the urge to harm him/herself. The contract reminds the client that there is a support network available if he/she becomes suicidal. Furthermore, the contract helps to mobilize significant other persons when the client is in distress. First, assess the client's suicidal risk and determine whether there is a need for inpatient hospitalization. The contract is not meant to take the place of inpatient hospitalization if that intervention is necessary. The client, parents, and therapist should sign the contract only after the client has given his/her verbal commitment not to engage in any acts of self-harm and has agreed to inform others when he/she experiences suicidal thoughts or urges. The client's refusal to sign the contract is a strong indicator that inpatient hospitalization is necessary, but willingness to sign should not be interpreted as a singular indication that hospitalization in not necessary to protect the client from self-harm. Obtain important phone numbers of agencies or individuals, such as a crisis hotline or the emergency room at a local hospital, in the event that the client becomes suicidal in the future.

NO SELF-HARM CONTRACT

This intervention is designed to keep you safe. You will be asked to sign a no self-harm contract in which you agree not to harm yourself in any way and/or to inform agencies or people important to you if you experience suicidal thoughts or urges to injure yourself. By signing the contract, you are recognizing that your life is important and that you are a person of worth. The contract also reminds you that there are other people or agencies that you can turn to in times of sadness or hurt.

1. The following suicide contract involves two important commitments on your part. First, you will pledge not to harm yourself in any way. Second, the contract calls for you to inform other important persons or agencies if you experience suicidal thoughts or urges in the future. The contract contains the names and phone numbers of important individuals or agencies who you can turn to if you experience suicidal thoughts. Place the contract in a private but easily accessible place where you can quickly locate the important telephone numbers if you need them. For example, place the contract in the top drawer of your desk or in a folder close to the telephone. Do not hesitate to contact the individuals or agencies identified on the contract if you experience suicidal thoughts or the urge to harm yourself.

2. After signing the contract, follow through by attending your counseling sessions. Your therapist or counselor may talk to you about the need for medication. Talk carefully with your therapist about this option and feel free to ask any questions.

    Therapy or counseling can be hard work, and sometimes requires you to get in touch with painful thoughts, feelings, or memories. Your therapist will explore the factors contributing to your suicidal thoughts or urges. By identifying these factors, you can find more effective ways to solve or handle your problems. Likewise, your therapist can help identify constructive ways to meet your needs. Although therapy or counseling can be hard work, it is hoped that in the end you will come out of it a stronger person.

NO SELF-HARM CONTRACT
PARENTS' INSTRUCTIONS

1. When an adolescent experiences despair to the point of suicide, his/her distress can have a ripple effect and create distress in his/her parents or significant others. Oftentimes, parents feel confused and uncertain as to what caused their child to experience suicidal thoughts or urges to harm him/herself. Parents may be even more confused as to how to respond to the suicidal crisis. Fortunately, there are steps you can take to provide support for your adolescent and reduce the risk of suicide or self-harm. You have already taken a very important step by contacting a therapist or local counseling center. In therapy, you and your child will learn positive coping strategies to help your son/daughter stop experiencing any suicidal thoughts or urges to harm him/herself.

   In this intervention, your son/daughter will sign a no self-harm contract, whereby he/she agrees not to harm him/herself in any way and to contact significant others if he/she becomes suicidal in the future. The suicide contract contains two important commitments on the part of your son/daughter: First, your son/daughter agrees not to harm him/herself in any way. Second, your son/daughter commits to telling other people or agencies if he/she becomes suicidal or has self-harm urges. The phone numbers of other important individuals or agencies are included on the contract. Place the contract in a private but easily accessible place where you or your son/daughter can easily locate the important telephone numbers in a time of crisis. For example, place the contract in the top drawer of a desk or in a folder by the telephone.

2. The suicide contract reminds your son/daughter that there are individuals or agencies available to offer help and provide support in a time of crisis or distress. If your son/daughter experiences suicidal thoughts or the urge to harm him/herself, then it is very important that you communicate this information to your therapist. Do not hesitate to call the therapist, crisis hotline, emergency room of a local hospital, or inpatient psychiatric unit if your child experiences a wish to die. Take your child immediately to the emergency room of a local hospital if he/she has made a serious suicide attempt. In the event of a medical emergency, call the police or emergency medical team.

3. Your son/daughter will need to be reevaluated for inpatient hospitalization if he/she makes a suicide attempt or experiences a strong urge to die. Your therapist and/or the admissions staff on the inpatient unit will inform you as to whether this step is necessary. If your son/daughter stabilizes and inpatient hospitalization is not needed,

then you are strongly encouraged to follow through with regular outpatient therapy or counseling sessions for your son/daughter. Your involvement and input in your child's therapy is important. Your therapist will assess the factors that contributed to your son/daughter's suicidal thoughts and urges to harm him/herself. Your input in this process can be very valuable. Please inform the therapist of any significant stressors or events that you feel may have contributed to your son/daughter becoming suicidal. Offer any suggestions or insights that may be helpful to the therapist in understanding your son/daughter.

4. At home, closely monitor your son/daughter's moods around the times of crisis. Listen carefully to your child's thoughts, feelings, and concerns. Offer empathy, concern, and hope after your child has verbalized his/her thoughts and feelings. Provide your child with a sense of hope that he/she can overcome the current problems. Encourage your child to talk to other individuals who he/she sees as sources of support. You should also encourage your son/daughter to engage in activities that have brought him/her pleasure or reward in the past. Relaxation and exercise can also help your child cope with his/her problems. If you have any questions as to how to provide help or support for your son/daughter, then ask your therapist.

NO SELF-HARM CONTRACT

I, _____, agree that I will not harm or hurt myself in any way.
(Name of client)

I, _____, further agree that I will successfully contact at least one
(Name of client)
of the agencies or individuals listed in the event that I experience suicidal thoughts
or the urge to injure myself.

_____   _____

Signature of Client   Signature of Parent

_____   _____

Signature of Parent   Signature of Teacher or Therapist

Names of Individuals or Agencies   **Telephone Numbers**

Mother: _____   Home: _____   Work: _____

Father: _____   Home: _____   Work: _____

Therapist: _____ Phone: _____
            (Name)

Crisis Hotline: _____   Phone: _____
                (Name of agency)

Emergency Room: _____   Phone: _____
                (Name of hospital)

Psychiatric Hospital: _____   Phone: _____

Significant Others: _____   Phone: _____
                    (Name)

_____   Phone: _____
(Name)

RENEWED HOPE

GOALS OF THE EXERCISE

1. Cease all suicidal ideation or passive death wishes, and return to highest previous level of functioning.
2. Reestablish a sense of hope in life.
3. Identify the significant factors contributing to the emergence of suicidal ideation or passive death wishes.
4. Renew interest and involvement in social activities and interpersonal relationships.

ADDITIONAL PROBLEMS FOR WHICH THIS EXERCISE MAY BE MOST USEFUL

- Anxiety
- Depression
- Low Self-Esteem
- Mania/Hypomania

SUGGESTIONS FOR PROCESSING THIS EXERCISE WITH THE CLIENT

In this assignment, the client is instructed to read a short story about a teenager, Jeremy, who experiences suicidal thoughts while enduring several life stressors. After reading the story, the client is asked to respond to a series of process questions. The client then brings his/her responses to the next therapy session for processing. The response to the questions will help the client and you gain greater insight into the factors contributing to the emergence of the suicidal thoughts or passive death wishes. This assignment should only be given after the client's suicide risk and need for hospitalization has been assessed. This assignment is not meant to take the place of hospitalization. It should be given to a client whose suicidal crisis has stabilized and who is now felt to be at low risk for suicide.

RENEWED HOPE

Sometimes life's problems seem to pile up all at once. The future may look bleak with little hope that things will turn around and get better. If you have ever experienced moments when you felt depressed to the point of wondering whether life was worthwhile, then it is important to step back and realize that there are people available to help you get through the rough times. There are steps that you can take to overcome or deal with life's problems. The purpose of this assignment is to help you step back, identify the factors contributing to your depression and suicidal thoughts, and develop a plan of action to cope or deal with your real life problems.

Read the following story of a teenager named Jeremy who feels so overwhelmed by his problems that he experiences suicidal thoughts. As you read the story, you may find that some of your experiences are similar to Jeremy's in some ways, but different in others. Whether or not Jeremy's experiences are similar to yours, your therapist has given you this assignment to reflect on the factors that have lead to your suicidal thoughts.

Please read the following story:

"Oh great," Jeremy muttered to himself as he glanced at the grade at the top of his algebra test. "Just what I needed, another D on my math test." Jeremy rubbed his forehead and leaned back in his chair. His algebra teacher, Mr. Hunt, began going over the correct answers with the class, but Jeremy tuned him out and began daydreaming. He had been daydreaming a lot lately. To Jeremy, it didn't seem as if anything was going right in his life. His grades had dropped from mostly Bs during his freshman year to Cs and Ds during his sophomore year in high school. His parents were constantly on his back about his declining grades. In his mind, he could hear his parents giving him the same lecture that they give him repeatedly when he brings home poor grades.

His relationships with his peers were not any better. He was more irritable and short-tempered with his friends. Jeremy's friends noticed the change in his moods and began to pull away or avoid him when he walked down the hall at school. This made him question whether his friends cared about him at all.

Jeremy noticed that his problems seemed to start piling up after he broke up with his girlfriend, Amber, about a month ago. Jeremy really liked Amber. He enjoyed spending time with her and found it very easy to talk to her. He was caught off guard when Amber stated out of the blue one day that she was interested in dating someone else. She expressed her wish to remain friends with Jeremy, but Jeremy was not interested in being "just friends." He tried to act as if it didn't bother him, but on the inside, he was hurting. Ever since then, Jeremy had a hard time concentrating on his schoolwork. He couldn't seem to stay focused. What's more, he experienced little enjoyment in going to the movies or basketball games with his friends. Jeremy had always enjoyed teasing and clowning around with his friends, but now he was quick to snap at his friends if they teased him in the slightest way.

Jeremy's relationship with his parents was very strained, and not just because his grades were dropping at school. His father was traveling a lot more since his promotion; he was often gone during the week. His mother was irritable and depressed because she had to assume even more responsibilities around the house. Jeremy was upset with his parents because he didn't think they were taking the time to listen to him. Since his breakup with Amber, Jeremy questioned whether his parents even cared about him. Yet, Jeremy wasn't helping matters at home, either. He often picked on his two younger sisters for no reason at all. He would tune his parents out and sarcastically reply "whatever" when his parents began to talk to him about his grades. Sometimes he would deliberately crank up the music in his room just to irritate his parents.

Jeremy stopped daydreaming when he heard Mr. Hunt give the class instructions, "Okay, now I want you to get your books out and turn to page 159. We're going to get started on a new section on integers." Jeremy sighed to himself and thought, "I don't care about going on to something new." Lately, he had been so down in the dumps that there were times when he felt like ending his life.

Jeremy began to daydream again, instead of listening to Mr. Hunt talk to the class. Halfway through the lecture, Mr. Hunt interrupted Jeremy out of his daydream when he said to the class, "Jeremy, don't you think that you, of all people, should be paying attention to this new material?" Jeremy was embarrassed and glumly replied, "I suppose."

His friend Aaron noticed that something was wrong and approached Jeremy after class. Aaron asked, "Hey, Jeremy, what's wrong with you? Something seems to be bothering you." Jeremy sarcastically replied, "Nothing's wrong, everything is just great." Aaron persisted, "I know better than that. Something's bothering you." Jeremy commented, "Don't worry about me. I'll be okay." But Aaron continued, "Lately you've seemed so down. It seems like you're not totally there when you're around the guys. It's like you've checked out or something." Jeremy then stated, "Sometimes I feel like checking out for good." Aaron alertly picked up on what Jeremy was trying to say and asked, "What do you mean? You're not thinking of killing yourself?" Jeremy hesitated before saying, "Yeah, sometimes I feel like that. Like I don't want to live anymore." Aaron asserted himself, "I really think you ought to talk to somebody, Jeremy. Mrs. Thompson, the school counselor, has helped a lot of kids who were so down that they thought about taking their life. Why don't you go down and talk to her?"

At first, Jeremy resisted the idea of going to talk to anybody, but with Aaron's encouragement, he reluctantly agreed to talk to the school counselor after school. Aaron went with him to Mrs. Thompson's office. To Jeremy's surprise, he found that she was easy to talk to and interested in what he had to say. Before too long, he found himself talking to Mrs. Thompson about his hurt and pain. He admitted that he experienced thoughts of suicide. After listening to Jeremy's concerns and pain, Mrs. Thompson stated that she thought his parents should know about his sadness. Jeremy did not want his parents to know about his suicidal thoughts at first, but agreed to allow Mrs. Thompson to call home after she explained that his parents would want to understand and help him if they heard how serious his problems were. His mother answered the phone and seemed very concerned while talking to Mrs. Thompson. His mother agreed to set up an appointment for Jeremy with a therapist at a local counseling center.

Jeremy walked out of the office feeling renewed hope. He realized for the first time in a while that there were people who truly cared and were willing to listen to him. The next day, Jeremy walked up to Aaron in the hallway and thanked him for his concern and friendship. Aaron said in return, "I'm just glad I could help a friend. I know that you've been there for me in the past when I needed someone to talk to." Jeremy smiled and walked down the hallway with Aaron to their algebra class.

Please respond to the following questions that relate to you. Take a few minutes to think about the question before you begin writing down your thoughts. Bring your responses back to the next therapy session to review with your therapist.

1. How were your experiences similar to Jeremy's?

_____

_____

_____

_____

_____

2. How were your experiences different than Jeremy's?

_____

_____

_____

_____

_____

3. At the beginning of the story, Jeremy's problems seemed overwhelming to him. What problems have you experienced that have seemed overwhelming or insurmountable to you?

_____

_____

_____

_____

_____

4. Jeremy was saddened and hurt by the breakup with his girlfriend. What hurt or pain have you experienced in your important interpersonal relationships?

_____

_____

_____

_____

_____

5. In the story, Jeremy begins to experience renewed hope after Aaron showed his concern and he talked with Mrs. Thompson. Who can you turn to for support and help? Identify at least three people.

   A. _____

   B. _____

   C. _____

6. How can other people support or be of help to you?

   _____

   _____

   _____

   _____

   _____

7. At the end, Jeremy thanks Aaron for being a good friend. Aaron responds by telling Jeremy that he knows Jeremy has been there for him in the past. What person(s) could use your help or support at the present time?

   _____

   _____

   _____

   _____

   _____

8. What positive things can you do to cope or deal with your life problems? Identify at least three positive ways you can help yourself be less depressed.

   A. _____

   _____

   _____

   _____

   B. _____

   _____

   _____

   _____

   C. _____

   _____

   _____

   _____

SYMBOLS OF SELF-WORTH

GOALS OF THE EXERCISE

1. Cease all suicidal ideation and return to the highest previous level of daily functioning.
2. Reestablish a sense of hope and meaning for life in the future.
3. Increase feelings of self-worth.
4. Regain interest and enthusiasm for social activities and relationships.

ADDITIONAL PROBLEMS FOR WHICH THIS EXERCISE MAY BE MOST USEFUL

- Anxiety
- Attention-Deficit/Hyperactivity Disorder (ADHD)
- Depression
- Low Self-Esteem
- Social Phobia/Shyness

SUGGESTIONS FOR PROCESSING THIS EXERCISE WITH THE CLIENT

This intervention is designed to provide the suicidal client with a sense of self-worth and a renewed interest and zest for living. The client is instructed to take an inventory of his/her strengths, interests, or accomplishments. Some clients will have difficulty identifying any strengths, interests, or accomplishments because of their despair and hopelessness, but remind them that all individuals have self-worth and are blessed with unique strengths or talents. After the client identifies his/her strengths, interests, or accomplishments, instruct the client to bring in objects or symbols that represent his/her strengths, interests, or accomplishments. The objects or symbols can give you some insight into what activities provide the client with a sense of meaning and reward. Then you can plan other homework assignments or interventions that will help stabilize the client's mood and further decrease the risk for suicide. This exercise is only to be given after the client's suicidal risk has been assessed. The exercise is not meant to take the place of hospitalization. This exercise can be modified to work with a number of different emotional or behavioral problems.

SYMBOLS OF SELF-WORTH

Every individual is unique or special in some way. We all have been blessed with some talent, strength, or interest that makes each one of us unique. At times, it is difficult to feel good about ourselves when we experience sadness and despair or feel overwhelmed by life's problems. Yet, it is especially important at these moments to step back and reflect on our own positive qualities or characteristics. By reflecting on our strengths, interests, or accomplishments, we gain a renewed sense of hope and interest in living.

1. The first step in this exercise is to step back and spend a few minutes thinking about your strengths, interests, or accomplishments. Find a quiet or peaceful place where you will have some time alone to think about this exercise. Ask yourself, "What are my strengths and interests?" and "What accomplishments have made me feel good about myself?" For example, you may feel really good about yourself because you have made good grades in school or have been on a winning basketball team. After identifying your strengths, interests, or accomplishments, write them down in the following spaces. Identify at least five strengths, interests, or accomplishments.

    A. _____

    _____

    B. _____

    _____

    C. _____

    _____

    D. _____

    _____

    E. _____

    _____

    F. _____

    _____

    G. _____

    _____

    H. _____

    _____

I. _____

_____

J. _____

_____

2. Next, think of an object or symbol that represents your strengths, interests, or accomplishments. Bring in these symbols or pictures of such objects to your next therapy session. The symbols or objects will help your therapist learn more about you and discover what your strengths and interests are. Again, think closely about what types of objects or symbols you would like to bring in. Several examples or suggestions follow to help you decide.

   • Girl Scout uniform with pins or badges reflecting membership in a group or past accomplishments

   • Football helmet demonstrating membership on a sports team

   • Instrument representing your musical talent

   • Ski boot reflecting your interest in downhill skiing

   • School report cards reflecting your academic accomplishments

   • Computer CD-ROM showing an interest in video games

   • Poetry or drawings reflecting your artistic talents

   • Medals, awards, or ribbons representing past accomplishments

   • Picture of household pets showing your interest in animals

   • Pictures from past vacations reflecting interests and positive memories

   Perhaps these examples or suggestions will give you some ideas. Remember to be yourself and select objects or symbols that reflect who you are as a person. Be creative and have fun with this exercise. At the same time, you are encouraged to be practical in selecting your symbols or objects. For example, if you have a strong interest in biking, then it would be very difficult to bring in your bicycle. However, your bike helmet or a picture of you riding your bike would be good symbols of your interest in biking.

3. Bring in three to five symbols or objects to your next therapy session. Be prepared to discuss these symbols or objects with your therapist. Your therapist will want to know how you developed your strengths and interests or how you achieved your accomplishments. Please respond to the following items or questions to help you prepare for the next therapy session.

   Name of first symbol or object:

   _____

What strength, interest, or accomplishment does this symbol or object represent?

_____

_____

_____

How are you using this strength or interest in your present life? If your symbol or object represents an accomplishment, how did you achieve this accomplishment?

_____

_____

_____

Name of second symbol or object:

_____

What strength, interest, or accomplishment does this symbol or object represent?

_____

_____

_____

How are you using this strength or interest in your present life? If your symbol or object represents an accomplishment, how did you achieve this accomplishment?

_____

_____

_____

Name of third symbol or object:

_____

What strength, interest, or accomplishment does this symbol or object represent?

_____

_____

_____

How are you using this strength or interest in your present life? If your symbol or object represents an accomplishment, how did you achieve this accomplishment?

_____

_____

_____

_____

Name of fourth symbol or object:

_____

What strength, interest, or accomplishment does this symbol or object represent?

_____

_____

_____

_____

How are you using this strength or interest in your present life? If your symbol or object represents an accomplishment, how did you achieve this accomplishment?

_____

_____

_____

_____

Name of fifth symbol or object:

_____

What strength, interest, or accomplishment does this symbol or object represent?

_____

_____

_____

_____

How are you using this strength or interest in your present life? If your symbol or object represents an accomplishment, how did you achieve this accomplishment?

_____

_____

_____

_____

Appendix

ALTERNATE ASSIGNMENTS FOR PRESENTING PROBLEMS

Attention-Deficit/Hyperactivity Disorder (ADHD)

Depression

Mania/Hypomania

Medical Condition

Mental Retardation

Negative Peer Influences

Obsessive-Compulsive Disorder

Oppositional Defiant

Panic/Agoraphobia

Parenting

Peer/Sibling Conflict

Physical/Emotional Abuse Victim

Posttraumatic Stress Disorder (PTSD)

Psychoticism

Runaway

School Violence

Sexual Abuse Perpetrator

Sexual Abuse Victim

ABOUT THE CD-ROM

INTRODUCTION

This appendix provides you with information on the contents of the CD that accompanies this book. For the latest and greatest information, please refer to the ReadMe file located at the root of the CD.

SYSTEM REQUIREMENTS

- A computer with a processor running at 120 Mhz or faster
- At least 32 MB of total RAM installed on your computer; for best performance, we recommend at least 64 MB
- A CD-ROM drive

Note: Many popular word processing programs are capable of reading Microsoft Word files. However, users should be aware that a slight amount of formatting might be lost when using a program other than Microsoft Word.

USING THE CD WITH WINDOWS

To install the items from the CD to your hard drive, follow these steps:

1. Insert the CD into your computer's CD-ROM drive.
2. The CD-ROM interface will appear. The interface provides a simple point-and-click way to explore the contents of the CD.

If the opening screen of the CD-ROM does not appear automatically, follow these steps to access the CD:

1. Click the Start button on the left end of the taskbar and then choose Run from the menu that pops up.
2. In the dialog box that appears, type **d:\setup.exe.** (If your CD-ROM drive is not drive d, fill in the appropriate letter in place of *d*.) This brings up the CD interface described in the preceding set of steps.

USING THE CD WITH A MAC

1. Insert the CD into your computer's CD-ROM drive.
2. The CD-ROM icon appears on your desktop, double-click the icon.
3. Double-click the Start icon.
4. The CD-ROM interface will appear. The interface provides a simple point-and-click way to explore the contents of the CD.

WHAT'S ON THE CD

The following sections provide a summary of the software and other materials you'll find on the CD.

Content

Includes all 79 homework assignments from the book in Word format. Homework assignments can be customized, printed out, and distributed to parent and child clients in an effort to extend the therapeutic process outside of the office. All documentation is included in the folder named "Content."

Applications

The following applications are on the CD:

Microsoft Word Viewer

Windows only. Microsoft Word Viewer is a freeware viewer that allows you to view, but not edit, most Microsoft Word files. Certain features of Microsoft Word documents may not display as expected from within Word Viewer.

USER ASSISTANCE

If you have trouble with the CD-ROM, please call the Wiley Product Technical Support phone number at (800) 762-2974. Outside the United States, call 1(317) 572-3994. You can also contact Wiley Product Technical Support at **http://support.wiley.com**. John Wiley & Sons will provide technical support only for installation and other general quality control items. For technical support of the applications themselves, consult the program's vendor or author.

To place additional orders or to request information about other Wiley products, please call (800) 225-5945.

For information about the CD-ROM, see the **About the CD-ROM** section on pages 351–352.

WILEY
Publishers Since 1807